PETERSON'S

GOLF

SCHOOLS

& RESORTS

GOLF SCHOOLS AND RESORTS
IN
THE UNITED STATES

JAMES M. LANE

Peterson's

Princeton, New Jersey

This book is dedicated to
Isabel, Will, Alex, and Mitchell
with high hopes for their
own adventures in golf.

Library of Congress Cataloging-in-Publication Data

Lane, James M. (James Max)
    Peterson's golf schools & resorts: a comprehensive guide to golf schools
and resorts in the United States / James M. Lane
    p.   cm.
    Includes index.
    ISBN 1-56079-476-3
    1. Golf—Study and teaching—United States—Directories.   2. Golf
resorts—United States—Directories.   I. Title.
GV981.L35   1995   95-7991
796.352'3—dc20   CIP

Cover and Interior Design by Kathy Kikkert.

Cover photo provided by Kiawah Island Resort, Kiawah Island, South
Carolina.

Printed in the United States of America

10 9 8 7 6 5 4 3 2 1

Visit Peterson's Education Center on the Internet (World Wide Web) at
http://www.petersons.com.

The Author

James M. Lane is author of *The Complete Golfer's Almanac* and is a longtime contributor to *LINKS Magazine*. His travels in golf have taken him from the Australian outback to the Russian countryside and the Scottish Highlands. He lives with his wife, Annie, daughter, Isabel, and nine-handicap in Los Angeles.

CONTENTS

CONTENTS

LOCAL SCHOOLS 121

ACKNOWLEDGEMENT

The following people rendered significant and otherwise uncredited assistance in bringing this book to completion:

Jimmy Ballard, Jim Flick, Marlene Floyd, Doc Giffin, Chuck Hogan, Dick Krull, Peter Jacobsen, Jack Kuykendall, Ann Rodewig Lane, Alex Miceli, Danny O'Neil, Arnold Palmer, Ed Seay, Tuzy Snyder, Dick Taylor, Don Trahan;

All the instructors and their dedicated staffs who provided complete and up-to-date information;

Mark Brown, George Fuller, Matt Sullivan, Randy Guyton, Chris Duthie, Pat Enochs, Cindy Spaulding, Brett Borton, and Ed Cherry—a great team of writers, editors, and researchers at LINKS Magazine;

Tim Pipher and WHHI-TV, who supported the television project that led to this book;

Peter de Savary and The Carnegie Club, who provided some much-needed rest and relaxation in the midst of things;

Jeff Stern, Chase Burns, Faye Burton, Howard Maat, Michelle Mendez-Eyraud, Eric Mollinedo, Lori Radcliff, Jeff Still, Jenny Sucov, and all of my team at JSA Publishing, who showed great patience while I was completing this book;

Terry Schneider, Julia White, and the other wonderful editorial, sales, and production staff at Peterson's;

Julie Merberg and Perigee Books, who gave me a sabbatical from The Complete Golfer's Almanac to undertake this book.

James M. Lane

Los Angeles
May 1995

FOREWORD

Anyone who can throw a ball or swing a bat can become a skilled golfer. That lesson was drilled home for me by my own teacher, Sam Byrd, who started out in sports as a New York Yankee and Babe Ruth's roommate, ending up years later as a winner on the PGA Tour.

Grantland Rice once approached Sam and said he'd like to do a book on the difference between the baseball swing and the golf swing. Sam told him it would be a pretty quick read. It turned out that the same technique that Babe Ruth taught Sam in the late 1920s (to put a towel under his left armpit and take a flat level swing) was the technique that Sam taught Ben Hogan in the mid-1940s, except that the towel had turned into a handkerchief, and the swing plane had changed.

So, if golf is so straightforward (and since equipment and course conditions have improved dramatically in recent years), why aren't the scores of the average golfer going down? The truth is that golfers haven't taken enough time to work on their game. Those who do are finding that they can make dramatic improvement, even if they took up golf as an adult. Why, Calvin Peete didn't take up the game until he was 24, and he went on to record many tournament wins including The Players' Championship!

I won't promise you those kinds of results, but I do know that the best thing you can do for your golf game is to enroll at a golf school and learn from someone who's had proven success with amateurs and professionals alike.

But it's not just advanced golf instruction that you'll receive at a golf school. You'll be learning from a teacher who knows people. How to communicate with them. How and when to push golfers to achieve the best results of their golfing lives. How to develop consistency and course management skills. Finally, how to win while having fun with the game of golf. No golf school instructor would last a season without developing these skills.

This book is the most in-depth guide to golf schools that has ever been written. And James M. Lane is not just writing as a golf journalist who knows his way around the golf business. He's learned his way around a golf swing through instruction programs just like you'll see in this book.

I just wish he would visit me down in my new offices at Palm Beach Polo. I have some advice for him to knock his handicap down to a five!

No matter what your handicap or ambition in golf, you'll find the answers to all of your questions about golf schools in *Peterson's Golf Schools and Resorts*. Enjoy!

Jimmy Ballard

INTRODUCTION

HOW TO USE THIS BOOK TO FIND SCHOOL BY NAME OR LOCATION

The major national golf schools are listed alphabetically, with their locations across the country described at the end of the listing. Major national schools are loosely defined as schools with locations in at least two states, or single-site schools under the direction of a nationally renowned instructor.

More locally oriented schools are listed in alphabetical order, by state. The national schools operating in each state are duly cross-referenced here.

ALPHABETICAL LIST OF ALL SCHOOLS:
All schools are listed alphabetically in Index A.

TO FIND SCHOOLS BY TYPE OF INSTRUCTION OFFERED:
Instruction type is listed in Indexes B–G.
SHOW-ME
I-AM-ME
REBUILDERS
SCHOOLS FOR WOMEN
HI-TECH
ON-COURSE EMPHASIS

RESORT LOCATIONS:
National schools located at golf resorts and hotels are listed in Index H.

ANSWERS TO YOUR QUESTIONS ABOUT GOLF INSTRUCTION

JAMES M. LANE

1. *What are the three most important things to learn when beginning with golf?*
The grip, the grip, and the grip.

2. *You have only 15 minutes for a golf lesson before heading out to play your first round. You are playing with your boss and very much want to make a good impression. What should you study?*
Etiquette! Golfers are quite willing, as a rule, to indulge even the rankest of beginners as long as they keep up, keep smiling, and keep to the rules.

3. *What's the most curable curse of the average golfer?*
A slice.

4. *What's next?*
The sand-blast.

5. *What are the most innovative ideas of the century in golf instruction?*
The Vardon grip, straight-line putting, and the connected swing.

6. *What's most responsible for the lower scoring we see today—the ball or the clubs?*
The grass! Advances in drainage and agronomy have produced dramatically better scoring conditions.

7. *What does a good golf teacher teach best?*
Confidence!

8. *Who are the best golf teachers?*
The ones you believe in. I can't tell you how many pros credit their parents as their greatest teachers. One of the best lessons I ever took was from a thirteen-year-old boy.

9. *Why should I enroll in a celebrity-teacher golf school if the celebrity rarely shows up?*

   Well, you probably shouldn't, if that's the way you look at it. A celebrity school offers some degree of certainty regarding the approach and goals of the program, and they have some of the best staff teachers in the country.

10. *What do all the great ball-strikers have in common?*

    Great club position at impact and tremendous swing velocity.

11. *What can I do to add distance to my drives?*

    Play a draw, hit it low, and swing the clubhead.

12. *What's the most important moment at a golf school?*

    The moment you relax!

13. *What are the five most important shots to practice in golf?*

    The tee shot, a three-iron off the back foot, the 120-yard pitch, the uphill chip from light rough, and the 15-foot putt.

14. *Why?*

    A good driver can score three on every hole. A bad driver can score thirteen. A good recovery-shot player can score par on every hole even if caught behind a tree, on hard pan, or far off the fairway. A bad recovery-shot play can score quadruple-bogey.

    The 120-yard pitch, if properly executed, can create a birdie opportunity; misfire and triple-bogey can sneak into the picture. The uphill chip from light rough reflects the fact that almost all greens are sloped toward the tee and most golfers end up short and right of the hole. This is a par-saving shot that, if missed, can lead to double bogey. The area within 15 feet of the hole is nine times greater than the area within 5 feet. Master this length and you will take enormous pressure off your iron game.

15. *Is summer a good deal for a Florida golf school? Their rates are quite low.*

    Yes, but only if you are off the course before noon. Plan to spend the afternoons near the pool.

16. *Do you prefer on-course or on-the-range instruction?*

    Personally, on-course. But as long as there are targets to hit at, practice ranges are fine.

17. *What about the new trend of designing practice holes at resort courses?*

    Courses like the Nicklaus practice course at The Hills of Lakeway and the Fazio practice course at World Woods are an awesome addition to golf.

18. *Is it true that you "drive for show and putt for dough"?*

    Yes. In the top ten for scoring on the Senior PGA TOUR in 1994, only three figured in the top ten for driving distance. Eight were among the top ten putters.

19. *What's the most important step a golfer can take before going to golf school?*

    Setting reasonable personal goals.

20. *How do today's pros hit the ball so much further than the generation before them?*

    They swing faster and the ball suffers less wind resistance at high velocities.

21. *Are regional junior competitions a good idea for junior golfers?*

    In many instances, yes. But remember, not all golfers develop physically at the same rate, and junior golf is largely dominated by early bloomers. But their best organizations, like the American Junior Golf Association, offer a realistic exposure to tournament venues and conditions for talented young players.

22. *What's the best length for a golf school?*

    Try a local one-day school to see if golf school is for you. Then enroll in a three- or four-day instruction program. That will give you a comprehensive drill-set. Five-day programs typically involve tournament play, which is fun but not always as good from an instructional point of view.

23. *Should a golf school have a follow-up program?*

    Yes! If the golf school helps to monitor your practice habits, fine. But 30-minute, twice-a-week practice sessions will help fine-tune your skills whether your club pro or golf school pro is doing the instruction.

24. *What do you need to succeed at golf school?*

    A love of practice, a set of goals, and a willingness to give anything an honest try.

25. *Why is videotape so important?*

    The eye cannot pick up your movements just before impact—the most critical moments in the swing.

26. *What extra equipment should I take to golf school?*

    Extra gloves. Try wearing them on both hands. Also bring plenty of sunblock and a good broad-brimmed hat.

27. *If I have free time to work on any aspect of my game, what should I work on first?*

    The sand-shot. This is the single greatest advantage that pros have over the average amateurs. With practice you can get up-and-down 40 percent to 50 percent of the time and never risk worse than three shots in. Average amateurs routinely take three or four shots to get in from the sand.

28. *How many shots can golf school take off my game?*

    A good rule of thumb is to set a goal of a minimum of three strokes and a maximum of a 33 percent reduction in your handicap. A thirty-six-handicapper should aim for twenty-four. A bogey golfer should aim for twelve. A nine-handicapper should reach for six!

29. *Are coed golf schools a good idea?*

    They're excellent as long as players are grouped by level of ability. The most important thing is to find a program you feel comfortable with.

30. *Are beautiful resorts a distraction from the work at golf school?*

    Not at all. Golf school shouldn't feel like work. A good resort can help you keep in a positive state of mind.

31. *Are golf schools more valuable for beginners, mid-handicappers, or experts?*

    They work for players of all abilities, for different reasons. For beginners they offer a logical, systematic approach to golf. For experts they offer exposure to the most advanced theories and best teachers in golf.

32. *What different personality types are there among golf students and golf instructors?*

    Roughly speaking, there are "show-me" golfers and "I-am-me" golfers. "Show-me" golfers are eager to try new ideas, new equipment, new teachers, and new locations. They are the golfers most willing to contemplate a wholesale rebuilding of a swing. Greg Norman would be an example of a "show-me" golfer. "I-am-me" golfers tend to be more conservative in their approach to new ideas and techniques, favor their old clubs and tested instruction techniques, and prefer tinkering with their swing rather than rebuilding it from scratch. Arnold Palmer is an example of an "I-am-me" golfer. Neither type is inherently more successful than the other. But it is vital to recognize what type you are when considering a golf school.

33. *What's the most underrated service a good golf pro provides?*

    Club fitting. Unsuitable clubs cost distance, accuracy, confidence, and strokes.

34. *What is the difference between long irons and lofted woods?*

    Long irons are more accurate and lofted woods are easier to hit.

35. *What is the most important skill in golf?*

    Controlling one's temper. A calm golfer plays better and is better to play with.

36. *If my home club has bent grass greens and my resort golf school has Bermuda grass, how should I practice my putting?*

    Start on a flat part of the green to become accustomed to the short roll. Then work on a slope to adjust to the reduced break.

37. *What's a good forty-ball warm-up routine?*

    The same proportion as you hit them on the course. Six wedge-shots, seven mid-irons, seven tee-balls, two sand shots, three chips, and fifteen putts.

38. *What's the best playing format for learning golf?*

    Scotch foursomes, also known as alternate-shot. You learn never to criticize your partner's shot, and eventually you learn not to criticize your own. Criticism is fatal on a golf course. Plus, one places more focus on strategy, which is also vital to good golf.

THE STORY OF
GOLF INSTRUCTION

Like almost every modern sport, golf had its roots in the madcap, chaotic banging of a ball around a field with what Winston Churchill described as "instruments singularly ill-suited to the purpose." Various authorities have credited any number of peoples—Celts, Romans, Huns, or a band of leisure-loving Visigoths—with the invention of golf in its earliest form. But the story of golf instruction begins rightly in the medieval era (no later than 1353), when golfers adopted the principle of allowing each team to hit a second uninterrupted shot. Previously, teams of players would alternate hitting a ball back and forth across a field, and strategy and technique went no further than devising the most efficient means of bashing a ball over the heads of the opposition, preferably in the direction of the goal line or at least into some abyss from which the other team could not extract itself.

With adoption of the second short (and with the principle of each team playing its own ball), this primeval game became golf and at the same time acquired a strategy, something that its medieval rival, football, did not acquire until the invention of the scrimmage in the 19th century. It also rapidly acquired such a popularity that it so utterly eclipsed the sport of archery (which was vital to Scotland's preparation for national defense) that the playing of golf in Scotland was made a criminal offense punishable by hanging. No idle threat that, for at least one poor golfer did pay this sorry price for his round—but ultimately a peace with England was achieved and the Scots devoted their renowned intensity to the study of what would become their national game.

Since that time there doesn't seem to be any aspect of ball-striking or mental technique that hasn't come in for scrutiny, particularly in our own highly scientific 20th century. Stance, grip, alignment, swing plane, waggle, wrist cock, shoulder turn, and angle of attack have all been addressed by the parade of teachers, quacks, visionaries, kinaesthetes, scientists, engineers, mystics, duffers, and well-meaning Uncle Bobs who have over the past 600 years plunked a ball on the turf and uttered the magic phrase "Let me show you . . ."

The Show-and-Tell of golf instruction took on new importance in 1848 when, with the invention of the gutta-percha ball (or "guttie"), golf became both exportable and cheap. Prior to 1848, golf ball construction was a laborious and costly art practiced by a handful of cottage manufacturers in the vicinity of Edinburgh—and if a ball was expensive, freight was prohibitive. Golf at this time simply had no chance to expand beyond the Scottish lowlands. Since all of golf was compacted into such a tiny area, golfers were able to learn simply by imitating the great players of the day on the handful of courses then in existence.

The guttie changed all that. By 1856, the game had expanded to England, Ireland, France, and India. These new clubs hired full-time professionals, many of them expatriate Scots, and with them came the first flowering of formal golf instruction as the canny professionals undertook the task of teaching golf in foreign lands and foreign conditions. The first book of golf instruction can be firmly dated to this period, with the publication in 1857 of *A Keen Hand* by H. B. Farnie.

The 19th century was a time of slow advancement in technique, with concentration primarily on a long-running disagreement as to whether an open stance or a closed stance was the better way to address the guttie, which for all its low cost was something of a dodo and difficult to put into the air. The controversy was only truly resolved when the modern wound (Haskell) ball appeared in the early 1900s and made the guttie obsolete.

At roughly the same point in time as the Haskell, golf instruction was advanced even more directly by the arrival of the touring professional golfer. Soaring popularity and plummeting travel costs ushered in the barnstorming era, when golfers such as Harry Vardon could earn a living from personal appearances, tournament purses, and exhibition matches and avoid the low status and even lower pay of the club professional.

Vardon's tournament successes and his proselytizing work in far-flung places such as Canada and the United States led to popular adoption of two of his innovative techniques—a steady, rhythmic, and utterly simple swing technique, and the overlapping (Vardon) grip, which is still the most popular method of gripping a club. Vardon did not personally invent either—but his success stamped them first with legitimacy and finally with a certain inevitability as he racked up six British Open crowns and the 1900 U.S. Open title.

Although both the first golf magazines and the Professional Golf Associations appeared early in the 20th century, barnstorming professionals and Bobby Jones would continue to dominate golf instruction right up to the Great Depression. Huge crowds flocked to see Jones and Hagen on both sides of the Atlantic, learning such secrets as Hagen's straight-line putting—drawing the clubface back from the ball in a straight line rather than in the slight arc popular at his time. His innovation was important in the 1920s and allowed him to win many tournaments—but it is even more important today with the increased emphasis on fast, difficult putting surfaces.

The modern sand wedge and modern bunker techniques were also a by-product of the era—this particular innovations the work of several golfers, most notably Gene Sarazen. But the Great Depression had a devastating effect on touring professionals, and the age of coast-to-coast exhibition tours came to a close.

The years between 1932 and 1956 are not celebrated in golf instructional lore, but that isn't to say that the instructors of the era weren't any good. In fact, club-level and local instruction was better in this era than at any time during golf's history, as aging tour pros such as Tommy Armour retired to club jobs while young pros like Claude Harmon decided not to join the nascent PGA Tour owing to its low purses and often appalling conditions. Ernest T. Jones was at his studio on Fifth Avenue in New York City, preaching the virtues of "swing the clubhead" at five dollars a lesson to all comers. In addition, the best northern pros would travel to Florida in the winter and pick up new teaching styles and techniques in winter PGA meetings or on the winter tournament circuit. Finally, modern golf range equipment began to appear, eliminating the need for a ball-shagging caddie and sparking a boom in driving-range construction. College-based instructional programs were also adopted by many major universities during these years, attracting future stars such as Arnold Palmer.

In the mid-1950s, a new golf boom began, and, with tournament purses soaring and golf acquiring a certain cachet, younger amateurs and club pros abandoned careers in insurance or on the practice tee for glory on the PGA Tour. Prize money and endorsement income made millionaires out of Arnold Palmer and Jack Nicklaus, and, with thousands of dollars now resting on the success of this putt in the Masters or that five-iron in the Open, leading professionals began to openly seek the advice of golf gurus such as Gardner Dickinson, Bob Toski, Harvey Penick, and Jack Grout. At the same time, Palmer, Nicklaus, and Gary Player parlayed their tournament successes into an empire of instructional publications—magazine articles, television tips, and ghost-written, handsomely illustrated books. National magazines such as *Golf* and *Golf Digest* capitalized on the new-found popularity of the game to achieve relatively massive circulations and a national forum for cutting-edge instructional techniques.

Golf instructors, too, found that the golf magazines and their increasingly visible work with touring professionals brought them more business than they could handle on a local level. So, although local golf schools had been in existence since just after the war, in 1968 the Ben Sutton and Craft-Zavichas Schools, which would evolve into the first national golf schools, opened for business.

Golf did not sustain in the 1970s the same level of popularity it enjoyed in the 1960s, but significant changes were looming for the game as golf's expansion had created a large enough golf economy to allow for substantial investment in research and development—the groundwork was laid in the 1970s for the radical transformation of turf preparation, golf club technology, and instructional technique. The cavity-backed iron, the metal wood, the graphite shaft, as well as revolutionary changes in irrigation technique and turf-laying, date to the 1970s. All would have substantial impact on the game as golfers achieved better and better control over the golf ball (in flight direction, overall distance, and spin characteristics).

Golf instruction and, in particular, golf schools would not enjoy a real economic boom until the 1980s, but the influential theory of connection, video analysis of the golf swing, and the emphasis on big-muscle leadership date to the pioneering work of David Leadbetter, Jimmy Ballard and others in the late 1970s and early 1980s. Golf instruction also became more specialized, as teachers by the mid-1980s began to emphasize their expertise with "practical instruction" (John Jacobs), "short-game instruction" (Dave Pelz), "women's instruction" (Penny Zavichas and Linda Craft), or "mental conditioning" (Bob Rotella and Chuck Hogan).

By the 1990s, golf instruction had boomed to the point that there are now forty national golf schools offering hundreds of programs across the country, with a cornucopia of techniques, price points, regimens, and training goals. The biggest of the golf schools, John Jacobs', now has its own travel division and a line of golf clubs. Virtually all of the national golf schools offer books and videotapes for sale. Prominent golf gurus such as Dave Pelz, Ken Venturi, Rick Smith, and Jim Flick are in demand not only with the touring pros but at skyrocketing master class rates at the finest resorts. Harvey Penick's *Little Red Book* became the biggest-selling sports book of all time. In short, golf instruction has expanded into one of the largest and most vibrant sectors of the substantial golf economy.

Looking back over the entire grand parade of gurus and journeyman instructors, if one were to assign a grade to golf instruction as a whole, even six centuries into it, one still has to pencil in "I" for "Incomplete." It's well worth noting that, even in this day of golf gurus and their technical wizardry, fewer than half the world's players can regularly break 100. It's also fitting to mention that when James Durham recorded a 94 at the Old Course in 1767, he set a course record that lasted 86 years. Golf has indeed come far, and has far to go.

THE ACADEMY OF GOLF

PALM BEACH GARDENS, FLORIDA; COLORADO SPRINGS, COLORADO

PROGRAM A three-day program.

ABOUT THE PROGRAM If there is a "hot seat" in golf instruction, the head instructor at PGA National, who teaches at the home of the PGA of America, has to be sitting on it. Mike Adams is the pro in question, and his program has not only passed muster for the PGA, it is one of the best-known programs in the country, with a summer program at The Broadmoor in Colorado in addition to the main campus at PGA National Resort and Spa.

The Academy of Golf is a three-day program with a price tag of $895 (four days for juniors). The programs run Tuesday through Thursday and Friday through Sunday throughout the year at PGA National (Monday through Thursday for juniors). The satellite school at The Broadmoor runs from June through mid-September.

The PGA National experience is high-tech by golf instruction standards. Biomechanical golf analysis, high-speed split-screen video, quadscreen video analysis, laser analysis for putting, a full-time sports psychologist, and a personal physiologist for muscle development and exercise design are all available.

It all sounds pretty forbidding—something like Dr. Frankenstein would think up. But Mike Adams actually emphasizes the individual and works with the golfer's strengths. The technology serves the student, not the other way around.

Each student is videotaped daily on the full swing and once on putting and pitching (these techniques are more individualistic; most reputable schools focus on teaching the repeatable full swing). The videotapes are recorded for personal take-home videos (graphics and computer swing analysis). Each student also receives a personal fitness analysis, a recommended program from the staff physiologist, instruction on mental toughness, and course management skills.

In short, PGA National offers a range of instruction activities that embrace technology yet insist on individualized instruction. This school offers a model for any aspiring golf school guru.

The Robb Report recently rated The Academy of Golf the finest program in the nation.

COSTS From $895 for the three-day program.

STUDENT/TEACHER RATIO 3:1.

HEAD INSTRUCTOR The head instructor is Mike Adams. "We treat each student as an individual. We take the good in each student's swing and build upon it." Adams personally teaches at both sites.

■ ABOUT THE LOCATIONS ■

PGA NATIONAL RESORT

PALM BEACH GARDENS, FLORIDA

The PGA National Resort and Spa was founded some fifteen years ago as the PGA of America's headquarters and as its statement in golf resort excellence. The amenity base is, to say the least, sumptuous. It has five golf courses, a European-style spa, nineteen tennis courts, three swimming pools, croquet, a health and racquet club, 335 rooms, and seven dining establishments. The resort has received a Four-Star rating from Mobil and

Four Diamonds from AAA for ten consecutive years—no small achievement in itself.

There are two golf seasons in Florida. First there is the warm season, which runs from November to March and features crowded hotels and courses, high prices, and the best weather in the country. Second, from April through October, is the hot season, which features empty courses and hotels, low rates, and the worst weather in the country. Use your best judgment. (Note: Palm Beach Gardens receives some temperature relief from the ocean breezes but is beset by thunderstorms on summer afternoons.)

PGA National is home to three courses designed by George and Tom Fazio (Haig, Champion, and Squire), one by Karl Litten (Estate), and a fifth course designed by Arnold Palmer and Ed Seay (The General). Each of the courses features water on at least thirteen holes, so accuracy and judgment will be at a premium.

If you have a free day at the beginning of your stay at PGA National, play Estate, Haig, or Squire. Haig gives more room off the tee for big hitters, while Estate and Squire are more friendly to short hitters. All three are good "tune-up" courses, especially if you are coming off a sabbatical.

On your final day at the resort, try to get out to Champion or The General. They're great aesthetic rewards for all the hard work you've been through at golf school, and both will test your new fount of golfing knowledge with a combination of tough landing areas, length, toughness, and emphasis on accuracy (The General more so off the tee; Champion on the approaches).

The course that receives the bulk of national attention is Champion, which hosted the 1983 Ryder Cup and the 1987 PGA Championship and is the annual site for the PGA Seniors Championship. Champion, re-modeled by Jack Nicklaus in 1990, features a trio of difficult opening holes and is not the ideal first-day course. Thus it is hard to generalize about the game that will succeed— Larry Nelson's precision game and Arnold Palmer's gambles have both netted major victories here.

The resort is built around a 26-acre lake and features a Mediterranean Revival architectural theme. Vaulted ceilings and tile floors abound throughout the resort. The spa is a late addition to the resort and inspired a renovation and remodeling effort in 1992. Several of the restaurants feature spa cuisine, but Explorers serves Continental cuisine in a formal setting for those seeking a more luxurious resort experience.

PGA National is billed as a complete resort, and it certainly doesn't disappoint. Values are certainly excellent in the off-season, but be prepared for some sweating on the range if you try the budget route.

THE BROADMOOR
COLORADO SPRINGS,
COLORADO

Perennial recipient of the Mobil Five-Star and AAA Five-Diamond awards (and one of the few true golf resorts to do so), The Broadmoor makes an excellent complement to PGA National as a summer site for The Academy of Golf. Well, let's go one step further. It is a better place to be.

The resort anchors the western edge of Colorado Springs, a few miles southwest of the Air Force Academy. The main road on the west side of the city leads right to The Broadmoor's main entrance.

The resort is designed in the Spanish revival style, which was popular during the

1920s, and it is simply enormous. Perhaps the only drawback to the resort is that the grandeur of the establishment may be off-putting to some who want to vacation in a more private setting. But the buildings are designed in a campus style, with interconnecting passageways and paths, which gives the hotel a manageable, human scale.

Before moving on to golf, let's have a quick word about some of the additional resort activities. Winter sports are the headline acts here; skiing and ice-skating are the sports most closely associated with The Broadmoor. In fact, the U.S. Olympic skating teams trained here for years. It's not hard to imagine Peggy Fleming, Dorothy Hamill, and Bonnie Blair wandering the resort grounds between sessions on the ice. In summer, there's hot-air ballooning and mountain-climbing for the daring; hang-gliding for the ultra-daring. Summer Olympians are also in the area; the bikers like the hills and the thin air for strength and stamina training.

For those of a more sedentary nature, the Broadmoor offers its own movie theater and a cornucopia of restaurants, with pub fare to southwestern cuisine in formal settings.

The Broadmoor's fame is derived from its famous East Course, designed by Donald Ross, which has hosted the U.S. Amateur, U.S. Women's Amateur, the Curtis Cup, and the NCAA Championship. Jack Nicklaus won his first U.S. Amateur here in a final against Deane Beman; Juli Inkster and Deb Richard won the Women's Amateurs here. The course played extremely long when it first opened in the 1920s but today is regarded, like Pinehurst No. 2, as a strategic course—in which placement (especially on the green) wins over raw power.

Two other courses are on the property. Robert Trent Jones designed the West Course during the early 1960s when he was redefin-ing the modern resort course with Golden Horseshow (Colonial Williamsburg) and Mauna Kea. It is monstrously long from the tips and features the exquisitely demanding par-threes that Jones became known for in his resort designs.

The Broadmoor has had a third course since 1976, the South Course; this demanding and hilly course was the first collaboration between Arnold Palmer and Ed Seay. The managing partner of Bear Creek Country Club, one of Colorado's top five courses, once told me that he first thought of Palmer to design Bear Creek because he was amazed that anyone could get any golf course put into the hills south of the Broadmoor, let alone a good one. The South Course is a few miles away from the resort proper; it features the best views of Colorado Springs and the surrounding plains.

The golf courses, incidentally, are still under the overall direction of Dow Finsterwald. The former PGA Championship winner left the PGA TOUR to become head pro. He's done a fine job in maintaining the quality of the golfing experience here. The courses are bentgrass from tee to green and well maintained throughout the year. If the winter is severe, however, consider delaying a visit until at least July to allow the grass to reestablish and thrive.

■ CONTACT ■

The Academy of Golf
PGA National Resort
1000 Avenue of Champions
Palm Beach Gardens, FL 32444
407-627-7593

ACADEMY OF GOLF DYNAMICS

COLORADO SPRINGS,
COLORADO; AUSTIN, TEXAS

PROGRAM Three-day schools, February–November. Midweek and long weekend options available.

ABOUT THE PROGRAM A number of fairly authoritative sources have rated this program one of the finest in the country, including *MONEY* magazine. Tom Kite went so far in *GOLF* magazine as to rate this number one! Both President Bill Moretti and Head Instructor Jay Bowden subscribe to the "Learning Styles" method of teaching, which acknowledges that different students learn in different ways. The trick is, of course, to design a program that caters to individual learning styles without tumbling into chaos, hence, the low student-teacher ratios and an emphasis on the student and teacher as a team. Mental aspects of the game, including course management skills, are also taught. High-speed, stop-action videotape analysis is employed as well as specialized swing training aids. The program includes a "Welcome" breakfast and a "Graduation" lunch. The school offers assistance for area accommodations, but (just in case) we recommend Texas Timeshares in Lakeway (800-826-1841), offering two-bedroom villas, swimming, tennis, a hot tub, and a marina on Lake Travis for boaters.

COSTS Colorado Springs, $695 to $995 per person; Austin, $600 to $825 per person.

ACCOMMODATIONS Not included in package price.

STUDENT/TEACHER RATIO 3:1.

HEAD INSTRUCTOR The head instructor is Bill Moretti, 1993 South Texas PGA Teacher of the Year and *GOLF* magazine contributor. All instructors are PGA professionals.

■ ABOUT THE LOCATIONS ■

GARDEN OF THE GODS RESORT/KISSING CAMELS GOLF CLUB

COLORADO SPRINGS,
COLORADO

Garden of the Gods is a spectacular series of rock formations in the hills above Colorado Springs. It is a must-see while in the area. This is a rather soothing and inspiring location for a resort. The course is down the road a stretch at the foot of Pike's Peak, where Press Maxwell (son of the noted designer Perry Maxwell) built one of the older and still more attractive Colorado courses. It's a shade over 7,100 yards from the tips, but at an elevation of 6,400 feet, there's plenty of extra carry in the thin air; the course will play like a 6,500 yarder at the seashore. The greens are huge and the fairways are invitingly broad.

Elegant dining is a tradition in Colorado Springs—stemming from The Broadmoor—and Garden of the Gods keeps up its end. Indoor and outdoor tennis, swimming, and hiking trails complete the offering. Definitely look into the hiking—the rock formations are truly a delight!

THE HILLS OF LAKEWAY
(COMMUTER ONLY)
AUSTIN, TEXAS

The lakes and rolling hills of the Austin area have proven to be a cradle of great golfers over the years. Jack Nicklaus designed a Learning Center here that takes full advantage of the conditions, complete with three practice holes (par-three, par-four, and par-five), a feature shared by perhaps only three other golf courses in the country. It's a relatively rare opportunity to practice in real-life situations and lies. Students, alas, do not have privileges at the Nicklaus-designed course. Two other courses in the area offer playing privileges.

■ CONTACT ■

Academy of Golf Dynamics
The Hills of Lakeway
45 Club Estates Parkway
Austin, TX 78738
512-261-3300

AL FRAZZINI'S SCHOOL OF GOLF
WESLEY CHAPEL, FLORIDA; LAKE GENEVA, WISCONSIN

PROGRAM Five-day golf schools: October–May, Tampa; May–September, Lake Geneva.

ABOUT THE PROGRAM Al Frazzini has been in the instruction business for over thirty years now, dividing his time almost equally between Wisconsin and Florida. His style is a hybrid of the range-oriented teachers and the on-course instruction pioneered by Ben Sutton. On-course instruction is part of the program, but so are long hours of work on the range along with high-speed, stop-action video analysis.

COSTS $175 per person per day.

ACCOMMODATIONS Accommodations are included in the package price.

HEAD INSTRUCTOR New head instructor, Robert Macmillan, a former European Tour player, carries on the tradition with extra focus on the mental side of the game and teaches anyone from the rankest beginner to the most ancient golf veteran. Classes are quite small, and include 40 hours of instruction (a hefty bonus over typical five-day programs), nine-hole playing lesson, golf cart and green fees, club cleaning and storage, daily breakfast and lunch, plus a cocktail party.

STUDENT/TEACHER RATIO 4:1. All instructors are PGA professionals.

■ ABOUT THE LOCATIONS ■

QUAIL HOLLOW COUNTRY CLUB
WESLEY CHAPEL, FLORIDA

An inviting 6,761-yard, par-seventy-two course is the scene for both after-hours play and on-course instruction. Wesley Chapel is somewhat better known as the home of the Four-Diamond rated Saddlebrook Resort and of tennis pro Jennifer Capriati, but Quail Hollow is just as close to Tampa and Busch Gardens and comes without the expense if you choose to stay at the Holiday Inn resort recommended by the school. Otherwise, Saddlebrook is right down the street with its two Arnold Palmer and Ed Seay-designed courses.

GRAND GENEVA RESORT

LAKE GENEVA, WISCONSIN

Lake Geneva is a long-time getaway favored by Chicago and Milwaukee business executives. In recent years, the former Playboy resort has been converted into one of the better resorts in the country. Blackwolf Run is nearby, but the resort has two outstanding courses of its own, which are routinely rated among the top resort courses in the country. The first is a Pete Dye and Jack Nicklaus course designed in the Scottish style, while the Brute course, designed by Robert Harris, is in the American parkland style. The facility as a whole features 1,400 acres of rolling hills and countryside, skeet and trap shooting, indoor and outdoor tennis, horseback riding, and canoeing.

■ CONTACT ■

Al Frazzini's Golf Course
Quail Hollow Country Club
6225 Old Pasco Road
Wesley Chapel, FL 33544
800-598-8127 or 414-248-8811

AMERICA'S FAVORITE GOLF SCHOOLS

SEDONA, ARIZONA; SAN DIEGO, CALIFORNIA; SANTA ROSA, CALIFORNIA; LITTLETON, COLORADO; COLORADO SPRINGS, COLORADO; MYSTIC CONNECTICUT; LAKE LANIER, GEORGIA; CRETE, ILLINOIS; FINDLAY, ILLINOIS; LAS VEGAS, NEVADA; GETTYSBURG, PENNSYLVANIA; BEAUFORT, SOUTH CAROLINA; FREEPORT, BAHAMAS; TORONTO, ONTARIO, CANADA

PROGRAM The headquarters is in Fort Pierce, Florida; there are twenty locations, including California, Nevada, Colorado, Arizona, Oklahoma, Illinois, Ontario, Connecticut, Pennsylvania, South Carolina, Florida, and the Bahamas.
ABOUT THE PROGRAM America's Favorite represents one of the most successful national instruction programs in the country. Their success is all the more remarkable because they have de-emphasized the role of the celebrity instructor. Instead, like John Jacobs' program, America's Favorite is centered around fundamental, practical instruction from highly trained, low-profile instructors, with low student-teacher ratios and the aid of straightforward devices such as videotape replays.

Each of the staff instructors teaches golf full-time on a year-round basis. Here there are no moonlighting club pros picking up a few quick bucks—they are all certified by the PGA or the United States Golf Teachers' Association. The programs are run at a variety of lengths in attractive locations throughout the country.

The typical program at America's Favorite includes 5 hours of lessons (on the range and playing lessons). Video analysis for analyzing swing faults and monitoring of progress is used. There are classroom sessions on theory and course management skills and on-course play with the instructing professional. All golfers are grouped by ability. Class size is limited to 4 golfers per professional.

Frankly, one of the prime advantages of the America's Favorite approach to golf schooling is the affordability. Considering the locations (which include Hilton Head, Palm Springs, Las Vegas, Tempe, Orlando, and the Bahamas), the rates are excellent. One note, however—rates do not include meals, so make allowances.

In addition to the regular programs, America's Favorite Golf Schools acts as a clearinghouse for the International Junior Golf Association (IJGA), a division of the USGTA that offers a series of one-week summer golf camps in four locations (Fort Myers in southwest Florida and Hilton Head Island, plus a spring break camp in Orlando). Both options are definitely worth a look, as junior golf instruction has been somewhat overlooked by the major national golf schools.

The philosophy of America's Favorite Golf Schools is extremely low-key. There isn't much advanced swing theory here. Analysis, instruction, and plenty of practice under close supervision is the whole program. The locations are excellent, the rates are very favorable, and as a basic golf instruction and vacation package this one is a winner!

All schools offer three or five nights accommodation, 5 hours of daily instruction that includes on-course play, daily videotape and critique, green fees and carts during and after class, unlimited range balls, all taxes, and full use of resort facilities.

STUDENT/TEACHER RATIO 4:1.

HEAD INSTRUCTOR There are 16 full-time instructors.

■ ABOUT THE LOCATIONS ■

BELLROCK INN & OAKCREEK COUNTRY CLUB
SEDONA, ARIZONA

Not a bad way to experience the Arizonan winter weather, which is bone dry and warm. Oakcreek is not exactly threatening the top-100 rankings, but the scenery around Sedona has to be seen to be believed. Sedona golf photography has graced the cover of many a magazine and book; the stark desert landforms and the lush green fairways are remarkable. As Brett Borton wrote of Arizona in *The Endless Fairway*, "you just want to bend down and touch the grass." Sedona is 2 hours north of Phoenix and 1 hour south of Flagstaff. The award-winning Bellrock Inn is less than 1 mile from the course.

PROGRAMS Three days (Monday-Wednesday or Friday-Sunday) and five days (Monday-Friday). October 15–May 31.

COSTS Three-day school $775 single, $655 double, $140 nonparticipating spouse, $535 commuter; five-day school $1295 single, $1095 double, $235 nonparticipating spouse, $895 commuter.

SAN VICENTE INN & GOLF CLUB
SAN DIEGO, CALIFORNIA

Actually situated in Ramona, about 30 minutes from San Diego, this program offers instruction and accommodations on one campus. The San Vicente is new to America's Favorite Golf Schools this year, but it is already considered one of their choicest options because of the proximity to a major city, the climate, and the tranquillity of the setting. The

San Vicente styles itself a country inn, so expect more personal service here than at the larger, group-oriented hotels.

PROGRAM Three days (Monday-Wednesday or Friday–Sunday) and five days (Monday-Friday). Year-round.

COSTS Three-day school $775 single, $655 double, $140 nonparticipating spouse, $535 commuter; five-day school $1295 single, $1095 double, $235 nonparticipating spouse, $695 commuter.

QUALITY INN & ADOBE CREEK GOLF CLUB
SANTA ROSA, CALIFORNIA

Santa Rosa is a gateway to the famed vineyards of the Napa Valley, originally known as the Valley of the Moon. Pebble Beach is more top of mind when it comes to Northern California golf, but there are jewels to behold in this region, such as Silverado and the Chardonnay Club. And you can't beat the wines.

Adobe Creek is probably the best-known Robert Trent Jones course in the state. As a bonus, Mr. Jones designed the practice areas, which makes for a unique golf learning experience. This is a program particularly recommended if there are nongolfers to be considered, because the Valley has so many additional sight-seeing options, from wine-tasting to giant redwoods to the ruins of Jack London's Wolf House. One cautionary note: the program is billed as available year-round, but spring and summer are the desired seasons. The weather can be downright nippy during the late fall and winter, and intensive practice with long irons on cold mornings is not highly recommended.

PROGRAMS Three days (Monday-Wednesday or Friday-Sunday) and five days (Monday-Friday). Year-round.

COSTS Three-day school $850 single, $660 double, $210 nonparticipating spouse, $460 commuter; five-day school $1400 single, $1095 double, $325 nonparticipating spouse, $750 commuter.

LONE TREE RESORT
LITTLETON, COLORADO

Colorado is vastly underrated for golf as a result of its popularity with skiers, but Lone Pine has done a lot of work to make believers out of the region's golfing crowd. It is located 20 minutes south of Denver on Route 25 and features large, luxurious rooms right on the course. The course is very highly regarded by locals (often the best judges in such matters), as are the practice facilities—a bonus for golf schoolers. Be careful about trying this school outside of June, July, and August, however—the weather can get unpredictable.

PROGRAMS Three-day school (Monday-Wednesday or Friday-Sunday) and five days (Monday-Friday), May 1-October 15.

COSTS Three-day school $636 single, $515 double, $125 nonparticipating spouse, $435 commuter; five-day school $1060 single, $855 double, $725 commuter.

WESTCLIFFE INN AND SAINT ANDREWS GOLF CLUB
COLORADO SPRINGS, COLORADO

This particular school is in the same neighborhood as The Broadmoor and the U.S. Air Force Academy (which offers a summer instruction program). All this makes Colorado

Springs one of the hot spots for golf instruction. Consider this the middle option in terms of resort accommodations. Alas, it is the third choice when it comes to golf because this course is only a nine-holer. It has great views of the mountains, though.

PROGRAMS Three days (Monday-Wednesday or Friday-Sunday) and five days (Monday-Friday). May 1-October 15.

COSTS Three-day school $625 single, $525 double, $100 nonparticipating spouse, $450 commuter; five-day school $1025 single, $860 double, $150 nonparticipating spouse, $725 commuter.

MYSTIC RAMADA INN AND STONINGTON COUNTRY CLUB
MYSTIC, CONNECTICUT

The seaport town of Mystic provided the setting for the motion picture *Mystic Pizza* and is within a half-day drive of nine states. It is scenic and, while hardly exotic, is a viable option in the summer months, especially for commuters. The town is home to resort casinos, Seaquarium, and some of New England's most memorable dining. One note: the Stonington Country Club is 3 miles from the Ramada and is only nine holes.

PROGRAMS Three days (Monday-Wednesday or Friday-Sunday) and five days (Monday-Friday). May 1-October 15.

COSTS Three-day school $650 single, $540 double, $150 nonparticipating spouse, $425 commuter; five-day school $1089 single, $889 double, $250 nonparticipating spouse, $695 commuter.

STOUFFER PINE ISLE RESORT
LAKE LANIER, GEORGIA

One of the key additions this year for America's Favorite is the Stouffer Pine Isle. It is one of the finest resorts in the country and quite convenient to a major city and airport. Lake Lanier is 45 minutes by car, northeast of Atlanta, and it is a fairly solid little golf mecca with Pine Isle and Reynolds Plantation, with the widely admired Great Waters course by Jack Nicklaus. The Pine Isle course is by Gary Player, which means it's a shorter course with emphasis on precision, and it has relatively flat greens. The course has an outstanding setting at Lake Lanier—both the lake and the nearby Blue Ridge mountains offer great vistas. Pine Isle is a full-service resort, and alternative activities abound, including horseback riding, tennis, and swimming.

PROGRAMS Three days (Monday-Wednesday or Friday-Sunday) and five days (Monday-Friday). Year-round.

COSTS Three-day school $815 single, $625 double, $225 nonparticipating spouse, $425 commuter; five-day school $1295 single, $1030 double, $375 nonparticipating spouse, $695 commuter.

BALMORAL WOODS COUNTRY CLUB
CRETE, ILLINOIS

This is a commuter school only, located 45 minutes from downtown Chicago in the scenic town of Crete. This location is new this year from America's Favorite and is an excellent idea for the Chicago metro market. The Balmoral Harness Race Track is directly across the street—now there is a unique after-school program!

PROGRAMS Three days (Monday-Wednesday or Friday-Sunday); and five days (Monday-Friday). May 1-October 15.

COSTS Three-day school $435 commuter; five-day school $935 commuter.

EAGLE CREEK RESORT

FINDLAY, ILLINOIS

While Findlay, Illinois, is slightly off the beaten path as far as top-grade resort experiences go, this course is magnificent! It was once voted "Best New Resort Course" by GOLF Digest. This is an excellent commuter option, convenient to several major Midwestern cities. The resort has 128 standard rooms and 10 suites, most overlooking the natural surroundings of Eagle Creek State Park or Lake Shelbyville. Boating is a popular resort activity.

PROGRAMS Three days (Monday-Wednesday or Friday-Sunday) and five days (Monday-Friday). May 1–October 31

COSTS Three-day school $650 single, $525 double, $135 nonparticipating spouse, $425 commuter; five-day school $1075 single, $875 double, $210 nonparticipating spouse, $690 commuter.

MAXIM HOTEL AND SAHARA COUNTRY CLUB

LAS VEGAS, NEVADA

Ah, Vegas. The Maxim Hotel offers the standard Las Vegas fare—its own casino, restaurants, and award-winning entertainment. Vegas is home to a handful of really strong courses, and the Sahara Country Club is one of them . . . not quite the Desert Inn, but good enough to have been a former host of the Tournament of Champions when that event was a permanent spring event in Las Vegas. Las Vegas is also home to the Desert Inn Country Club and Shadow Creek, the new course from Tom Fazio that's been both highly praised and is practically impossible to get on.

In addition to golf and the Strip, Las Vegas is convenient to the Lake Mead National Recreation Area and, somewhat further away, the Grand Canyon. The school is year-round, but stay away in summer. They say it is a dry heat, but 110 degrees is just too hot for golf.

PROGRAMS Three days (Monday-Wednesday or Friday-Sunday) and five days (Monday-Friday). Year-round.

COSTS Three-day school $595 single, $525 double, $125 nonparticipating spouse, $425 commuter; five-day school $975 single, $875 double, $165 nonparticipating spouse, $695 commuter.

GREEN VALLEY DRIVING RANGE

LAS VEGAS, NEVADA

The Maxim Hotel program is apparently hot—because America's Favorite has added a new Las Vegas option this year for commuters. These are fairly humble surroundings—it is really just a driving range—but the lack of a resort golf course makes the staff all the more concentrated on instruction and game improvement. Master Teaching Professional Paul Dionne heads the local operations and has invested in a state-of-the-art facility. It is a year-round school, but try to avoid the summers if you can.

PROGRAMS Three days (Monday-Wednesday or Friday-Sunday) and five days (Monday-Friday). Year-round.

COSTS Three-day school $395 commuter; five-day school $655 commuter.

PENN NATIONAL GOLF CLUB & INN
GETTYSBURG, PENNSYLVANIA

Well, this location answers the question of what else there is to do in Gettysburg besides seeing the battlefield and President Eisenhower's home. Penn National is ranked among the state's top ten courses, high praise considering the proliferation of classic courses in Pennsylvania. This is another America's Favorite school—with the accommodations right on the golf course—a major plus. Gettysburg is convenient to Washington, Baltimore, Harrisburg, and of course Philadelphia.

PROGRAM Three days (Monday-Wednesday or Friday-Sunday) and five days (Monday-Friday). May 1-October 15.

COSTS Three-day school $690 single, $585 double, $225 nonparticipating spouse, $460 commuter; five-day school $1150 single, $975 double, $375 nonparticipating spouse, $750 commuter.

DAYS INN AND THE GOLF PROFESSIONALS CLUB
BEAUFORT, SOUTH CAROLINA

Beaufort is virtually unknown for golf, but there are many similarities to neighboring Hilton Head Island, so golfers shouldn't be too surprised by the thirty-six holes of splendid marshside golf here. Beaufort compares favorably to Hilton Head in traffic and authentic history (prior to the Civil War Beaufort was the wealthiest town in America, and many buildings survive from the period). Beaufort has become a favorite haunt of Hollywood filmmakers, who have shot *The Big Chill*, *The Prince of Tides*, and *Forrest Gump* here, among many other notable films.

PROGRAMS Three days (Monday-Wednesday or Friday-Sunday) and five days (Monday-Friday). October 15–May 31.

COSTS Three-day school $655 single, $575 double, $115 nonparticipating spouse, $465 commuter; five-day school $1095 single, $955 double, $170 nonparticipating spouse, $750 commuter.

QUALITY ATLANTIK BEACH GOLF RESORT AND THE LUCAYA GOLF & COUNTRY CLUB
FREEPORT, BAHAMAS

This is one of the more notable Caribbean resorts and one of the best locations for America's Favorite schools.

PROGRAMS Three days (Monday-Wednesday or Friday-Sunday) and five days (Monday-Friday). October 15–May 31.
COSTS Three-day school $660 single, $555 double, $165 nonparticipating spouse, $425 commuter; five-day school $1100 single, $925 double, $260 nonparticipating spouse, $695 commuter.

HOLIDAY INN AND ANNANDALE GOLF AND COUNTRY CLUB

TORONTO, ONTARIO, CANADA

PROGRAM Three-day (Monday-Wednesday or Friday-Sunday). May 1–October 15.
COSTS Three-day school $625 single, $535 double, $110 nonparticipating spouse, $485 commuter.

■ CONTACT ■

America's Favorite Golf Schools
P.O. Box 3325
Fort Pierce, FL 34948
800-365-6640
In Florida 407-464-3706

ARNOLD PALMER GOLF ACADEMY

ORLANDO, FLORIDA; TARPON SPRINGS, FLORIDA

PROGRAMS Three- and five-day Academies, Alumni Progress, Academy for Young Golfers, Corporate Packages, Individual Lessons, Mastering Fundamentals, and Annual Lesson Plan.

ABOUT THE PROGRAMS Three- and five-day Academies: The Palmer philosophy is to work with the individual's skills rather than forcing a new technique, and to stress fundamentals, the scoring zone, practicing like a pro, course strategy, and attitude over complex mechanics. Academies are available at three ability levels—beginners (twenty handicap and above), intermediates (ten-nineteen handicap), and advanced (nine handicap and below). Special programs are also available for executive men and women, seniors, parents and children, and disabled golfers. All academies include daily instruction from 9 a.m.-5 p.m., drills, exercises, video analysis, the Arnold Palmer golf instruction book and tape, daily playing lessons, gifts, and awards. All prices include accommodations, cocktail party and farewell dinner, club cleaning and storage, unlimited use of resort facilities, and a special rate for extended resort vacation packages. Please note that Arnold Palmer does not personally instruct at or attend his academies. He develops the programs and techniques and selects his instructors. Arnold does give frequent clinics and exhibitions to coincide with grand openings and anniversaries at Arnold Palmer-designed golf courses. To see Palmer at work personally, follow his playing schedule (selected Senior events, the Senior Skins, and The Masters) and look for announcements by Palmer courses in the area for a Monday or Tuesday clinic. He gives a good clinic and is worth seeing, especially for his analysis of the golf grip.

APGA also maintains an Alumni Progress Program. Alumni submit a videotape thirty days after leaving the school, and the instructor prepares a free Progress Analysis Report with a detailed practice plan and suggestion list for continued improvement.

The Saddlebrook Academy for Young Golfers: Students in grades 9–12 combine a full-time accredited college-prep education program with instruction from APGA. Each student receives 5 hours of classroom study and 4 1/2 hours of golf and fitness practice daily. On-premises housing matches 5 students with a qualified live-in house parent. They are comfortable lodgings, and there is a full meal plan seven days a week. The Saddlebrook Academy for Young Golfers is available at Saddlebrook Resort only under the direction of Greg Riehle.

COSTS Individual lesson (1 hour includes video analysis and tape) $75, individual playing lessons (includes Charger nine-holes) $100, one-half day academy session (per student, includes 4 hours of instruction, 5:1 student/teacher ratio, video analysis, and Arnold Palmer Instructional book and tape) $200, mastering the fundamentals seminar (1 1/2 hours of instruction, shot-making exhibition, and concentration on basic fundamentals) $30 per person with minimum of 5 students, annual lesson plan (24 hours of one-on-one instruction, club fitting session, Academy notebook, and personalized bagtag) $1200.

CORPORATE PACKAGES Package A (twenty-four half-day Academy Sessions, 20 percent discount on Arnold Palmer Golf Academy merchandise, 20 percent discount on ProGroup Golf Equipment) $3600, Package B (twelve half-day Academy Sessions, 10 percent discount on Arnold Palmer Golf Academy merchandise) $1920, Package C (eight half-day Academy Sessions, 10 percent discount on Arnold Palmer Golf Academy merchandise) $1360.

THREE AND FIVE-DAY SCHOOLS Three-day school (three nights) single occupancy $1150, commuter $750; five-day school (five-night) single occupancy $1850, commuter $1250.

JUNIOR PROGRAM Five-day school (commuter) $500 (includes daily instruction from 9 a.m. –12 p.m., lunch, daily competition, video analysis, gifts, and awards). APGA also operates the only state high school accredited

boarding school for young golfers. For current rates and dates call 813-973-1111.

STUDENT/TEACHER RATIO 5:1.

HEAD INSTRUCTOR The head instructor is Brad Brewer. Brad heads the APGA program from the world headquarters at Saddlebrook Resort. Brewer has competed in over 100 international tour events and has taught courses, written golf articles, and coordinated golf programs around the world. He currently instructs PGA TOUR pros Steve Lowery, Tom Garner, Todd Barringer, and Arnold Palmer, as well as top-ranked women's amateur Sara Ingram. Dick Tiddy, a former college teammate of Palmer's who heads instruction at the Bay Hill site, was voted North Florida PGA Professional of the Year in 1993.

■ ABOUT THE LOCATIONS ■

BAY HILL CLUB & LODGE

ORLANDO, FLORIDA

Site of the Nestle Invitational Golf Tournament, the breathtaking Bay Hill course sweeps across 270 acres along the shores of the Butler chain of lakes. The twenty-seven-hole course is one of the favorites on the PGA TOUR and one of the toughest; 7 U.S. Open champions (Julius Boros, Hale Irwin, Tom Kite, Arnold Palmer, Payne Stewart, Lee Trevino, and Fuzzy Zoeller) as well as Paul Azinger, Fred Couples, Nick Faldo, and Ben Crenshaw are among the winners at Bay Hill since the TOUR arrived in 1967. The club includes a seventy-room lodge, which looks out onto the course—with casual dining for breakfast and lunch and continental cuisine for dinner. The Lodge includes a cocktail lounge, tennis courts, waterskiing, fishing, and swimming and is 15 minutes from Walt Disney World, Sea World, and Universal

Studios Orlando. The Clubhouse accommodates meetings for groups of up to 100.

SADDLEBROOK RESORT
TARPON SPRINGS, FLORIDA

Saddlebrook is an AAA Four-Diamond resort near Tampa that became famed as the home to the APGA, the Harry Hopman International Tennis Center . . . and a young tennis prodigy named Jennifer Capriati. Two Arnold Palmer-designed courses, superb restaurants, tennis, a 500,000-gallon super pool, and lake (stocked with bass) are all situated within a stroll from the central walking village. The 480-acre resort is a first-class, friendly establishment that places emphasis on active resort vacations and on learning experiences such as the APGA, the Tennis Center, and the Saddlebrook Sport Science Center, which teaches mental and physical toughness techniques to Jim Courier, Pete Sampras, Dan Jansen, and numerous resort guests.

The golf is not as strong at Saddlebrook as at Bay Hill, but it is still a notable golf facility in its own right. Multiple pin placements on the large greens put the emphasis on club selection and accuracy on approaches, and there is plenty of water to enforce discipline from tee to green.

■ CONTACT ■

Arnold Palmer Golf Academy
9000 Bay Hill Boulevard
Orlando, FL 32819-4899
800-523-5999
In Florida 407-876-2429

AVIARA GOLF ACADEMY
CARLSBAD, CALIFORNIA;
CARMEL VALLEY, CALIFORNIA

PROGRAMS Half-day schools twice a month, year-round (adults in the mornings, juniors in the afternoons). Weekend schools twice a month except November (once). Three-day schools weekly except December (twice). Four-day schools: three in January, two schools per month February-September, one in October, and one in December. Short game school: three-day schools in February, April, and July.

ABOUT THE PROGRAMS The Aviara Golf Academy philosophy is to work with the golfer's current swing and to give practical instruction for correcting both minor and major swing flaws as well as tips for stance, alignment, and execution in the short game. Playing lessons are videotaped and analyzed in the Learning Center to pinpoint specific areas for additional work in practice sessions. While the instructors view tapes and make notes, students are free to play extra holes at Aviara, a finalist for "Resort Course of the Year" honors from both GOLF Digest and GOLF magazine when it opened in 1991.

The practice range was designed by Arnold Palmer and Ed Seay to incorporate fairway-quality tee areas, pitching greens, practice bunkers, and specifically designed slopes for practice in uphill, downhill, and sidehill lies.

The Half-Day School begins with an opening clinic on the fundamentals of the golf swing followed by full-swing work moving from irons to driver and high-speed, stop-action videotape sessions with playback and analysis, including graphics, audio overlays, and side-by-side comparisons with the world's best players.

The Junior Clinics include swing work, video analysis, side-by-side comparisons of the student's swing with the world's top players (emphasized here especially because of a junior golfer's ability to mimic physical motion), teaching how to construct a productive practice session, plus drills on putting, chipping, pitching, and sand play.

The Weekend Schools come in two styles: 1 1/2 days or two full days (you may elect to use the second afternoon for play on the Aviara course). Instruction begins with a clinic on the fundamentals of the golf swing, video analysis of past and current tour players' swings, demonstration of alignment and preshot routine, plus videotaping and analysis of each student's swing. Following lunch, students take on full-swing work plus a session with pitch shots, involving videotaping and working on pitch shot corrections. The second morning begins with full-swing work and video analysis before a session about putting and chipping before lunch. The afternoon session involves special instruction in handling poor lies, a final long game, and a short game wrap-up session with the instructor, identifying specifics for continued work at home.

The full three- and four-day schools divide into two types—beginners and experienced players. The three-day beginners' school covers the fundamentals of putting, chipping, and pitching on the first day and rules, full swing, exercises, and instruction on creating a practice plan on the second day, followed by a third day with on-course instruction on rules and etiquette, video analysis of the full swing, bunker-play, and a review.

The regular four-day school begins on the first day with a clinic on the fundamentals of the golf swing, video analysis of past and current tour players' swings, and videotaping

and analysis of each student's swing. Following lunch, full-swing work, instruction, and video analysis of pitch shots are undertaken. The second day begins with instruction on the mental aspects of the game, including visualization of the shot, followed by full-swing work and putting and chipping sessions until lunch. After lunch there is a clinic about handling poor lies, full swing, and short game instruction. The third morning includes a playing lesson on the Aviara course, with a playing lesson review, full- swing work, bunker play, pitching instruction, a personal equipment evaluation, and a closing session for the three-day school attendees. The optional fourth day is spent with a morning playing lesson and an afternoon playing lesson review, question and answer session on trouble shots, and individual practice in areas of the game that require extra work.

All three- and four-day programs include a take-home video, daily lunch in the Argyle Restaurant, unlimited range balls, private locker, cart rental, bag tag and notebook, the Aviara Golf Academy instruction manual, videotape, and optional reduced-fee golf course play after school hours.

COSTS Half-day schools (alumni) $125; weekend school 1 1/2 days $595, 1 1/2 days plus eighteen holes $695; two full days $695, three-day school $995; four-day school $1295.

STUDENT/TEACHER RATIO 5:1.

HEAD INSTRUCTOR The head instructor is Kip Puterbaugh. Kip has been named by *GOLF* magazine as one of the top fifty teaching pros in the country on the strength of his programs at Aviara. Puterbaugh is a noted student of the game; he is apt to quote swing gurus from an earlier era (Harvey Penick, Norm von Nida, George Knudsen) in the course of his sessions. Puterbaugh has authored many articles on golf instruction, including a recent cover story for *GOLF Digest*. He is author of *The Body Swing*, published in Japan and Korea, and has created a three-part video series with NBC commentator Charlie Jones. Among his students are PGA TOUR players Dennis Paulson and Scott Simpson. All instructors are PGA members.

ACCOMMODATIONS Not included in the package prices. Accommodations are available at extra cost at La Costa Resort & Spa ($195 per room), L'Auberge-Del Mar Resort and Spa ($119 per room), the Inn at Rancho Santa Fe ($95 per room), the Radisson Inn ($65 per room), or the Olympic Resort ($61 per room). The Aviara Golf Academy staff will handle all reservations.

■ ABOUT THE LOCATION ■

AVIARA GOLF CLUB
CARLSBAD, CALIFORNIA

Aviara was rated as one of the country's best new resort courses at its opening in 1991. It capitalizes on its setting on rolling land overlooking Batiquitos Lagoon, home to 133 species of wildlife, to create a particularly dramatic and natural golf setting. Besides being one of the best courses to emerge from the design shop of Arnold Palmer and Ed Seay, it is also blessed with sheer beauty. Photos of Aviara have graced many a magazine cover. Aside from wildlife and naturally rolling land, Palmer and Seay incorporated much of the rock they found while clearing the course into extensive rockwork bordering the on-course lagoons and streams.

One of the most striking aspects of Aviara is the whopping differential in the yardages for each of the four sets of tees. The forward tees play to just 5,007 yards, manageable for even

the shortest hitter, while the tips crest at a shade over 7,000 yards. The hole that gets the most attention is the finishing hole, which ranges from 309 to 443 yards. Note, a variation of 43 percent! It is quite a design feat to create a course with such variation yet with hazards close to, but not smack in the middle of, each of the landing areas. The task was carried off with style here. The hole is played as a dogleg right to a green surrounded by Batiquitos Lagoon with a waterfall rushing nearby. Arnold Palmer was once asked why he liked to design a lot of moving streams and rivers near his greens. The sound of rushing water, he explained, helps golfers concentrate while putting. Nice touch at the close.

QUAIL LODGE & GOLF CLUB
CARMEL VALLEY, CALIFORNIA

Twice a year the Aviara Golf Academy decamps to the only golf resort in the Monterey area with a Mobil Five-Star rating—and it is not Pebble. It is Quail Lodge. That's not to say that the Lodge has a better golf course. But it is a pretty good experience all the same from soup to nuts. The course was designed by Robert Muir Graves, a regional architect best known for Port Ludlow up in Washington State. The course has hosted the 1975 U.S. Senior Open and the 1991 Spalding Invitational Pro-Am, which doesn't quite match the AT&T for star power, but it's a pretty well regarded tournament all the same. The course is short—only 6,515 yards from the tips and 6,141 from the regular tees. But it is a good test and has absolutely knockout mountain views. Ten lakes are on the property; most of them work their way into the course. The course conditioning, by the way, is one area where Quail Lodge beats Pebble Beach hands down.

The Lodge itself is obviously one of the very best. Its success is due to an unusual dedication to personal service and the wide range of activities. A chilled bottle of champagne awaits your arrival. Fresh coffee and newspapers arrive each morning. Fresh flowers appear in each suite daily. The Covey restaurant is rated right up there with perhaps five or six restaurants on the Pacific Coast for service and cuisine.

One other thing—the guy who looks like Clint Eastwood on the 600-acre ranch across the street is the high plains drifter himself—not a bad recommendation for the quality of the area!

■ CONTACT ■

Aviara Golf Academy
7447 Batiquitos Drive
Carlsbad, CA 92009
800-433-7468
In California 619-438-4539

BEN SUTTON GOLF SCHOOLS
SUN CITY CENTER, FLORIDA

PROGRAMS Three-day school; five-day school; eight-day school.

ABOUT THE PROGRAMS Ben Sutton Golf Schools is the "granddaddy of them all." It pioneered the concept of the national golf school back in 1968. Experience has its advantages, as shown when a recent survey revealed that 98 percent of former Sutton students said their game improved as a result of Sutton instruc-

tion, 99 percent said it was worth their investment of time and money, 97 percent said they would recommend Sutton to their friends, and 93 percent said that they would return for more instruction.

The 42-acre Ben Sutton learning facility is the largest I'm aware of except for the World Woods facility in western Florida (which does not have a golf school). The facility has more than the usual driving range, practice bunkers, and chipping and putting greens. It has entire holes constructed with real situations ripe for instruction—the uneven lies, guarded greens, pesky bunkers, impenetrable rough, sprawling forced carries over water, and an assortment of trees to learn to hit through, over, or around with confidence.

Ben Sutton primarily shies away from quick fixes and emphasizes repetition and building muscle memory under real course conditions. The full-swing instruction puts a premium on development of a consistent preshot routine for proper set-up and alignment, shoulder turn, weight shift, and wrist cock for maximum distance and control. Short-game instruction emphasizes practice not only in familiar putting, chipping, and sand situations but also on the pitching game from the odd distances, 73, 98, or 129 yards—typical of game conditions.

The three-day school includes 16 hours of instruction; high-speed, stop-action video analysis and instant replay; graph-check sequence photographs of the student's swing; instructional films; free golf after classes; club cleaning and storage; and green fees and cart for nonschool spouse. The five-day school is much the same except that instruction bumps up to 26 hours, while the eight-day school (the longest duration for any golf school in the country) features 31 hours of instruction plus two tournaments, including a pro-am with instructors. Several "Beat-the-Pro" putting and chipping clinics help to break up the routine throughout the week.

COSTS Accommodations are included in the package price. Three-day school, January–May (double occupancy) $635, (single occupancy) $715, (double occupancy with one nonparticipating resort guest) $960, (commuter) $475.

Three-day school, June–December (double occupancy) $625, (single occupancy) $685, (double occupancy with one nonparticipating resort guest) $875, (commuter) $450.

Five-day school, January–May (double occupancy) $1075, (single occupancy) $1195, (double occupancy with one nonparticipating resort guest) $1630, (commuter) $750.

Five-day school, June–December (double occupancy) $1035, (single occupancy) $1115, (double occupancy with one nonparticipating resort guest) $1520, (commuter) $685.

Eight-day school, January–May (double occupancy) $1695, (single occupancy) $1895, (double occupancy with one nonparticipating resort guest) $2550, (commuter) $1200.

Eight-day school, June–December (double occupancy) $1475, (single occupancy) $1635, (double occupancy with one nonparticipating resort guest) $2225, (commuter) $1000.

STUDENT/TEACHER RATIO 7:1.

HEAD INSTRUCTOR The head instructor is Dick Sutton. All instructors are PGA or LPGA professionals. Ben Sutton's philosophy (1900-1991) remains the driving force behind the Ben Sutton golf schools. His primary innovation was to take golf instruction off the driving range and onto the golf course, noting that range-based instruction often failed to translate into real scoring improvements in actual playing conditions. Sutton was also the first to commit to a practice facility larger than the usual assortment of range, practice greens, and practice bunkers. Golf course architects such as Jack Nicklaus, Tom Fazio, Arnold Palmer, and Ed Seay are now intimately involved with the design and construction of practice holes and facilities as a result of Sutton's influence and success.

■ **ABOUT THE LOCATION** ■

SUN CITY CENTER COUNTRY CLUB
SUN CITY CENTER, FLORIDA

The Sun City Center Inn, 25 miles southeast of Tampa on the road to Sarasota and Naples, offers comfortable guest quarters and a restaurant with a contemporary and healthful menu. Forty courtside rooms are reserved for the Golf School. Each room features two double beds and cable TV. The Inn itself has a swimming pool and tennis as alternative recreation.

The Sun City Center Country Club is a twenty-seven-hole facility constructed with the needs of the average golfer in mind. The design is standard for western Florida. Wetlands abound and water hazards have been constructed for aesthetics and also to assemble enough earth to provide a rolling terrain on what is essentially flat land. Holes are typically set at a friendly length and offer a spirited if not overwhelming challenge. Green fees and cart come complimentary with the golf school package.

■ **CONTACT** ■

Ben Sutton Golf School
2920 Market Avenue North
Canton, OH 44714
800-225-6923 or 216-453-4350

BERTHOLY-METHOD GOLF SCHOOL

FOXFIRE VILLAGE,
NORTH CAROLINA

PROGRAMS Three-day schools, March-November, and personal private instruction.

ABOUT THE PROGRAM The irrepressible Paul Bertholy, once described as "the best [instructor] in golf history" holds court adjacent to Foxfire Golf Course in Jackson Springs, in the Pinehurst area. It is one of the most interesting programs around. The instructors sometimes outnumber the students, and students will experience the Bertholy-Method Isotonic Swing Trainer, one of the earliest swing trainers developed and still one of the best.

Bertholy is a PGA master teacher and a former instruction editor of *GOLF* magazine. He works with one full-time assistant.

The Bertholy-Method refers to the swing that Paul Bertholy "cloned" from observation of Ben Hogan during the early and mid-1940s and his efforts to teach that swing to golfers. (An interesting note: Bertholy's own swing is, in still photography, an almost perfect reproduction of the great Hogan's.) The program begins with Progressive Precise Intensified Conditioning, or sensitizing and training the muscles for the golf swing. A swing pipe developed by Bertholy is utilized to produce a sense memory of a correct swing. The program's aim is to reduce and contain the instinctive right hand cast, right arm thrust, and right shoulder roll we all naturally manifest.

Bertholy also teaches the short game and putting techniques; the distinctive putting jab stroke used most famously by Arnold Palmer is the type taught here. Also, command and control of emotion on the course is addressed during the sessions.

Bertholy gives personal private instruction only during December and January. Note: thirty-handicappers and higher and left-handers must take personal private instruction. They love beginners and left-handers, explains Bertholy, but the other students become confused. In short, as the school's name implies, Bertholy teaches a system of golf, not modest improvement.

COSTS Three-day school Monday-Wednesday, $950 for regular school; $1500 for personal private instruction.

STUDENT/TEACHER RATIO 1:2 to 4:1.

HEAD INSTRUCTOR The head instructor is Paul Bertholy. Bob Toski, who would know, calls Bertholy "unquestionably the finest teacher of the golf swing that I have encountered." Leo Fraser, the legendary PGA President, agrees. So did *MONEY* magazine in a two-year study.

Bertholy is now 80 years of age, but he remains an active teacher and a force in the game. Since he has taught legions of PGA teaching professionals and over 100,000 students, his system may well have the most adherents among teaching professionals of any in the country, save perhaps Jimmy Ballard's.

■ ABOUT THE LOCATION ■

Foxfire is in the Pinehurst area, which means that there are many options for accommodations and great golf. Note that Bertholy-Method is a commuter school only. There are twenty-eight hotels and motels in the Pinehurst area, and a full list can be obtained by calling the

Pinehurst Area Convention and Visitors Bureau at 800-346-5362. Aside from Pine Needles, the Pinehurst Resort, and Mid-Pines, which are described in this book, the Pine Crest Inn at 910-296-6121 and the Holly Inn at 800-533-0041 are conveniently located in the Village of Pinehurst. Foxfire itself offers golf course villas with fully equipped kitchens, as well as a restaurant and grill room, night putting greens, tennis, fishing, a swimming pool, and a lounge. Foxfire has two courses designed by Gene Hamm, East and West. Both are challenging courses; East was selected as one of the top ten public courses in the Pinehurst area. But a visit to Pinehurst wouldn't be considered complete without a visit to the beautiful walking village of Pinehurst, designed by Frederick Law Olmstead (of Central Park fame), or a round on one of the famed Pinehurst area courses. Pinehurst No. 2 and No. 7, Pine Needles, The Legacy, The Pit, and Talamore are the most highly recommended. Also consider a stop for dinner or cocktails at the Pine Crest Inn, where many of golf's legendary players and scribes hang out. If you think you've seen Bob Drum or Dick Taylor at a nearby table . . . well, you probably have.

■ CONTACT ■

Edgewood Drive I
Foxfire Village, NC 27281
910-281-3093

BILL SKELLEY SCHOOL OF GOLF

GOLD CANYON, ARIZONA;
COPPER MOUNTAIN,
COLORADO; MIAMI LAKES,
FLORIDA; NICEVILLE,
FLORIDA; FAIRFIELD GLADE,
TENNESSEE

PROGRAMS Three- and five-day schools at Gold Canyon Ranch, Arizona, January–March; three- and five-day schools at Copper Mountain Resort, Colorado, June–September; three-, four- and five-day schools at Miami Lakes, Florida; November–May; three- and five-day schools at Bluewater Bay Resort (Niceville), Florida, March–July, September–November; three- and five-day schools at Fairfield Glade, Tennessee, June–September.

ABOUT THE PROGRAMS The Bill Skelley method is a fairly regimented program taught by staff professionals who have gone through a two-year training program themselves. It is a program that has its focus on the mechanics of the swing rather than mental aspects of the game. High-speed, stop-action video analysis is utilized in conjunction with a Bill Skelley instruction handbook and swing training aids to communicate a correct swing sequence for the upper body, leg, and arm muscles. A special bonus for corporate clients: TOUR veteran Bruce Fleischer is associated with the school and makes appearances at corporate schools and clinics by special arrangement.

The three-day program includes 15 hours of on-course and range-based instruction, green fees and cart, two breakfasts and lunches, a welcome reception, and a farewell dinner. The four-day program adds an additional breakfast, lunch, and 5 hours of instruction, including on-course work. The five-day program adds an additional breakfast and lunch, a second dinner and reception, and 5 hours of instruction.

COSTS From $1500.

STUDENT/TEACHER RATIO 4:1.

HEAD INSTRUCTOR The head instructor is Bill Skelley. All instructors are PGA professionals.

■ ABOUT THE LOCATIONS ■

GOLD CANYON RANCH

GOLD CANYON, ARIZONA

Hardin and Nash combined with Ken Kavanaugh to design the 6,398-yard Gold Canyon Ranch course, which plays to a very pleasant 4,876 yards from the forward tees, and thus is heartily recommended for women golfers. It's a lush, well-maintained course set against Superstition Mountain. The course is of the modern desert type, so precision is very much the key.

The resort itself is apparently located in the vicinity of the Lost Dutchman Mine, so bring a metal detector! But if something more relaxing is called for, there's tennis, biking, and a series of quite intimate and attractive casitas, a number of which have a private spa. Not a bad place for a couple's golf school retreat.

COPPER MOUNTAIN RESORT/COPPER CREEK GOLF CLUB

COPPER MOUNTAIN, COLORADO

Best known as a ski resort, an hour and a half out of Denver and through the Eisenhower Tunnel, the AAA Four-Diamond rated Copper Mountain resort is also home to a 6,094-yard, Pete and Perry Dye-designed course. It is a short course and presented a tricky design problem for the Dyes, but Pete Dye is the leading practitioner of the short-par-four among American course architects. One or two of his better examples are at the twisting Copper Mountain course. In addition, it is the highest course in North America at slightly over 9,000 feet. Balls will go at least 10 percent further, and the greens will be quite dry and fast.

The resort as a whole is home to tennis, swimming, biking, hiking, rafting, and horseback riding, with nice rooms and spectacular views of the Rockies throughout. Vail is about 20 minutes away by car.

DON SHULA'S HOTEL AND GOLF CLUB

MIAMI LAKES, FLORIDA

Don Shula's Hotel is about what you would expect—loaded with memorabilia and quite decent golf. It is not five-star, but there is a choice between the 200-room hotel and the 100-room Golf Club. Additional activities include tennis, racquetball, swimming, dining, and a fitness center. The Miami climate was rated third-best in the nation by Retirement Places Rated.

The 7,055-yard course is water, water everywhere on the finishing stretch and can be a ball-muncher. But it is fairly dry and pleasant on the front.

BLUEWATER BAY RESORT
NICEVILLE, FLORIDA

One of the best resorts on the northwest coast of Florida, Bluewater Bay offers a special bonus for golf owing to the twenty-seven holes designed by Tom Fazio and Jerry Pate with Bob Cupp. The resort is roughly halfway between Pensacola and Panama City on Choctawhatchee Bay, a growing resort area that also includes the resort town of Destin. Fazio was here in a quiet stretch in his career and did quite a lot with low-lying ground, putting plenty of movement into the land with well thought out mounding and superior bunkering. Plenty of other resort activities are available, including a deepwater marina, swimming, tennis, a private beach, racquetball courts, and a health and fitness center. The accommodations are in studio-sized to three-bedroom villas, which are in sparkling condition.

FAIRFIELD GLADE
FAIRFIELD GLADE, TENNESSEE

One hour from Knoxville in the Cumberland Plateau area of central Tennessee is Fairfield Glade, a ninety-seven-room resort hotel and condominium complex offering two championship-length golf courses (Heatherhurst and Stonehenge), a marina, swimming, equestrian and tennis centers, and 12,000 acres of wilderness for hiking. Fishing and boating are a main activity here. Morning often brings a dense fog and a mysterious aura to the courses. Near the resort is the Catoosa Wildlife Reserve.

■ CONTACT ■

Bill Skelley School of Golf
Main Street
Miami Lakes, FL 33014
305-828-9740

CHUCK HOGAN GOLF SCHOOLS
BIRMINGHAM, ALABAMA; SEDONA, ARIZONA; TEMPE, ARIZONA; DALLAS, TEXAS; BRAINERD, MINNESOTA; WAIKOLOA, HAWAII

PROGRAMS Experts Only, Golfers' School, Sedona Experience, Pebble Beach Workshop, Hawaii Experience, Players' School.

ABOUT THE PROGRAMS This is the school where Chuck Hogan used to hang his hat. Although Chuck has now returned to Oregon to teach, the Chuck Hogan Schools retain his unique approach to instruction, placing the emphasis on mental conditioning as much as physical mechanics. Peter Jacobsen recalled a session with Hogan in which the coach pretended to toss five golf balls on the putting surface, telling Jacobsen, "Here, putt these first for me," and only accepted Jacobsen as a student after Jake reported making every one of the five imaginary putts.

Chuck Hogan schools offer three distinct curriculums. The Expert Schools are designed for the low handicap golfer who is primarily interested in exploring the mental side of the game. The Golfers' Schools provide a well-rounded approach to the game encompassing mental, mechanical, physical fitness, and club fitting instruction. In the Players' School, students are paired with an instructor who actually takes the group on the course for "playing" instruction.

COSTS Experts Only April 7-10 Sedona, Arizona $1495; April 14-17 Dallas, Texas $1495; June 23-26 Birmingham, Alabama $1495; October 20-23 Birmingham, Alabama $1495; November 17-20 Tempe, Arizona $1495; December 1-4 Birmingham, Alabama $1495; December 8-11 Location TBA $1595. Golfers' School April 7-10 Sedona, Arizona $895; May 26-29 Birmingham, Alabama $695; June 23-26 Birmingham, Alabama $795; July 21-24 Braynard, Minnesota $1295; August 11-14 Location TBA $895; August 18-21 Location TBA $895; September 8-11 Birmingham, Alabama $795; October 20-23 Birmingham, Alabama $795; November 17-20 Tempe, Arizona $795; December 1-4 Birmingham, Alabama $795; December 8-11 Location TBA $795. Sedona Experience (all located in Sedona, Arizona) April 21-25 $1195; April 28-May 2 $1195; May 5-9 $1695; October 6-10 $995. Pebble Beach Workshop August 21–September 4 Pebble Beach, California $2995 (double occupancy). Hawaii Experience November 5–13 Waikoloa, Hawaii $2095 (double occupancy). Players School September 22–25 Location TBA $995.

STUDENT/TEACHER RATIO 3:1.

HEAD INSTRUCTOR Chuck Hogan, president of Sports Enhancements Associates, has taught more than 60 PGA and LPGA tour players, including Johnny Miller, Peter Jacobsen, and Colleen Walker. He has produced videos such as "Nice Shot" and "Aim to Win." He has written five books, is a contributing writer for more than ten magazines (including *GOLF* magazine and *Golf For Women*), and has worked with professional athletes in baseball, tennis,

gymnastics, and track and field. Hogan is a consultant to the golf teams at the University of Arizona, Arizona State, and UCLA, among others. The instructor is Billy McDonald.

■ ABOUT THE LOCATIONS ■

Chuck Hogan Golf Schools are commuter-only schools. Nonresidents must make their own arrangements for accommodations.

TOUR GOLF'S PRACTICE TEE
BIRMINGHAM, ALABAMA

SEDONA GOLF RESORT
SEDONA, ARIZONA

Excellent Gary Panks-designed eighteen-hole golf course, with lush green fairways spread amongst the red rocks. Subtle elevation and terrain changes are the rule here, as well as some of the prettiest scenery of any course in the United States. Certainly this is the most striking of all the desert courses. Sedona is part of a residential and resort community.

KARSTEN GOLF CLUB
TEMPE, ARIZONA

The outstanding Pete Dye course design on the Arizona State University campus is now edging onto many top-100 course rankings for the United States. Named in honor of Karsten Solheim, founder of Karsten Manufacturing and Ping clubs, the course hosted the 1992 Women's NCAA Championship. It has a tough finishing stretch, particularly the 212-yard, par-three sixteenth and the 471-yard, par-four eighteenth. Karsten is located on Rural Road, anchoring the southern end of perhaps the most memorable street for golf in America, with Camelback, Gainey Ranch and the Hyatt Regency Scottsdale, McCormick Ranch, the TPC of Scottsdale, The Registry, and Mountain Shadows, offering resort accommodations and golf par excellence.

BEAR CREEK GOLF CLUB

DALLAS, TEXAS

MADDENS RESORT

BRAINERD, MINNESOTA

KINGS COURSE, WAIKOLOA

WAIKOLOA, HAWAII

The lava-field courses of Hawaii's Kohala Coast are Hawaii's great gift to golf architecture. Waikoloa, with three such courses, is one of the best-kept secrets among Hawaiian resorts. The Kings Course, where the Hogan school is located, is the latest of the three courses, the longest, and the most memorable. Designed by Tom Weiskopf and Jay Morrish, Kings is rendered in the links style with wide fairways, sublime bunkering, and the trade winds to contend with. The 327-yard par-four fifth hole is just barely driveable in a tail wind. Two tall pincers of lava guard the green—a reminder that Weiskopf and Morrish designed not only for tradition's sake, but for exhilaration.

■ CONTACT ■

Chuck Hogan Golf Schools
4880 Valleydale Road
Birmingham, AL 35242-9981
800-345-4245
In Alabama 205-991-FORE

CRAFT-ZAVICHAS GOLF SCHOOLS

PUEBLO, COLORADO; PALM COAST, FLORIDA; BELLAIRE, MICHIGAN

PROGRAMS Sheraton Palm Coast five-day school: one in January, four in February, four in March, and three in April; women-only schools in February, March, and April; alumni-only school in March.

Pueblo West 2 1/2-day school: two in May.

Pueblo West four-day school: three in May, one in June, and one in August; women-only schools in May, June, and August;

Shanty Creek four-day women-only school: one in June and in July. Both schools are for women only.

ABOUT THE PROGRAMS A pioneer among golf schools, this school has operated continuously since 1968. The instruction concentrates on building leverage with the body for a powerful swing, maximizing the release of that energy for power, and proper rotation of the club face through the swing for a squared clubface at impact and straight shots. A special emphasis is placed on instruction for women, with women-only schools featuring female instructors. Personalized attention and care is the rule here, not the exception. Craft-Zavichas prides itself as a "non-factory-assembly golf school" and a good starting place for beginners, lefties, and women—three groups somewhat ignored by several large golf schools (which should know better).

The 2 1/2-day program includes four days and three nights accommodations, daily lunches and one dinner, 15 hours of instruction, green fees and cart for after-class play, practice facilities, unlimited range balls, club cleaning and storage, the Craft-Zavichas Instruction Manual, video analysis (two camera, strobe effect, split-screen system for simultaneous viewing from two angles), and a take-home tape. Instructors add personalized comments and optics to the student's tape for follow-up study. Bunker play and other trouble shots are covered in depth. Short- game and long-game instruction alternate every 75 minutes to keep energy at a high level throughout the day.

The four-day program expands to 20 hours of instruction and six days and five nights accommodations, plus Welcome and Farewell banquets. The five-day school includes 25 hours of instruction with seven days and six nights accommodations, plus a third dinner and two receptions.

COSTS Sheraton Palm Coast five-day school (double occupancy) $1535, (single occupancy) $1865, (double occupancy with nonparticipating resort guest) $2025, (commuter) $1205.

Pueblo West 2 1/2-day school (double occupancy) $700, (single occupancy) $765, (double occupancy with nonparticipating resort guest) $825, (commuter) $625.

Pueblo West four-day school (double occupancy) $1050, (single occupancy) $1155, (double occupancy with nonparticipating resort guest) $1275, (commuter) $925.

Shanty Creek four-day school (double occupancy) $1325, (single occupancy) $1535, (commuter) $1055.

STUDENT/TEACHER RATIO 4:1.

HEAD INSTRUCTOR The head instructor is Penny Zavichas. "We didn't just get into women's golf. We helped elevate it and encourage it." So reports owner Penny Zavichas (the niece of women's golfing pioneer and Olympic champion Babe Didrickson Zaharias). Zaharias introduced Zavichas to golf in the 1950s and since then she has amassed a pile of credentials, including a Master Professional rating from the LPGA and the LPGA Teacher of the Year Award. She has taught now since 1959—thirty-six years in the business—and has certainly found her way around a golf swing. Zavichas still makes cameo appearances at most of the LPGA and PGA Teaching Summits as one of the two or three leading golf teachers for women. She has one of the most credible endorsements in golf—from Karsten Solheim, designer of Ping golf equipment and founder of Karsten Manufacturing. All teachers are PGA or LPGA Class A professionals. Many are PGA and LPGA TOUR veterans.

ACCOMMODATIONS Included in the package price.

■ ABOUT THE LOCATIONS ■

PUEBLO WEST
....
PUEBLO, COLORADO

Pueblo isn't exactly a major metropolitan center, but the views of the Rockies stretch as far as the eye can see. There's something to be said for the absolute tranquillity that is guaranteed in southeastern Colorado. Approximately an hour south of the relative hubbub of Colorado Springs, the Craft-Zavichas school has its headquarters in Pueblo. Students stay at the Best Western Inn at Pueblo West, adjacent to the Pueblo West course where instruction is held.

The Three-Diamond facility has golf, tennis, biking, hiking, and swimming, as well as a full-service restaurant and lounge. Rooms are oversized and have private patios. Hunting, fishing, windsurfing on nearby Lake Pueblo, and, if the timing is right, the Colorado State Fair, are all available as additional activities. Pueblo West bills itself as the point where the West and Southwest meet, and, with a nod to Durango and the Tamarron Resort, that is a fairly believable claim.

SHERATON PALM COAST RESORT

PALM COAST, FLORIDA

About halfway between Jacksonville and Orlando is one of the most interesting development plans ever launched, the 100-square-mile ITT Palm Coast. Its resort anchor is the Sheraton Palm Coast Resort, home to a cornucopia of golf courses (five in all) and one of the more intelligently designed marinas on the East Coast. If you have a boat and want to sail or motor into golf school, Palm Coast and Harbour Town are your choices without a doubt.

The Sheraton is one renovation short of becoming a truly outstanding hotel. But there is no doubt about the golf, which is hard to top. There is Palm Harbor—tight and testy. There is Cypress Knoll, designed by Gary Player—picturesque, tight, and testy. There is Pine Lakes from the design shop of Arnold Palmer and Ed Seay—wet, picturesque, tight, and testy. Finally, Matanzas Woods, also from Palmer and Seay, is long, wet, picturesque, tight, and testy. Across the causeway is Hammock Dunes from Tom Fazio, which is not technically in the resort line-up. But try to find a way onto the course because it is the best of the lot and one heck of a golfing experi-

ence—a links-style course and smartly done. Hammock Dunes narrowly missed snatching a top-100 ranking from a few of the national magazines in the early 1990s.

The Sheraton also offers tennis, a full-service restaurant, biking, a beach club, swimming, and three whirlpool spas. Historic Saint Augustine is nearby as well as Marineland. Sheraton recently named the Sheraton Palm Coast resort its Resort of the Year, which if you've ever seen the Sheratons in Hawaii, takes on significant meaning.

SHANTY CREEK RESORT

BELLAIRE, MICHIGAN

Forty miles north of Traverse City in the northwest quadrant of Michigan's lower peninsula is Shanty Creek Resort, part of the tempting palette of Michigan resorts (Treetops and Grand Traverse and such courses as The Bear, Treetops, and the Donald Ross Memorial). The three courses at Shanty Creek are all well done, but most of the publicity goes to The Legend designed by Arnold Palmer and Ed Seay. This course has their customary emphasis on hefty length from the tips and subtle course strategy from all points on the course. Each of the layouts is heavily wooded with superb conditioning and bentgrass greens.

In addition to golf, the resort offers tennis, swimming, mountain bike trails, a private beach, a fitness center, racquetball, lake and stream fishing, boating, and hiking. Canoeing, skeet shooting, orchard tours, and hayrides are some of the resort activities of an earlier era that are still offered at Shanty Creek. A children's program is also available.

The 600 rooms at the resort are built with design themes that blend into the lake and woodland views. Casual to formal dining is available at several restaurants, as well as a lounge.

■ CONTACT ■

Craft-Zavichas Golf School
600 Dittmer
Pueblo, CO 81005
800-858-9633
In Colorado 719-564-4449

DAVE PELZ SHORT GAME SCHOOL

BOCA RATON, FLORIDA;
LA QUINTA, CALIFORNIA

PROGRAMS Boca Raton: regular schools, two in January, three in February, two in March, one in April, three in November, and two in December; Signature sessions, one in January, one in February, one in March, one in April, and one in October.

PGA West: regular schools, two in January, one in February, two in March, and two in April; Signature sessions, one in February, one in March, and one in April; alumni session, one in January.

ABOUT THE PROGRAMS Dave Pelz is on most short lists of the top golf instructors, as his rates reflect. This school is concentrated on the short game, where three strokes can be turned into two, and where improvement has the most direct impact on scoring. Noting that the short game accounts for 65 percent of the total shots per round, Pelz combines theory and outdoor execution sessions for wedge play, pitching, chipping, sand play, and putting. Pelz structures his teaching to players of all ability levels;

thus on occasion amateurs are learning side-by-side with PGA and LPGA TOUR pros! Pelz has a putting robot on-site, plus Wedgy the mechanical wedge robot, video analysis, laser alignment, and practice aids, all grouped into a Short Game Center designed to house the Short Game School.

There are three programs at the Pelz school. The Premier sessions are conducted by the highly skilled professional instruction team trained by Dave Pelz. The Executive sessions follow the same format as the Premier sessions but include personal instruction from Dave Pelz (or in a few cases PGA TOUR professional Tom Jenkins). In addition, there are four Alumni sessions per year which are priced at a slight discount off the Premier rate. They are restricted to graduates of the Dave Pelz Short Game School.

One of the most striking success stories for Pelz in the 1990s has been the resurgence of Peter Jacobsen's career. The crown prince of the PGA TOUR put himself under Pelz's tutelage and went on to record one of the most impressive spring campaigns ever seen on the TOUR, with over $800,000 in prize money through the end of April.

COSTS Boca Raton: Regular school, January–September: (double occupancy) $2080, (single occupancy) $2475; Signature sessions (with Dave Pelz) (double occupancy) $2580, (single occupancy) $2975.

Regular School, October-December (double occupancy) $2010, (single occupancy) $2335, (commuter) $1810; Signature Sessions (with Dave Pelz) (double occupancy) $2510, (single occupancy) $2835.

PGA West: Regular school (double occupancy) $2055, (single occupancy) $2430, (commuter) $1685; Signature Sessions (with Dave Pelz) (double occupancy) $2555, (single occupancy) $2930, (commuter) $2185; Alumni school (double occupancy) $1680, (single occupancy) $2055, (commuter) $1310.

STUDENT/TEACHER RATIO 4:1.

HEAD INSTRUCTOR The head instructor is Dave Pelz. After fourteen years as a NASA research scientist at Goddard Space Center, Dave recommitted his career to the science of golf. For the past sixteen years, he has studied the game full-time—from testing and developing equipment to manufacturing to teaching the finest players in the world. To his successful students, such as Tom Kite, D.A Weibring, Tom Sieckmann, Beth Daniel, and many others, Dave Pelz is known as "Professor Putt." His book *Putt Like the Pros* is considered the definitive book on putting in the world. Prior to 1985, Pelz worked primarily with PGA and LPGA TOUR professionals but in the past ten years has restructured his short game instruction to include small groups of amateurs. All instructors are PGA certified.

ACCOMMODATIONS Accommodations are included in the package price. Rates include room, service charges, and taxes. Beach Club and Tower rates are available on request. There is no additional charge for an additional nonparticipating guest accompanying a student enrolled at the single occupancy rate.

■ ABOUT THE LOCATIONS ■

THE BOCA RATON RESORT AND CLUB
BOCA RATON, FLORIDA

The Boca Raton Resort is one of the handful of resorts given the Mobil Five-Star rating (The Greenbrier in West Virginia is the only other eastern United States golf resort with Five Stars), and to say that guests are drowned in luxury is to understate the matter. Students at the Dave Pelz Short Game School stay at The Cloister of the Boca Raton Resort. The resort includes a Beach Club, fitness center, tennis, and two courses designed by the vastly underrated Joe Lee, who was for many years the chief design associate of Dick Wilson. He had a hand in many of Wilson's best-known designs, including Doral and Cog Hill.

PGA WEST
LA QUINTA, CALIFORNIA

It would be hard to imagine a serious golfer who has not heard of The Stadium Course at PGA West. This infamous course by Pete Dye serves as the hub of a golfing complex in La Quinta, just minutes from the famed La Quinta Hotel and within an hour's drive of over seventy courses that blanket the Palm Springs area. The Stadium Course is the one described by Tom Fazio as "the greatest triumph by an architect over a given piece of property," and it is rated in the top 100 in the world. So why all the controversy?

For starters, it is hard. As in grinding, gnashing, jitters-inducing hard. The developers, Landmark Land, wanted an uncompromising test of golf; Dye responded with a design that stretches to 7,261 yards and a 77.1 rating from the tips. But it is actually very playable from the forward tees and the regular men's box.

Secondly, it is different. It's target golf, where relentless accuracy is the only road to birdie.

The trick at the Stadium Course is to get the ball in play and to keep it there. The fact that most golfers take foolish risks explains the high rating at PGA West. The course will mercilessly discipline you for overambitious play. The eleventh hole, dubbed "Eternity" by the local wags, is 618 yards from the tips and plays off the tee to a two-tiered fairway. Every shot on this hole—as with the course—requires perfect accuracy. Blind shots, water, and miles of sand are the penalties meted out for straying from the appointed line.

There is also the easier and more forgiving Jack Nicklaus Resort course at PGA West (in addition to two private courses, the Nicklaus Private and the Palmer course), although don't expect a traditional golf experience here, either. It is also target golf, with a high emphasis on accuracy off the tee.

Accommodations at PGA West include one- to three-bedroom condominiums; premium rates are in the winter months, but they're well worth it. Also consider making a reservation around May, as the cactus will be in bloom, and there's nothing prettier than a flowering desert.

■ CONTACT ■

Dave Pelz Short Game School
1200 Lakeway Drive
Suite 21
Austin, TX 78734
800-833-7370
In Texas 512-261-6493

DAVID LEADBETTER ACADEMY OF GOLF

ORLANDO, FLORIDA; NAPLES, FLORIDA; BIDDENDEN, KENT, ENGLAND; MIJAS-COSTA, MALAGA, SPAIN

PROGRAMS Half-day sessions, one-day schools, three-day schools, two-day retreats.

ABOUT THE PROGRAMS Just about as high-priced as instruction gets, but Leadbetter is, after all, perhaps the most prominent golf guru in the world. He has had phenomenal success with players such as Nick Price, David Frost, Ernie Els, and Nick Faldo, who have been extravagant in their praise of his observations and advice. His success with some players, such as Ian Baker-Finch, has been mixed. Leadbetter is known not only as a celebrity instructor but as one of the top theoretical teachers. His swing theories focus on movement of the big muscles of the torso and taking the hands out of the action. Video swing analysis, the David Leadbetter Putting System, The Right Angle, Swing Mirror, Swing Links, and the Powerball are employed as teaching devices. Students are encouraged not only to improve their game but to come to understand it better and to become their own best teachers.

Leadbetter has, like most major teachers, a stable of staff instructors who handle the bulk of the instruction. Leadbetter himself is available at super-premium rates for those who want advice from the Guru himself.

COSTS From $125–$200 per hour; half-day sessions from $175–$250; one-day schools $550; three-day-schools (Naples only) $1375; two-day retreats from $1200–$2000; prices do not include accommodations.

STUDENT/TEACHER RATIO 2:1.

HEAD INSTRUCTOR David Leadbetter has built his reputation over the past ten years on the basis of his outstanding success as a "pro's pro," first with Nick Price, later with Nick Faldo, and today with practically everyone, it seems. Leadbetter is a native of England who played on the African mini and junior circuits years ago. He became noted among the players for his ferocious interest in swing theory and mechanics. He met Nick Price during this period. Nick remembers him as always having his head in a book. It was

Price's slump in the mid-1980s that marked Leadbetter's rise to prominence as an instructor. Price has always given great credit to Leadbetter for the improvements in his swing. Leadbetter was also behind the rebuilding of Nick Faldo's swing and was criticized for his suggestion to Faldo that he should embark on a weight-training program to build the large upper-body muscles.

Leadbetter's book *Faults and Fixes* is one of the minor classics of instruction. Since the late 1980s he has also been associated with International Management Group to expand the scope of his activities into the golf school, has had an expanded publishing schedule, and has also moved into broadcasting. Leadbetter was perhaps the first instructor to be retained as a color commentator for a major golf broadcast when he worked the 1993 World Cup at Lake Nona.

Leadbetter makes his home at Lake Nona Golf Club, and the school is headquartered there. But rapid expansion has brought his Academy to nine locations in six countries.

■ ABOUT THE LOCATIONS ■
LAKE NONA GOLF CLUB
ORLANDO, FLORIDA

Lake Nona is the World Headquarters of the David Leadbetter Golf Academy, and no more fitting location could have been selected, as a transplanted Briton such as Leadbetter fits right in at the club, which is a delightful mix of the European and American golfing lifestyles.

If pressed to identify one feature of the Tom Fazio-designed course at Lake Nona that has elevated it to a ranking among the world's top-100 courses, it would have to be the sand. He has used more sand on other courses, but

rarely has anyone sprinkled bunkers around with such intelligence and brought them so neatly into scale with the surrounding terrain. The lesson of the Old Course at St. Andrews is that a flat piece of land makes for an exhilarating round of golf if the bunkering is superior and the turf is rippled. It's a lesson Fazio took to heart, and the result is a course that is, for the money, among the five finest in the southeastern United States. The course has hosted both the Solheim Cup (1990) and The World Cup (1993) and is an exciting experience to play. Accommodation at Lake Nona is in the form of some elegant guest lodges adjoining the club house (used by the out-of-town members). They are well appointed and overlook both the course and Lake Nona itself.

QUAIL WEST GOLF AND COUNTRY CLUB
NAPLES, FLORIDA

Quail West was nominated two years ago for *GOLF Digest*'s best new private course award. Designed by Arthur Hills, the course probably lost out by a nod because it's relatively easy for the expert player. But for sheer beauty there are few that can touch it in Florida. The course is built into a wildlife preserve, and deer, alligators and otter are among the animals that can be seen around the course. The design is the traditional Floridian lowland style with elevated greens and plenty of water and wetlands areas with required carries. Hills' most simple device here was in making the larger greens multi-tiered to enforce discipline on the approach shot and experimenting with significant cross-bunkering on the longer holes. Generous fairways abound, and Hills' well-known flair for wetlands design makes this such a remarkably pretty course that it's almost a shame to put divots in.

If you have a moment, sneak into the awesome Quail West clubhouse, the focal point of the ultra-exclusive Quail West community. There's a hint of British style amidst all the Floridian splendor. Plenty of stucco and a few flamingos and it is very, very large and expensively furnished.

*For the following Leadbetter international locations, please enquire for specific rates and times, as school offerings are more limited and subject to currency exchange fluctuations.

CHART HILLS GOLF CLUB
BIDDENDEN, KENT, ENGLAND

A new club in the Southeast of England designed by Leadbetter student Nick Faldo with American architect and Anglophile Steve Smyers, the traditional, rolling course at Chart Hills will serve as Leadbetter's European headquarters. Chart Hills is not far from Maidstone and is less than an hour by car from the English coast and from London. The clubhouse has a particularly striking view of the course and of the Kentish Downs. It is a rather stirring addition to the fine roster of courses in southeastern England.

LA CALA GOLF & COUNTRY CLUB
MIJAS-COSTA, MALAGA, SPAIN

The newest addition to the Leadbetter roster is La Cala along the Mediterranean coast of Spain. The club opened in 1991 with a pair of courses by Robert Trent Jones Jr. associate Cabell Robinson. The North Course is a championship layout with a par of seventy-three and measuring 6,160 metres from the white tees. The par-seventy-one South Course is in the target-golf style and measures 5,960 metres. The practice facilities are reported to be outstanding, with a range, practice greens, and a six-hole par-three course for on-course instruction work. The club does not offer accommodation, but the school can assist. The club does offer swimming, tennis, sauna, and squash.

■ **CONTACT** ■

David Leadbetter Golf Academy
Lake Nona Golf Club
9100 Chiltern Drive
Orlando, FL 32827
407-857-8276
　　Additional Leadbetter locations:
Bad Tatzmannsdorf
Bad Tatzmannsdorf, Austria
　　Golf Club de Montpelier
Massane, France
　　Mt. Juliet
Thomastown, County Killarney, Ireland
　　Thana City Golf and Country Club
Bangkok, Thailand

DORAL GOLF LEARNING CENTER
MIAMI, FLORIDA

PROGRAMS One-day school with Jim McLean; two-day school with Jim McLean; two-day school with Master Instructors; three-day school with Jim McLean; three-day school with Master

Instructors; five-day Players' School with Jim McLean; Junior Schools; two-day Pro School; two-day Junior School; three-day Junior School; special nostalgia schools also available with New York Jets coach Bruce Coslet and former Yankee great Bobby Murcer.

ABOUT THE PROGRAMS The basic program includes full-swing instruction, video analysis, breakfast, range balls, a gift package, an instructional videotape, and workbook. The Jim McLean schools have a 2:1 student/teacher ratio and a maximum of 6 students (Jim works with two additional instructors). The Master Instructor schools feature up to 20 students and a 4:1 student to teacher ratio. Each program option includes approximately 5 hours of instruction in the Learning Center per day—but with the three- and five-day schools the program includes personalized on-course instruction (carts and green fees included).

The five-day Players' School is the most expensive format—for a good reason. This premium offering is for accomplished players only—men with handicaps of twelve or under; women with handicaps of eighteen or under. The five-day program includes 35 hours of golf instruction at The Learning Center, video analysis, and extensive on-course work. Students play eighteen holes per day for four days with Jim and Master Instructors, and there is a 3:1 student to teacher ratio and a limit of 12 students. This option is offered typically only twice a year and fills up quickly.

In addition to the regular schools, Doral offers several special schools worth a mention. There are two Junior Clinics offered at Thanksgiving (two-day) and Christmas (three-day), which includes 6 hours of instruction, video analysis, and a workbook. Yankee great Bobby Murcer and NFL coach Bruce Coslet attend one three-day school each per year, answering questions and socializing with the students. Finally, Doral offers a two-day pro-only school once a year, offering expert diagnosis and individual improvement suggestions; the program features Jim McLean, 2 Master Instructors, and a maximum of 9 students.

COSTS One-day school with Jim McLean $625; two-day school with Jim McLean $1250; two-day school with Master Instructors $500; three-day school with Jim McLean $1275; three-day school with Master Instructors $975; Junior Schools two-day Pro School $900; two-day Junior School $300; three-day Junior School $450.

STUDENT/TEACHER RATIO 2:1 to 4:1.

HEAD INSTRUCTOR The head instructor is Jim McLean. Jim McLean has been called "one of the top three teachers in the game today" by PGA TOUR veteran Peter Jacobsen. He is one of the 300 Master PGA Professionals out of 22,500 PGA members and has taught a large number of successful touring professionals and prominent amateurs over the years, including Steve Elkington, Bill Murray, Tom Kite, and Bruce Lietzke. Brad Faxon relates, "Jim has taught me more about golf than any other teacher," while 1993 United States Women's Open champion Laurie Merten says, "Jim and his staff helped me with my attitude while reinforcing the mechanics I needed to succeed on tour."

■　ABOUT THE LOCATION　■

DORAL RESORT & SPA
MIAMI, FLORIDA

Doral has five superb championship golf courses. The famous "Blue Monster" is home of the Doral-Ryder Open, a fixture on the PGA TOUR since 1962 that has been won by

United States Open champions Billy Casper, Jack Nicklaus, Lee Trevino, Hubert Green, Raymond Floyd, and Tom Kite, as well as major championship winners Ben Crenshaw, Greg Norman, Lanny Wadkins, and Tom Weiskopf. The back nine on the Blue Monster is one of the most intimidating finishes in golf if the winds are right and strong. The 437-yard, par-four eighteenth has water stretching from the tee box all the way to a green half encircled by the lake. The par-three ninth hole is also a monster, with 180 yards of carry to the green from the tips.

In addition to the five courses, Doral is also a Four-Star resort hotel and Five-Diamond spa—the only one in the United States. If you wake up in the morning in one of the 650 guest rooms and think you're in Pebble Beach, well, you can be forgiven because they're designed in a similar style. It's been awarded a Gold Medal by *GOLF* magazine as one of "America's Best Resorts." Although the resort is completely self-contained and no one need leave the premises, it is convenient to Miami's South Beach area for nightlife as well as top restaurants such as Mark's Place, Chef Allens, the original Tony Roma's, and Joe's Stone Crab on the Beach, which is simply one of the best restaurants in the country!

■ CONTACT ■

The Doral Golf Learning Center
4400 N.W. 87th Avenue
Miami, FL 33178
800-723-6725

GALVANO INTERNATIONAL GOLF ACADEMY

WISCONSIN DELLS, WISCONSIN;
GREEN LAKE, WISCONSIN;
STURGEON BAY, WISCONSIN;
FORT MYERS, FLORIDA

PROGRAMS Fort Myers: four-day schools January-March; two-day school in February. Wisconsin sites: three-day programs April-August; five-day schools for Juniors only June-August.

ABOUT THE PROGRAMS Galvano, the longest running golf school in the nation, was founded in 1941. Notable students have included Bob Hope, Johnny Carson, Carol Burnett, Morey Amsterdam, Milton Berle, Willie Mosconi, and Dwight Eisenhower. The school doesn't attract quite a high-octane crowd now that Phil Galvano Sr. is getting on in years, but it has kept up with the latest technology, adding high-speed, stop-action video analysis to its usual techniques. Mental conditioning and course strategy are strongly emphasized. The program alternates morning instruction on the range with afternoon playing lessons.

COSTS One-day commuter school $125; two-day school $389; three-day school (double occupancy) $435, (commuter) $315; private half-day analysis with Phil Galvano II $500.

HEAD INSTRUCTOR The head instructor is Phil Galvano Sr. All instructors are PGA professionals.

STUDENT/TEACHER RATIO 4:1.

■ ABOUT THE LOCATIONS ■

CHULA VISTA RESORT

WISCONSIN DELLS,
WISCONSIN

A nine-holer is all that's here, but the resort itself is an award-winning 235-room family-style resort. Don't expect too many frills, but there is a pool, tennis, live entertainment in the lounge, and a nice site above the Wisconsin River. Boat trips and numerous craft stores are area attractions worth investigating.

HEIDEL HOUSE

GREEN LAKE, WISCONSIN

One of perhaps the best ten places to stay in Wisconsin, though not quite up to Lake Geneva, Green Lake has a water-oriented charm all its own. Heidel House has 200 rooms and suites and is rather well appointed. Live entertainment is available in the lounge, as well as all the good dining, boating, and fishing activities one could require. Heidel House has access to three courses.

CHERRY HILLS LODGE

STURGEON BAY, WISCONSIN

Along the canal between Lake Michigan and Green Bay is the rather overlooked but ruggedly charming town of Sturgeon Bay. It's a tad remote, but that's the charm. Cherry Hills isn't all that big, with just thirty rooms, but there's an eighteen-hole course wrapped around the Lodge and a whole lot of service.

GATEWAY GOLF CLUB

FORT MYERS, FLORIDA

A sparkling and underrated Tom Fazio course that has one of the most unusual modern holes in the country, a blind par-three on the front nine. It is one of Fazio's flatter courses, but there are a number of interesting marsh-side holes, and it is all kept very natural and secluded from the sprawling surrounding residential community. The Gateway option is commuter only, but if you don't mind a half-hour drive, the Sanibel Harbor resort is quite a place and offers tempting opportunities to explore Sanibel and Captiva Islands—which preserve a Floridian resort aura of an earlier, quieter age. Both islands are excellent for beachcombing.

■ CONTACT ■

Galvano International Golf Academy
P.O. Box 119
Wisconsin Dells, WI 52965
800-234-6121 or 608-254-6361

GILLETTE LPGA GOLF CLINICS

PHOENIX, ARIZONA; LOS ANGELES, CALIFORNIA; SAN FRANCISCO, CALIFORNIA; WASHINGTON, D.C.; ATLANTA, GEORGIA; CHICAGO, ILLINOIS; BOSTON, MASSACHUSETTS; DETROIT, MICHIGAN; NEW YORK, NEW YORK; DALLAS, TEXAS

PROGRAMS One-day golf clinics for women, one day in each city: Phoenix in February, Los Angeles in April, Washington and Chicago in May, Boston in July, Detroit in August, New York in August, San Francisco in September, Atlanta and Dallas in October.

ABOUT THE PROGRAM When Jane Blalock was last heard from, she was doing veteran time on the LPGA TOUR following a spectacular career that included a victory in the inaugural Dinah Shore Classic. She has returned in the guise of a golf instruction impresario with this ambitious series of one-day clinics for women only, sponsored by Gillette, Chase Manhattan, the LPGA, American Airlines, Budget, and many other companies.

Who attends? A combination of women business executives, female leaders in the golf industry, and celebrated LPGA veterans. It's intended to be a bit of a zoo, with over 150 attendees per clinic, marshalled by 22 instructors into smaller groups by ability and experience. The day features 6 1/2 hours of instruction, including full-swing, putting, and chipping practice. The advanced and intermediate groups play a scramble in the morning with instructors, identifying areas of improvement for afternoon range sessions, while advanced beginners and beginners work on fundamentals on the range in the morning and apply new-found skills in an afternoon scramble session.

One would venture to say that this is a little less than a golf school and a lot more than a networking session for women golfers, particularly women executives eager to brush up their games. It's a pretty good idea and a nice combination of two goals that are important to the growing segment of women golfers. For more intensive and personal instruction, there are better programs around (even one-day workshops), but this is probably a lot more fun and you will meet a larger group of peers and pros.

COSTS $200, a continental breakfast, lunch, cocktail reception, awards, instruction, green fees, and a cart are all included in the cost.

HEAD INSTRUCTOR The head instructor is Jane Blalock. All instructors are PGA or LPGA professionals.

STUDENT/TEACHER RATIO 8:1.

■ CONTACT ■

Gillette LPGA Golf Clinics
c/o The Jane Blalock Company
Flagship Wharf
197 Eighth Street
Boston, MA 02129
800-262-7888

THE GOLF CLINIC

PEBBLE BEACH, CALIFORNIA; WAIKOLOA, HAWAII

PROGRAMS Two-, 2 1/2-, three-, 3 1/2- and five-day programs. Pebble Beach offers all programs year-round. Waikoloa offers the five-day clinics each March and November. A Juniors Program is offered.

ABOUT THE PROGRAMS Small classes and personalized, fundamental instruction are the hallmarks of the program. The methods of instruction are outlined by John Geertsen in his book *Your Turn For Success!* and roughly speaking offer a balance of basic mechanics along with a positive mental approach, which brings consistency to sound technique.

The basic three-day program is based at Poppy Hills, one of the sites of the AT&T National Pro-Am, and offers daily instruction, video analysis, videotape instruction, on-course instruction in the full swing and short game, a copy of Geertsen's book, and daily lunches. Daily rounds at the resort courses are offered, which is a decided advantage at Waikoloa, with three outstanding Hawaii courses, and a positive boon at Pebble Beach, with Poppy Hills, Spyglass Hill, and Pebble Beach rounds thrown into the package.

COSTS Please call The Golf Clinic at 800-321-9401 to obtain current cost information.

STUDENT/TEACHER RATIO 4:1.

HEAD INSTRUCTORS The head instructors are John Geertsen and Ben Alexander. All instructors are PGA professionals.

ACCOMMODATIONS Included in three- and five-day programs

■ ABOUT THE LOCATIONS ■

THE LODGE AT PEBBLE BEACH
PEBBLE BEACH, CALIFORNIA

Well, here it is. Pebble Beach is the resort everyone wants to stay at! It's not a Five-Star property, but if golf and a golfer's require-ments were the only criteria, then Pebble might have to have a sixth star.

Is there anyone who doesn't know the Pebble Beach story? Jack Nicklaus' victory in the 1972 Open to record his second step in the Grand Slam. Watson's only Open victory, in 1982? Kite's only major championship, the great blowdown of 1992. The Crosby and the now AT&T Pro-Am, which have reeled in the celebrities and great players over the years?

The course is subject to 6-hour rounds these days and is often in rough shape, and the tariff is so far beyond outrageous ($250 a pop) that the course has come in for some criticism as a bad value for the dollar, but it certainly is still one of the best five courses in the world. The awesome par-three seventeenth and par-five eighteenth get the bulk of the attention, but the tiny par-three seventh has seen its share of heroics, and the stretch from eight to ten is widely considered the finest triumvirate of par-fours in the world.

Five statements will probably suffice regard-ing Spyglass. "Spyglass makes you want to go fishing" (Jack Nicklaus). "They ought to shoot the man who designed this course" (Lee Trevino). "A 300-acre unplayable lie" (Jim Murray) "76.1 rating." (United States Golf Association). "Ranked number twenty-six in the United States" (*GOLF Digest*).

The Lodge at Pebble Beach is built around the old Del Monte Lodge, and several build-ings now house the 160-odd rooms. Pebble Beach's biggest claim to fame, aside from the courses themselves, is the Tap Room, perhaps the most famous nineteenth hole in the world, an English-style pub practically drowning in golf memorabilia. The dining is pretty darn good, too. Club XIX, pun intended, I suppose, offers a particularly satisfying French cuisine and has reaped a few awards.

ROYAL WAIKOLOAN HOTEL/WAIKOLOA BEACH CLUB

WAIKOLOA, HAWAII

If "Why play golf on the Kohala Coast?" is the question, "Waikoloa" is the answer. That's how the summary of Waikoloa begins in *The Endless Fairway*, and it still holds true today. The lava-field course of the Big Island is Hawaii's great gift to golf course architecture, and Waikoloa, with its three lava-based courses, is a logical starting place for a golfing trip through the Islands. The best action at Waikoloa is on the Tom Weiskopf and Jay Morrish–designed Kings Course, which emulates the links style through a couple of gimmicks, such as a double green at the third and the sixth, but also through some fairly sublime bunkering and intelligent routing that makes the most of the wind. And in Hawaii, there is plenty of wind.

The Royal Waikoloan Hotel is not the snazziest in the Waikoloa Resort—that honor goes to the Hyatt Regency Waikoloa, which at the time of its construction was the most expensive hotel ever constructed in the islands. The Royal Waikoloan offers 500 rooms, great hospitality, and great prices. A winning trio . . . just like the courses.

■ CONTACT ■

The Golf Clinic
P.O. Box 1129
Pebble Beach, CA 93953
800-321-9401 or 408-624-5421

GOLF DIGEST SCHOOLS

NORTH SCOTTSDALE, ARIZONA; CARMEL, CALIFORNIA; FALLBROOK, CALIFORNIA; LA QUINTA, CALIFORNIA; VAIL, COLORADO; TARPON SPRINGS, FLORIDA; BRASELTON, GEORGIA; SEA ISLAND, GEORGIA; SUN VALLEY, IDAHO; CHICAGO, ILLINOIS; BEND, OREGON; WILLIAMSBURG, VIRGINIA

PROGRAMS One-day, weekend commuter, three-day, four-day, and five-day schools available as follows:

North Scottsdale, Arizona
Mini-schools in January to February, May, October, November, and December; weekend commuter school in March; three-day schools in January, February, April, May, and October; three-day commuter (playing) in December.

Carmel, California
Three-day schools in June and September.

Fallbrook, California
Mini-schools in January, February, March, April, June, September, October, and November; three-day schools in June and November.

La Quinta, California
Mini-schools in February, March, April, and November; three-day schools in February.

Vail, Colorado
Three-day schools in July and August.

Tarpon Springs, Florida

Three-day schools in February, March, April, October, and November; three-day short-game schools in March and October; three-day low handicap school in March; three-day couples school in March; three-day playing schools in April, May, and November.

Braselton, Georgia

Mini-schools in May, June, August, September, and October.

Sea Island, Georgia

Mini-schools each month; three-day schools in February, March, April, May, August, September, October, and November; three-day couples schools in April and May; three-day ladies' school in September; four-day school in October; five-day parent and child school in July.

Sun Valley, Idaho

Mini-schools June–September; three-day commuter school in July.

Chicago, Illinois

Mini-schools May-August.

Bend, Oregon

Mini-schools June; mini-schools for couples in June and July; three-day commuter in June and August.

Williamsburg, Virginia

Three-day schools in March-May, September, and October; three-day ladies' school in April.

ABOUT THE PROGRAMS Along with John Jacobs, this is the biggest and best known of the golf schools worldwide . . . although far from the first. In 1971 Bob Toski and Dick Aultman started instruction under the *GOLF Digest* banner, with one school that year. *GOLF Digest* really hit its stride in the mid-1970s

■ Golf Digest Schools.

when future top instructors such as Jim Flick and Jack Lumpkin joined the staff. Legendary coach and two-time PGA champion Paul Runyan joined the staff in 1976. Jim McLean became associated with the schools in the 1980s, by which time annual attendance had passed 2,000 students.

So what is a *GOLF Digest* School? Well, firstly it is a school about fundamentals—posture, grip, and alignment. But more than basic fundamentals and drills, *GOLF Digest* succeeded in the golf instruction market for the same reason that IBM succeeded in the computer market: While everyone else sold gizmos and miracle cures, *GOLF Digest* sold service. As in "individual solutions for individual golfers." As in credibility and a proven, reliable training philosophy. As in listening.

As golf schools proliferate, *GOLF Digest* has lost some of the celebrity aura that surrounded the instruction staff. At times the teaching breakthroughs seem to come from other schools faster, but these schools still have the corner on name-brand recognition and the personal, student-driven style that built the empire.

Like all the major golf schools, *GOLF Digest* is heavily into videotaping golf swings for analysis. An innovative feature is that they store the images on a computer to compare on a student's return engagement—a tactic pioneered for touring pros that *GOLF Digest* has extended to the ordinary amateur golfer. Students also receive a take-home tape with voice-over analysis from their personal instructor.

The basic program includes full swing, chipping, putting, pitching, bunker instruction, mental conditioning, and course strategy. Students are tested in each of these areas, and an assessment is made for potential improvement. Each student also receives on-course instruction (except in mini- and two-day school

formats), daily lunches, gift packages, a notebook, and unlimited range balls.

Program length runs the full gamut from two half-days to five days. There are five specialty schools in addition to the basic program: low-handicap (with an emphasis on shotmaking and scoring strategies); ladies; short game; couples; and parent and child (a five-day program designed for learning and interaction between parent and child).

COSTS Two-day mini school (half-days, commuter) $500; three-day mini school (half-days, commuter) $675, (commuter—Sea Island) $725; two-day weekend (commuter) $1000; three-day (commuter) $1525; three-day commuter (plus eighteen holes of golf) $1750; three-day regular school with eighteen holes of golf (commuter) $1910, (commuter—Sea Island) $2000, (double occupancy) $2795, (double occupancy—Sea Island) $2885; three-day regular school (commuter) $1650, (commuter—Sea Island) $1750, (double occupancy) $2575, (double occupancy—Sea Island) $2685; four-day regular school Sea Island only, (commuter) $2450, (double occupancy) $3425; five-day parent/child school with rates for two golfers (commuter) $3350, (double occupancy) $4500.

STUDENT/TEACHER RATIO 3:1.

INSTRUCTORS All instructors are PGA professionals. Several are frequent contributors to *GOLF Digest* on instruction and training subjects; two (Jack Lumpkin and Scott Davenport) have been named PGA Section Teacher of the Year. *GOLF Digest* instructors have taught Dicky Pride, Robert Wrenn, Steve Lowery, Missie Berteotti, Brandel Chamblee, Howard Twitty, Davis Love III, Beth Daniel, Donna Andrews, and Billy Mayfair, in addition to many amateurs, including regional and national champions.

■ **ABOUT THE LOCATIONS** ■

TROON NORTH GOLF CLUB
NORTH SCOTTSDALE, ARIZONA

At the base of Pinnacle Peak Mountain, Troon North Golf Club features eighteen championship holes designed by Tom Weiskopf and Jay Morrish. Part of an 1,800-acre residential community, Troon North provides an excellent practice facility and atmosphere for learning. The course is just outstanding, and in 1993 earned *GOLF Digest* and *GOLF* magazine recognition as one of the top 100 courses in the country. Spectacular high desert landscape speckled with saguaros, mesquite, ocotillo, tons of boulders, and some eye-catching rock formations.

Resort Suites of Scottsdale has developed a special accommodations package for *GOLF Digest* School students. Rates vary throughout the year, but begin at about $200 per person double occupancy for a three-night stay.

PALA MESA RESORT
FALLBROOK, CALIFORNIA

A full-service destination resort, Pala Mesa Resort is located just 40 minutes north of downtown San Diego in the Temecula Valley wine country. Its well-established traditional golf course was renovated in 1984 by Ted Robinson. It is short, but generally a delight, although narrow at times. (So work on that driver!)

The Pala Mesa is the newest addition to the *GOLF Digest* line-up of resorts and offers a special package at the site with rates begin-

ning at about $320 per person double occupancy for a four-night lodging and meal package.

QUAIL LODGE & GOLF CLUB
CARMEL VALLEY, CALIFORNIA

It is the only golf resort in the Monterey area that has earned a Mobil Five-Star rating, and it is not Pebble. It is Quail Lodge. That is not to say that the Lodge has a better golf course. But it is a pretty good experience all the same from soup to nuts. The course was designed by Robert Muir Graves, a regional architect best known for Port Ludlow in Washington State. The course has hosted the 1975 U.S. Senior Open and the 1991 Spalding Invitational Pro-Am, which doesn't quite match the AT&T for star power, but it is a pretty well regarded tournament all the same. The course is short, only 6,515 yards from the tips and 6,141 from the regular tees. But it is a good test and has absolutely knockout mountain views. Ten lakes are on the property and most of them work their way into the course. The course conditioning, by the way, is one area where Quail Lodge beats Pebble Beach hands down.

The Lodge itself is obviously one of the very best. Its success has come from an unusual dedication to personal service plus a wide range of activities. A chilled bottle of champagne is waiting in the room. Fresh coffee and newspapers arrive each morning. Fresh flowers appear in each suite every day. The Covey restaurant is rated up there with perhaps five or six restaurants on the Pacific Coast for service and cuisine.

One other thing. The guy who looks like Clint Eastwood on the 600-acre ranch across the street is the high plains drifter himself. Not a bad recommendation for the quality of the area.

RANCHO LA QUINTA/GOLF CLUB LA QUINTA

LA QUINTA, CALIFORNIA

Rancho La Quinta is a new course designed by Robert Trent Jones Jr. Nestled within the La Quinta Cove at the base of the Santa Rosa Mountains, the course features lush rolling fairways enhanced by date groves and citrus orchards. The practice facility includes bunkered target greens, putting greens, and a chipping green with bunkers.

A special lodging package is available at The New Inn at Bermuda Dunes for *GOLF Digest* students. Rates begin at around $270 for a three-night stay.

SONNENALP RESORT

VAIL, COLORADO

The Sonnenalp Resort is in the heart of Vail Village, close to quaint shops and restaurants. An atmosphere of European warmth and charm pervades. The golf course is rated by *GOLF Digest* as one of the top seventy-five resort courses in the United States.

INNISBROOK RESORT

TARPON SPRINGS, FLORIDA

The Innisbrook, headquarters for the Golf Institute, offers one of the most extensive golf course conglomerations in all of Florida. With sixty-three holes, Innisbrook is topped only by the Sawgrass complex in Jacksonville, the Doral Resort in Miami, PGA National in Palm Beach, and Disney World in Orlando for sheer numbers of golf holes. Certainly Innisbrook has the most on Florida's west coast. The course that everyone knows is the famed Copperhead Course, rated in the nation's top 100, and a perennial in everyone's rankings of top resort courses. Copperhead was once rated the number one course in Florida, ahead of Seminole, the TPC, and Doral! Copperhead is home to the PGA TOUR/LPGA JC Penney Classic each November. Davis Love III, Fred Couples, Tom Kite, Beth Daniel, and Pat Bradley are among the players who have won the tournament. In addition to Copperhead, the Island Course has also been ranked in the nation's top fifty resort courses by *GOLF Digest.* The Sandpiper Course is a shorter and precision-oriented twenty-seven-hole complex.

This Hilton Resort offers spacious suite accommodations (included in the golf school package), fully-equipped kitchens, private patios, and balconies. Recreation at the resort includes not only golf, but Terry Addison's Australian Tennis Institute, a Zoo Crew children's program, swimming, fitness facilities, lake or sport fishing, bicycling, and beach shuttles. The resort is also home to shopping, six restaurants, two snack bars, and the Copperhead nightclub.

THE CHATEAU ELAN GOLF CLUB

BRASELTON, GEORGIA

The Chateau Elan, well known for its winery, is now known for its tournament-quality golf course and extensive practice facility. The course achieved some worldwide prominence in 1994 when it hosted the initial Gene Sarazen World Championship, which attracted top professionals from around the globe. Sarazen and Kathy Whitworth both worked on the design of the Sarazen course. Larry Nelson designed the other. Chateau Elan is just 40 minutes north of Atlanta. You may add accommodations at The Inn at Chateau Elan, a French-style country inn. Packages begin at around $350 for a three-night stay.

THE CLOISTER AND SEA ISLAND GOLF CLUB

SEA ISLAND, GEORGIA

Combine The Cloister, a five-star resort, and the Sea Island Golf Club, and you have one of the world's most superb golf destination resorts. Located on Georgia's beautiful coastline, the Sea Island Golf Club is set on what was once the site of an eighteenth-century cotton plantation. Along with fifty-four holes of championship golf, Sea Island is the site of the GOLF Digest Learning Center, a state-of-the-art learning and teaching facility that is GOLF Digest's pride and joy, complete with two multiple-camera video studios, video editing capabilities, covered practice stations, 300 yards of teeing area, five target greens with simulated practice fairways, chipping and putting greens with multiple bunkers, a practice fairway bunker, and uneven lie stations. Sea Island head professional Jack Lumpkin is known not only as the director of the Sea Island version of the GOLF Digest School but also as a GOLF Digest contributor and as the teacher of Davis Love, Beth Daniel, and Donna Andrews.

SUN VALLEY RESORT

SUN VALLEY, IDAHO

Idaho's most popular resort area provides a relaxing and informal atmosphere, with temperatures in the seventies and eighties during the summer. The eighteen-hole course has been recently redesigned by Robert Trent Jones Jr. The resort became known in the late 1960s as a skiing destination in the great Northwest resort boom of the era, but golf has come up a long way in this resort's priority list, and the scenery is also quite grand.

PINE MEADOW GOLF AND COUNTRY CLUB MUNDELEIN

CHICAGO, ILLINOIS

Located just 22 miles north of Chicago's O'Hare Airport in the heart of Lake Country, Pine Meadow is an outstanding teaching facility with ideal practice areas. Not a bad choice at all for a fast golf school getaway out of Chicagoland.

Lodging packages are available at the Holiday Inn at Gurnee beginning at about $255 for a three-night stay.

SUNRIVER RESORT

BEND, OREGON

Nestled among the pines along the Deschutes River, the Sunriver Resort is the Northwest's largest and most complete destination resort. Sunriver has thirty-six holes of golf, including the North Course designed by Robert Trent Jones Jr., and it is ranked among the top twenty-five resort courses in America. Sunriver provides the ultimate in mountain golf. A special accommodations package is available for GOLF Digest students with a four-night stay beginning at $300 per person double occupancy.

THE WILLIAMSBURG INN

COLONIAL WILLIAMSBURG, VIRGINIA

With two eighteen-hole courses and an executive nine-hole course, Williamsburg is well respected as a full-destination golf resort.

The Gold and Green courses were designed by Robert Trent Jones and Rees Jones. Accommodations are at the Williamsburg Inn, a Five-Star resort and part of the largest living history museum in the United States. The Green course is fine; the Gold course is one of the most difficult and exhilarating resort courses in the country. The course record on this short, par-seventy track is still only sixty-seven . . . and that was achieved by Jack Nicklaus in his prime. The par-threes are, in general, set atop virtual cliffs and require extreme precision to hit the lilypad-sized island greens below. It is an arduous and quite beautiful experience. Try to get here when spring is abloom, around late April when both courses are radiant.

■ CONTACT ■

GOLF Digest Schools
5520 Park Avenue, Box 395
Trumbull CT 06111-0395
800-243-6121 or 203-373-7130

THE GOLF INSTITUTE

TARPON SPRINGS, FLORIDA

PROGRAMS The four-day program is offered seven times in January, eight times in February and in March, seven times in April and in May, and then again in September with two schools late in the month, five more in October, and four in November and in December to round out the year; five-day school is offered twice in January, four times in February, five times in March, four times in April, twice in May and October, three times in November, and twice again in December; Playing School is offered once a month for 13 to 24 handicappers only in February, March, October, and November with two schools in April. Zero to twelve handicappers have two playing schools in February-March and one each in April-May and October-December; Junior School is offered twice during July; Summer Institute is offered twice in June and once in August and in September.

ABOUT THE PROGRAMS Founded by legendary instructor and PGA TOUR veteran Jay Overton, this has been one of the top-ranked programs in the country for fifteen years. The unique teaching methods feature intensive on-line sessions and on-course instruction, providing golfers with both confidence and consistency in their games. The philosophy is summed up by Jay Overton as "P.G.A. Posture, Grip, and Alignment." .It was awarded a "Best of the

South" award by *Links* magazine in 1992, and is well deserving of the honor. This program is really among the elite, and it is one of the best managed as well.

The basic program is the four-day, three-night program, which includes breakfast and lunch daily, 16 hours of instruction with drills and exercises, on-course play and instruction, videotape analysis, green fees, golf club and locker room service, social functions, gifts, and transfers.

The five-day school is the same except for three full rounds of golf and an additional 4 hours of instruction.

The Playing School offers on-course instruction with host professional Jay Overton, three afternoon sessions of on-line instruction, and all the other amenities offered at the Golf Institute. Dinners are also included with the Players School.

The Junior School is restricted to golfers ages 10–17 of all skill levels. The program covers fundamentals, rules and etiquette, and team competitions. Each student receives one-on-one instruction and plays on course with the professional staff. Schools are limited to 16 students and include 30 hours of individual instruction, videotape analysis, all meals, and one resident counselor per two-bedroom suite.

The condensed summer program covers all of the fundamentals of the game in 12 hours of instruction and 2 hours of on-course instruction. The Summer Institute includes breakfast and lunch daily and videotaped swing analysis, as well as gifts and transfers.

COSTS Summer Institute (three-day) (resort) $700, (commuter) $600; Junior Golf Institute (six-days) (resort) $900 (commuter) $575; Golf Institute (four days) (resort) $1200, (commuter) $925; the Golf Institute (five-days) (resort) $1500, (commuter) $1150; Playing School (resort) $2000, (commuter) $1450.

STUDENT/TEACHER RATIO 4:1.

HEAD INSTRUCTORS The head instructors are Jay Overton and Lew Smither III. Jay Overton founded the Golf Institute in 1979 and might still be running it today if not for his playing schedule; he is one of the elite club professional players winning any number of PGA sectional events and in 1993 playing the PGA TOUR full-time after becoming the oldest player ever to qualify for the TOUR via the grueling Q-School experience.

■ ABOUT THE LOCATION ■

INNISBROOK RESORT
TARPON SPRINGS, FLORIDA

Innisbrook is headquarters for the Golf Institute. It is one of the most extensive golf course conglomerations in all of Florida—with sixty-three holes, Innisbrook is topped only by the Sawgrass complex in Jacksonville, the Doral Resort in Miami, PGA National in Palm Beach, and Disney World in Orlando for sheer numbers of golf holes. Certainly Innisbrook has the most on Florida's west coast. The course that everyone knows is the famed Copperhead Course, which has been rated in the nation's top 100 and is a perennial in everyone's rankings of top resort courses.

Copperhead was once rated the number one course in Florida, ahead of Seminole, the TPC, and Doral! Copperhead is home to the PGA TOUR/LPGA JC Penney Classic played each November. Davis Love III, Fred Couples, Tom Kite, Beth Daniel, and Pat Bradley are among the players who have won the tournament. In addition to Copperhead, the Island Course has also been ranked in the nation's top fifty resort courses by *GOLF Digest*, and the Sandpiper Course is a shorter and precision-oriented twenty-seven-hole complex.

The Hilton Resort offers spacious suite accommodations (included in the golf school package), fully-equipped kitchens, and private patios and balconies. Recreation at the resort includes not only golf, but Terry Addison's Australian Tennis Institute, a Zoo Crew children's program, swimming, fitness facilities, lake or sport fishing, bicycling, and beach shuttles. The resort is also home to shopping, six restaurants, and two snack bars, as well as the Copperhead nightclub.

■ CONTACT ■

The Golf Institute
Innisbrook Hilton Resort
P.O. Drawer 1088
Tarpon Springs, FL 34286
813-942-2000

THE GOLF SCHOOL

OCEAN CITY, MARYLAND;
MOUNT SNOW, VERMONT

PROGRAMS Two-, three-, four-, and five-day programs. Ocean City: five schools in April, nine in May, eight in June, ten in July, eight in August, nine in September, and four in October. Mount Snow: six schools in May, eight in June, ten in July, eight in August, and nine in September.

ABOUT THE PROGRAMS Jay Morelli has polished his method to the point that it is now trademarked The Accelerated Method (TM). It is a process of speeding up the process of golf instruction to the point that swing fundamentals and finesse tactics can be effectively covered in the one school. It is an interesting idea, one that makes you wonder why other pros haven't given so much thought as to how their techniques will stay with the student after school.

Posture, grip, and alignment are the foundation of the instruction. High-speed, stop-action video is then brought in to address timing, balance, and rhythm. On-course instruction is then added to the mix. The final goal is the elusive repeating swing—that same effortless flow first developed by Harry Vardon at the turn of the century and exemplified by Fred Couples today.

The basic program package includes 5 hours of instruction daily, video analysis, green fees with cart for after-school play, club fitting, welcome reception, farewell banquet, and lunch daily (daily breakfast included at Ocean City).

COSTS Ocean City (April-May after Labor Day) two-day (double occupancy) $460, (commuter) $389; three-day (double occupancy) $601, (commuter) $510, four-day (double occupancy) $797, (commuter) $677; five-day (double occupancy) $998, (commuter) $861. (June-Labor Day) two-day (double occupancy) $499, (commuter) $389; three-day (double occupancy) $679, (commuter) $510; four-day (double occupancy) $902, (commuter) $677; five-day (double occupancy) $1143, (commuter) $861.

Mount Snow (April–May after Labor Day) two-day (Snow Lake Lodge) $459, (condominium) $491–$510; three-day (Snow Lake Lodge) $552, (condominium) $617–$640; four-day (Snow Lake Lodge) $725, (condominium) $809–$839; five-day (Snow Lake Lodge) $920, (condominium) $1024–$1062. Value dining plan (daily breakfast and dinner) two-day $29; three-day $70; four-day $93; five-day $99.

Military and school alumni take off ten percent for weekend schools, 15 percent for mid-week, ten percent discount after Labor Day at Mount Snow (except dining).
STUDENT/TEACHER RATIO 4:1.
HEAD INSTRUCTOR The head instructor is Jay Morelli. All instructors are PGA professionals.
ACCOMMODATIONS Included in package rates.

■ ABOUT THE LOCATIONS ■

RIVER RUN GOLF CLUB/COMFORT INN GOLD COAST
OCEAN CITY, MARYLAND

On Maryland's Atlantic Coast, the city has its own Boardwalk with arcades and amusements and white sand beaches. Nice town, but this particular option is a little strung out, with practice, after-practice play, and accommodations in three separate locations.

River Run is a typical Gary Player design, which means that it is relatively short at 6,705 yards, has multiple tees, is generally quite friendly from the forward tees, has a strong emphasis on precision, and has fairly flat greens. Player also is probably the strongest architect for straight aesthetics.

The accommodations are in a 202-room inn right on the beach. The course is 15 minutes down the road. Teaching is done at the Plantation Golf Center, a 16-acre practice area that attempts to capture actual course conditions.

MOUNT SNOW RESORT
WEST DOVER, VERMONT

Nice name for a golf resort, eh? But it's in the Green Mountains, so there's a plus. Quite obviously this is a ski resort that has added golf as a summer activity. They've done themselves well by forming an association with Mount Snow Country Club, a few minutes down the road, a rather pretty golf course that hosted the New England Open in years past.
ACCOMMODATIONS Accommodations are in the form of rooms at the Snow Lake Lodge or the spacious, luxury townhouses at the base of Mount Snow. Tennis, swimming, a health club, and biking are also available at the resort.

■ CONTACT ■

The Golf School
9301 West Fort Island Trail
Crystal River, FL 34423
800-632-6262 or 904-795-4211

GRAND CYPRESS ACADEMY OF GOLF
ORLANDO, FLORIDA

PROGRAMS Mini-schools are run throughout the year, four times a month during the summer and eight times a month during the peak winter and spring seasons. The Grand Cypress series runs October through May, twice a month (three times a month February-April). The Phil Rodgers series runs twice in February and March and three times during April and November. Phil Rodgers and Fred

Griffin jointly conduct an alumni school during April.

ABOUT THE PROGRAMS One of the most highly regarded programs in the country, it is situated at the elegant Grand Cypress Resort southwest of downtown Orlando. The Academy offers a private and natural setting alongside the highly regarded Grand Cypress courses designed by Jack Nicklaus.

The Academy is based on an unusual technology developed by Dr. Ralph Mann called CompuSport. Mann studied and recorded the swings of 50 top PGA TOUR pros (including Nicklaus, Palmer, and Norman) to create a computer model of a perfect golf swing. It is then adjusted by the computer to allow for the student's size and body type. By comparing the computer model with a high-resolution, slow-motion video of the student's swing, the instructors perform swing analysis and design a program to accent the student's strengths while correcting weaknesses. CompuSport also performs in-depth analysis of the putting stroke.

The Academy has its own 21-acre practice course, one of a few such facilities in the world, with par-three, par-four, and par-five holes designed specifically by Jack Nicklaus to offer every challenge of the game for learning purposes. Uneven lies, fairway bunkers, and rough shots pose realistic tests for the learning process. Club fitting is also offered to analyze the ideal length, lie of club, swing weight, and shaft flex for each student.

The standard school, the Grand Cypress series, offers three full days of instruction, accommodations at the Villas at Grand Cypress or the Hyatt Regency Grand Cypress, unlimited golf on the forty-five-hole Jack Nicklaus-designed courses, lunch and beverages, welcome reception, comprehensive full-swing and short-game instruction, on-course playing instruction, CompuSport computer video analysis to take home with model overlay and instructor comments recorded live, club fitting, unlimited use of the practice range, three practice holes, club cleaning and storage, gifts, books, and a locker. The mini-schools offer most of the above, with the prominent exception of on-course instruction. Students attending the premium-rate Phil Rodgers series also receive a copy of Phil Rodgers' book *Play Lower Handicap Golf.*

Only the best teach at Grand Cypress, including longtime director Fred Griffin, PGA Senior TOUR player Phil Rodgers, and biomechanics expert Dr. Ralph Munn.

COSTS Individual lessons $85 per hour ($95 per hour with Fred Griffin); full-swing computer lesson $200 per hour; nine-hole playing lesson $170 ($190 with Fred Griffin); eighteen-hole playing lesson $340 ($380 with Fred Griffin).

October–February three half-day mini-schools $1400, (double occupancy), $1650 (single occupancy), $1125 (commuter); three-day school (Grand Cypress Series) $2080 (double occupancy), $2350 (single occupancy), $1825 (commuter); three-day school (Phil Rodgers Series) $2330 (double occupancy), $2600 (single occupancy), $2060 (commuter).

March–April three half-day mini-schools $1450 (double occupancy), $1700 (single occupancy), $1125 (commuter); three-day school (Grand Cypress Series) $2150 (double occupancy), $2425 (single occupancy), $1885 (commuter); three-day school (Phil Rodgers Series) $2400 (double occupancy), $2675 (single occupancy), $2150 (commuter).

May–September three half-day mini-schools $1250 (double occupancy), $1425 (single occupancy), $1125 (commuter); three-day school (Grand Cypress Series) $1950 (double occupancy), $2125 (single occupancy), $1750 (commuter); three-day school

(Phil Rodgers Series) $2200 (double occupancy), $2375 (single occupancy), $2025 (commuter).

STUDENT/TEACHER RATIO 3:1

HEAD INSTRUCTOR The head instructor is Fred Griffin. Phil Rodgers is an adviser and instructor to the Academy of Golf. Recognized by *GOLF* magazine as one of the 50 best instructors in America, Fred Griffin is a Class A PGA professional with twelve years of teaching experience. He has served as the Director of the Academy since it opened in 1986. Griffin was formerly an instruction adviser for *GOLF Illustrated* and was voted Teacher of the Year by the PGA's North Florida section. Griffin is a frequent speaker as PGA educational programs and currently coaches several PGA and LPGA tour players.

Phil Rodgers has also been recognized by *GOLF* magazine as one of the 50 best instructors in America, making Grand Cypress one of a handful of schools with 2 top-ranked teachers. Rodgers has been a Class A PGA professional for over twenty-five years and prior to his teaching career was a noted touring professional with six PGA victories and a second-place finish in the 1963 British Open, losing in a playoff to Bob Charles at Royal Lytham. Like Charles, Rodgers has gone on to a successful career on the Senior Tour, but in recent years he has become best known as an instructor. He has several PGA and LPGA players among his students, most notably Jack Nicklaus. Nicklaus, in fact, recommended Rodgers to the Academy, where he serves as an adviser and instructor for the occasional Phil Rodgers series of advanced instruction.

■ **ABOUT THE LOCATION** ■

GRAND CYPRESS RESORT AND GOLF CLUB
··
ORLANDO, FLORIDA

Grand Cypress shows a more peaceful, exclusive side of Orlando to those who know the city primarily for Disney World. Although Grand Cypress is located in the same southwestern quadrant of the city as Disney and Universal Studios, the 1,500- acre facility has become known as an upscale retreat, especially for golfers. Grand Cypress has forty-five holes of Jack Nicklaus-designed golf, including the particularly interesting New Course, which is designed as an homage to Scottish golf and incorporates many of the design elements of famed links courses (and actually recreates Swilcan Burn from the Old Course). Grand Cypress is also home to an Equestrian Center and the Grand Cypress Racquet Club, racquetball, seven restaurants, five bars and lounges, swimming, bicycling, a health club, fitness and jogging trail, shopping, a 45-acre wildlife preserve designed with the Audubon Society, and fishing opportunities at 21-acre Lake Windsong. The golf shop was named one of the 100 best in America by Golf Shop Operations, and the facility as a whole has been awarded a Golf Medal by *GOLF* magazine.

Guests at the Grand Cypress Resort have two options for accommodations, the swank Hyatt Regency Grand Cypress or the courseside villas of Grand Cypress. Although the hotel is one of the best-run Hyatts in the entire chain, definitely choose the villas. They're spacious, closer to the golf facilities, and have a wonderful golf-oriented ambience that really puts a cap on a good golf school experience.

■ **CONTACT** ■

The Grand Cypress Academy of Golf
One North Jacaranda
Orlando, FL 32836
800-835-7377

JIMMY BALLARD GOLF WORKSHOP

PALM BEACH, FLORIDA

PROGRAM All programs are offered throughout the year. Two-day workshops begin each Tuesday and the three half-day workshops begin Thursday.

ABOUT THE PROGRAMS Despite the fact that Jimmy is still only in his early fifties, this is one of the pioneering golf school programs in the country. Only the fact that so many teachers and schools now accept Jimmy's theories and emulate his methods disguises exactly how revolutionary a teacher Jimmy was and is. This program is not for the faint at heart!

The seminar begins with a videotape of your golf swing, which is used as a reference point throughout the program. Ballard then launches into a seminar demolishing most of what you knew or thought you knew about golf instruction terminology. From there he introduces his theory of swing connection, and then students work on establishing connection throughout their swings via one-on-one instruction on the practice range. At the end of the workshop, each student is given a videotape record of his or her original swing, a 5- to 6-minute segment of personal instruction from Jimmy Ballard on areas of potential improvement, and finally the students' reconstructed golf swing is taped at the end of the workshop.

Sounds simple? Let's go back to the Theory of Connection for a minute. "Connection" is based on two statements. First, Ben Hogan's contention that the golf swing is as simple as making an underhanded tossing motion. Second, Ballard mentor Sam Byrd's contention that the golf swing that brought him fifteen PGA TOUR victories wasn't any different than the baseball swing, which won him, earlier in his career, a slot with the New York Yankees— the plane changed, but not the swing. Ballard formulated the theory that there is a strong position that every athlete, regardless of the sport, gets into in order to propel a ball forward—golf, baseball, tennis, or football. Athletes, goes the theory, use the large muscles of the legs, torso, and shoulders to deliver the powerful blow. This motion, this fundamental action common to athletes in many sports, is what Jimmy Ballard calls connection, and connection is what the Jimmy Ballard Golf Workshop is all about.

In addition to video analysis, the workshop is the home of the Jimmy Ballard Swing Connector, a patented contraption Jimmy uses to teach the connected swing. The Swing Connector "connects" the left arm to the left breast in a soft but restrictive manner. It prevents the left arm from running out of the left shoulder socket, which according to Jimmy, causes over 95 percent of all inconsistencies in hitting the golf ball. It is an unusual and highly effective device and makes the Jimmy Ballard Golf Workshop one of the best and most interesting programs in the country.

COSTS Private 1-hour lesson (staff) $60; private 2-hour lesson (1 hour with staff; 1 hour with Jimmy Ballard) $250; 2-hour playing lesson (staff) $125; 4 hours playing Lenox (staff) $250; two-day golf workshop (staff) $500; two-day golf workshop (Jimmy Ballard) $795; three half-days golf workshop (staff)

$500; three half-days golf workshop (Jimmy Ballard) $795.

STUDENT/TEACHER RATIO 5:1

HEAD INSTRUCTOR The one, the only, the inimitable Jimmy Ballard—he swept into national recognition on the basis of his articles on the "Seven Common Denominators" of the golf swing and instruction's "Misleading Terms," which gained a certain notoriety in the late 1970s and are widely accepted today. Jimmy's two early innovations were an emphasis on videotaped swing analysis instead of stop-action photography, and his expansion of the definition of great ball strikers beyond golf—identifying great "golf" swings by looking at Joe DiMaggio and Arthur Ashe, for instance.

After teaching amateurs for several years, Ballard leapt into national prominence on the basis of his reconstruction of Mac McLendon's swing in the late 1970s, which led to three tour victories for the veteran pro. Since then almost 200 tour professionals have made the trek to Jimmy's teaching facilities in Alabama, Florida, and South Carolina. Curtis Strange, Seve Ballesteros, Hal Sutton, Jerry Pate, Johnny Miller, Hubert Green, and Sandy Lyle are among his major championship winning students. Ballard is also the "guru" who has worked consistently with Jesper Parnevik in helping the unknown Swede to a runner-up finish in the British Open.

Ballard is the author of *How to Perfect Your Golf Swing* and is a former ESPN swing analyst.

■ ABOUT THE LOCATION ■

PALM BEACH POLO & GOLF CLUB

PALM BEACH, FLORIDA

One of the most prestigious resort clubs in all of Palm Beach (and that is saying something), Palm Beach Polo is much more than just a polo club. It has outstanding resort accommodations and the demanding courses, from Pete Dye, Ron Garl, Jerry Pate, and Tom Fazio. The Dye course is the one to play if you only have time for one. Palm Beach Polo was previously a part of the Landmark Land group of golf resorts (which included PGA West and The Ocean Course at Kiawah Island) and today offers golf; twenty-four tennis courts with clay, grass, and Har-Tru surfaces; the Equestrian Center with polo events; squash; croquet; full health spa; rowing clinics and swimming, as well as a children's program, three remarkable restaurants situated at the three clubhouses, two lounges, and over 120 condominiums and villas (one to three bedrooms).

■ CONTACT ■

The Jimmy Ballard Golf Workshop
Palm Beach Polo Club
11809 Polo Club Road
West Palm Beach, FL 33414
407-798-7233

JOHN JACOBS' PRACTICAL SCHOOL OF GOLF

POINT CLEAR, ALABAMA;
LITCHFIELD PARK, MESA,
SCOTTSDALE, TUCSON,
ARIZONA; NAPA, PALM
DESERT, RANCHO LAS
PALMAS, CALIFORNIA;
SKYLAND, COLORADO; FORT
LAUDERDALE, ORLANDO,
MARCO ISLAND, VERO
BEACH, FLORIDA; TRAVERSE
CITY, MICHIGAN; OSAGE
BEACH, MISSOURI; LAS
VEGAS, NEVADA; ATLANTIC
CITY, NEW JERSEY;
MARGARETVILLE, HAUPPAGE,
NEW YORK; PORTLAND,
OREGON; SOUTH PADRE
ISLAND, TEXAS; HEBER
VALLEY, UTAH; DELAVAN,
WISCONSIN; JACKSON HOLE,
WYOMING; GRAZ, AUSTRIA;
CADIZ-GIBRALTAR, SPAIN;
HAMBURG, GERMANY;
OESCHBERGHOL, GERMANY;
ZHONGSHAN CITY, CHINA

PROGRAMS

Point Clear, Alabama, Marriott Grand Hotel
Two-day schools: two in March, two in April, three in September, and one in October; four-day schools: one in August, four in September, and four in October; five-day schools: one in February, four in March, and four in April.

Litchfield Park, Arizona, The Wigwam Resort
Two-day schools: one in January, two in February, two in March, three in April, and two in May. Four-day schools: three in October, five in November, and four in December; five-day

■ Jacobs' Golf Group.

schools: five in January, four in February, four in March, five in April, and two in May.

Mesa, Arizona, Rodeway Inn/Painted Mountain Golf Club

Two-day schools: four in January, one in May, three in June, four in July, four in October, four in November, and five in December; five-day schools: five in January, four in February, four in March, five in April, four in May, four in June, four in July, five in October, four in November, and four in December.

Scottsdale, Arizona, Marriott Mountain Shadows Resort

Two-day schools: four in January, two in February, two in March, two in April, two in May, three in June, two in July, two in August, two in September, four in October, four in November, and three in December; four-day schools: four in June, five in July, and four in August; five-day schools five in January, four in February, four in March, five in April, three in May, four in September, five in October, four in November, and four in December.

Scottsdale, Arizona, Marriott's Fairfield Inn (nonresort)

Five-day schools: five in January, four in February, four in March, five in April, three in May, five in October, four in November, and four in December.

Tucson, Arizona, Tucson National Golf & Conference Resort

Two-day schools: one in January, two in February, two in March, three in April, two in May, three in June, two in July, two in August, one in September, one in October, two in November, and three in December; four-day schools: four in June, five in July, and four in August; five-day schools: four in January, four in February, three in March, five in April, and four in May.

Napa, California, Inn at Napa Valley/Chardonnay Club

Two-day schools: three in June, two in July, two in August, two in September, and one in

October; four-day schools: one in May, four in June, five in July, four in August, four in September, and two in October.

Palm Desert, California, Marriott Desert Springs Resort

Two-day schools: two in January, two in February, two in March, three in April, two in May, one in October, two in November, and three in December; five-day schools: five in January, four in February, four in March, five in April, three in May, three in October, four in November, and four in December.

Rancho Mirage, California, Marriott's Rancho Las Palmas Resort

Two-day schools: two in January, two in February, two in March, two in April, and one in May; five-day schools: five in January, four in February, four in March, and five in April.

Crested Butte, Colorado, Skyland Mountain Golf Resort

Two-day schools: two in June, two in July, two in August, and two in September; four-day schools: four in June, five in July, and four in August; five-day schools: four in June, five in July, four in August, and two in September.

Fort Lauderdale, Florida, Bonaventure Resort & Spa

Two-day schools: two in January, two in February, two in March, three in April, two in October, two in November, and three in December; five-day schools: five in January, four in February, four in March, four in April, five in October, four in November, and four in December.

Orlando, Florida, Marriott's Orlando World Center

Two-day schools: two in January, two in February, two in March, three in April, two in September, two in October, two in November, and two in December; five-day schools: five in January, four in February, four in March, five in April, four in September, five in October, four in November, and four in December.

Marco Island, Florida, Marriott's Marco Island Resort

Two-day schools: two in January, two in February, two in March, two in April, two in May, two in June, two in July, two in August, two in September, two in October, two in November, and two in December; four-day schools: four in June, five in July, four in August, and four in September; five-day schools: five in January, four in February, four in March, five in April, four in May, five in October, four in November, and four in December.

Vero Beach, Florida, Grand Harbor Golf & Beach Club

Two-day schools: two in January, two in February, two in March, two in April, two in May, two in October, two in November, and two in December.

Traverse City, Michigan, Grand Traverse Resort

Two-day schools: one in May, two in June, two in July, two in August, and one in September; four-day schools: one in May, four in June, five in July, and four in August.

Osage Beach, Missouri, Lake of the Ozarks, Marriott's Tar-Tan-A Resort & Golf Club

Two-day schools: one in May, three in June, four in July, two in August, and one in September; four-day schools: three in May, four in June, five in July, four in August, and one in September.

Las Vegas, Nevada, Angel Park Golf Club (commuter only)

Two-day schools: two in March, two in April, two in May, one in June, one in September, two in October, and one in November; five-day schools: two in February, four in March, four in April, five in May, two in June, two in September, five in October, and two in November.

Atlantic City, New Jersey, Marriott's Seaview Resort

Two-day schools: one in May, three in June, two in July, two in August, and one in

September; four-day schools: four in June, five in July, and four in August; five-day schools: three in May, four in June, five in July, four in August, and one in September.

Margaretville, New York, Hanah Country Inn & Golf Course

Two-day weekend schools: one in April, four in May, five in June, four in July, four in August, five in September, and one in October; four-day schools: one in April, four in May, four in June, five in July, four in August, four in September, and two in October.

Hauppage, New York, Wind Watch Hotel & Golf Club (commuter only)

Two-day schools: one in May, two in June, two in July, two in August, and two in September; four-day schools: one in May, four in June, five in July, four in August, and four in September.

Portland, Oregon, Langdon Farms (commuter only)

Two-day schools: two in July, two in August, and two in September; five-day schools: five in July, four in August, and four in September.

South Padre Island, Texas, Rancho Viejo Resort

Two-day schools: one in January, two in February, two in March, and three in April; five-day schools: one in January, four in February, four in March, and three in April.

Park City Area, Utah, Homestead

Two-day schools: one in May, two in June, two in July, two in August, and two in September; four-day schools: three in May, four in June, five in July, four in August, and two in September.

Delavan, Wisconsin, Lake Lawn Lodge

Two-day schools: three in June, two in July, two in August, and two in September; four-day schools: one in May, four in June, five in July, four in August, and four in September.

Jackson Hole, Wyoming, Jackson Hole Golf & Tennis Club/The Wort Hotel

Two-day schools: three in June, five in July, and four in August; four-day schools: four in June, five in July, and four in August.

ABOUT THE PROGRAMS This is the big enchilada of golf schools—the largest of all golf schools worldwide and over three times as large as the second-largest company (*GOLF Digest*), with over 10,000 students graduating annually from Jacobs' schools. Founded in 1971 by former British Ryder Cup captain, John Jacobs, and PGA professional Shelby Futch, the basis of the program has always been practical, result-oriented instruction, primarily in correcting the swing plane and in developing consistency.

Since 1971, the schools have grown to thirty sites, from the United States to Austria, Spain, Germany, and mainland China. The schools today are the official golf schools of Marriott Resorts and *GOLF* magazine (where Futch doubles as a teaching editor). The schools boast that 40 percent of their schools today are composed of repeat students. Jacobs offers corporate group schools, custom-designed incentive programs, convention clinics, a club-making and club-fitting subsidiary, a travel and tour company devoted to golfing getaways, a golf course ownership, and a management subsidiary.

The school offers instruction via international, junior, low-handicap, short-game, and playing school options. A typical program will focus on teaching straight driving, a balanced and fluid swing, accuracy in the short game, playing trouble shots with confidence, approaching and reading greens like a pro, aligning and stroking putts with greater accuracy, and developing a winning course strategy.

The standard school runs for two to five days and includes 6 hours of daily golf instruction, the Jacobs' Golf Manual, high-tech visual analysis with high-speed, stop-action video, equipment analysis, gift package, accommodations, breakfast and lunch daily, opening and closing dinners, nightly cocktail parties, plus green fees and carts for after-hours golfing. Nonresort programs do not typically include cocktail parties and dinners and breakfast may be continental style. Golf course privileges typically begin at 1 p.m.

The short-game school focuses on the putting, chipping, pitching, and sand play aspects of the game. Two five-day sessions are also available for juniors, offered in conjunction with Texas A&M University, with five days of instruction, accommodations at the Texas A&M dorms, all meals, and an eighteen-hole tournament. The junior schools are limited to boys and girls ages 13 to 16.

All classes are led by PGA and LPGA professionals. John Jacobs' is one of the handful of schools with two of the Best 50 Teachers in America (as selected by *GOLF* magazine) on staff (Shelby Futch and Co-Director of Instruction Craig Bunker).

COSTS

Point Clear, Alabama, Marriott Grand Hotel.

Two-day school (commuter) $275; four-day school (double occupancy) $1075, (single occupancy) $1375, (double occupancy plus nonparticipating resort guest) $1580, (commuter) $715; five-day school (double occupancy) $1215, (single occupancy) $1625, (double occupancy plus nonparticipating resort guest) $1820, (commuter) $865.

Litchfield Park, Arizona, The Wigwam Resort

Two-day school (commuter) $395; four-day school (double occupancy) $1095, (single occupancy) $1555, (double occupancy plus nonparticipating resort guest) $1650, (commuter) $710; five-day school January (double occupancy) $1350, (single occupancy) $2015, (double occupancy plus nonparticipating resort guest) $2230, (commuter) $895; five-day school February-April (double occupancy) $1475, (single occupancy) $2115, (double occupancy plus nonparticipating resort guest) $2355, (commuter) $895; five-day school May (double occupancy) $1320, (single occupancy) $1985, (double occupancy plus nonparticipating resort guest) $2200, (commuter) $895.

Mesa, Arizona Rodeway Inn/Painted Mountain Golf Club

Two-day school January, October-December (double occupancy) $395, (single occupancy) $440, (double occupancy with nonparticipating resort guest) $495, (commuter) $225; two-day school June-July (double occupancy) $245, (single occupancy) $295, (double occupancy plus nonparticipating resort guest) $315, (commuter) $175; five-day school January-February 12, April 16-May 21, October-December (double occupancy) $895, (single occupancy) $970, (double occupancy plus nonparticipating resort guest) $1275, (commuter) $545; five-day school February 12-April 16 double occupancy) $945, (single occupancy) $1050 (double occupancy plus non-participating resort guest) $1325, (commuter) $595; five-day school May 21-July 31 (double occupancy) $695, (single occupancy) $770, (double occupancy plus nonparticipating resort guest) $995, (commuter) $395.

Scottsdale, Arizona, Marriott Mountain Shadows Resort

Two-day school January–February (commuter) $285; two-day school March–May (commuter) $295; two-day school September–December (commuter) $255; two-day school June–August (double occupancy) $340, (single occupancy) $410, (double occupancy plus nonparticipating resort guest) $465, (commuter) $255; four-day school (double occu-

pancy) $760, (single occupancy) $985, (double occupancy plus nonparticipating resort guest) $1250, (commuter) $505, five-day school January, May (double occupancy) $1375, (single occupancy) $1895, (double occupancy plus nonparticipating resort guest) $2185, (commuter) $895; five-day school February–April (double occupancy) $1525, (single occupancy) $2085, (double occupancy plus nonparticipating resort guest) $2340; (commuter) $895; five-day school September (double occupancy) $1115, (single occupancy) $1575, (double occupancy plus nonparticipating resort guest) $1600, (commuter) $505; five-day school October–December (double occupancy) $1220; (single occupancy) $1795, (double occupancy plus nonparticipating resort guest) $1895, (commuter) $895.

Scottsdale, Arizona, Marriott's Fairfield Inn (nonresort)

Five-day school January–May (double occupancy) $945, (single occupancy) $1145, (double occupancy plus nonparticipating resort guest) $1145, (commuter) $895; five-day school October–December (double occupancy) $925, (single occupancy) $1095; (double occupancy plus nonparticipating resort guest) $1095, (commuter) $895.

Tucson, Arizona, Tucson National Golf & Conference Resort

Two-day school July–August (commuter) $285; two-day school January-May, September–December (double occupancy) $295, (single occupancy) $455, (double occupancy plus nonparticipating resort guest) $475, (commuter) $225; four-day school June–August (double occupancy) $795, (single occupancy) $1065, (double occupancy plus nonparticipating resort guest) $1145, (commuter) $595; four-day school September–December (double occupancy) $865, (single occupancy) $1145, (double occupancy with nonparticipating resort guest) $1220, (commuter) $595; five-day school January-April (double occupancy) $1325, (single occupancy) $1745, (double occupancy plus nonparticipating resort guest) $1845, (commuter) $885; five-day school May (double occupancy) $1095, (single occupancy) $1545, (double occupancy plus nonparticipating resort guest) $1600, (commuter) $885.

Napa, California, Inn at Napa Valley/ Chardonnay Club

Two-day school (double occupancy) $605, (single occupancy) $755, (double occupancy plus nonparticipating resort guest) $785, (commuter) $385; four-day school (double occupancy) $915, (single occupancy) $1220, (double occupancy plus nonparticipating resort guest) $1265, (commuter) $715.

Palm Desert, California, Marriott Desert Springs Resort

Two-day school (commuter) $295; five-day school January, October–December (double occupancy) $1475, (single occupancy) $2185, (double occupancy plus nonparticipating resort guest) $2390, (commuter) $1095; five-day school February–April (double occupancy) $1710, (single occupancy) $2395; (double occupancy plus nonparticipating resort guest) $2695, (commuter) $1095; five-day school May (double occupancy) $1575, (single occupancy) $2290, (double occupancy plus nonparticipating resort guest) $2540, (commuter) $1095.

Rancho Mirage, California, Marriott's Rancho Las Palmas Resort

Two-day school $255; five-day school (double occupancy) $1425, (single occupancy) $2035, (double occupancy plus nonparticipating resort guest) $2240, (commuter) $1045.

Crested Butte, Colorado, Skyland Mountain Golf Resort

Two-day school (double occupancy) $495, (single occupancy) $635, (double occupancy plus nonparticipating resort guest) $695, (commuter) $395; four-day school (double occupancy) $965, (single occupancy) $1220, (double occupancy plus nonparticipating resort guest) $1320, (commuter) $660.

Fort Lauderdale, Florida, Bonaventure Resort & Spa

Two-day school (commuter) $285; five-day school January, October–December (double occupancy) $995, (single occupancy) $1375, (double occupancy plus nonparticipating resort guest) $1995, (commuter) $845, five-day school February–April (double occupancy) $1095, (single occupancy) $1475, (double occupancy plus nonparticipating resort guest) $1595, (commuter) $865.

Orlando, Florida, Marriott's Orlando World Center

Two-day school January–April (commuter) $295; two-day school September–December (commuter) $260; five-day school January, September (double occupancy) $1325, (single occupancy) $1835, (double occupancy plus nonparticipating resort guest) $2035, (commuter) $915; five-day school February–April, October–December (double occupancy) $1425, (single occupancy) $2025, (double occupancy plus nonparticipating resort guest) $2220, (commuter) $915.

Marco Island, Florida, Marriott's Marco Island Resort

Two-day school January–May (commuter) $285; two-day school June-August (commuter) $195; two-day school September–December (commuter) $135; four-day school (double occupancy) $865, (single occupancy) $1165, (double occupancy plus nonparticipating resort guest) $1220, (commuter) $555; five-day school January–May (double occupancy) $1710, (single occupancy) $2395, (double occupancy plus nonparticipating resort guest) $2555, (commuter) $815; five-day school October–December (double occupancy) $1295, (single occupancy) $1785, (double occupancy plus nonparticipating resort guest) $1900, (commuter) $815.

Vero Beach, Florida, Grand Harbor Golf & Beach Club

Two-day school January (commuter) $245; two-day school February–December (commuter) $275.

Traverse City, Michigan, Grand Traverse Resort

Two-day school (double occupancy) $585, (single occupancy) $765, (double occupancy plus nonparticipating resort guest) $795, (commuter) $395; four-day school (double occupancy) $995, (single occupancy) $1375, (double occupancy plus nonparticipating resort guest) $1480, (commuter) $765.

Lake of the Ozarks, Osage, Missouri, Marriott's Tar-Tan-A Resort & Golf Club

Two-day school (double occupancy) $555, (single occupancy) $740, (double occupancy plus nonparticipating resort guest) $795, (commuter) $405; four-day school (double occupancy) $1055, (single occupancy) $1320, (double occupancy plus nonparticipating resort guest) $1490, (commuter) $645.

Las Vegas, Nevada, Angel Park Golf Club (commuter only)

Two-day school (commuter) $325; five-day school (commuter) $815.

Atlantic City, New Jersey, Marriott's Seaview Resort

Two-day school (double occupancy) $760, (single occupancy) $965, (double occupancy plus nonparticipating resort guest) $995, (commuter) $555; four-day school (double occupancy) $1195, (single occupancy) $1675, (double occupancy plus nonparticipating resort guest) $1885, (commuter) $845.

Margaretville, New York, Hanah Country Inn & Golf Resort

Two-day weekend school (double occupancy) $445, (single occupancy) $480, (double occupancy plus nonparticipating resort guest) $620, (commuter) $335; two-day midweek school (double occupancy) $400, (single occupancy) $425, (double occupancy plus nonparticipating resort guest) $565, (commuter) $310; four-day school (double occupancy) $750, (single occupancy) $850, (double occupancy plus nonparticipating resort guest) $1015, (commuter) $545.

Hauppage, New York, Wind Watch Hotel & Golf Club (commuter only)

Two-day school (commuter) $555; four-day school (commuter) $760.

Portland, Oregon, Langdon Farms (commuter only)

Two-day school (commuter) $325; five-day school (commuter) $815.

South Padre Island, Texas Rancho Viejo Resort

Two-day school (double occupancy) $405; (single occupancy) $555, (double occupancy plus nonparticipating resort guest) $585, (commuter) $245; five-day school (double occupancy) $995, (single occupancy) $1375, (double occupancy plus nonparticipating resort guest) $1500, (commuter) $710.

Park City Area, Utah, Homestead

Two-day school (commuter) $345. Four-day school (double occupancy) $925, (single occupancy) $1145, (double occupancy plus nonparticipating resort guest) $1295, (commuter) $725.

Delevan, Wisconsin, Lake Lawn Lodge

Two-day school (double occupancy) $555, (single occupancy) $655, (double occupancy plus nonparticipating resort guest) $735, (commuter) $435; four-day school (double occupancy) $865, (single occupancy) $1115, (double occupancy plus nonparticipating resort guest) $1270, (commuter) $695.

Jackson Hole, Wyoming, Jackson Hole Golf & Tennis Club/The Wort Hotel

Two-day school (commuter) $435, four-day school (double occupancy) $1165, (single occupancy) $1625, (double occupancy plus nonparticipating resort guest) $1875, (commuter) $710.

STUDENT/TEACHER RATIO 5:1

HEAD INSTRUCTORS John Jacobs, called "the father of European golf," is one of the most widely known and respected golf instructors in the world. Born in Yorkshire, England, he is well known throughout Europe and is recognized in the United States as "Doctor Golf." His most famous pupil in recent years is Jose-Maria Olazabal. As a player, Jacobs won the Dutch Open and the South Africa Match Play Championship (defeating Gary Player in the final). Jacobs has captained two Ryder Cup teams and coached a Walker Cup team to victory.

Shelby Futch is Jacobs' American partner who serves as President and CEO of the Jacobs empire. Shelby is the driving force behind the phenomenal success that the schools have enjoyed. Voted one of the "Best 50 Teachers in America" by *GOLF* magazine, Futch has been published in magazines throughout the world. As a player, he is best known for professional tournament play on the Far East and South American Tours and as a past winner of the Illinois PGA Championship.

■ ABOUT THE LOCATIONS ■

MARRIOTT GRAND HOTEL
POINT CLEAR, ALABAMA

Since 1847, Marriott's Grand Hotel has been regarded as "The Queen of Southern Resorts." Its secluded setting, and 550 acres along Alabama's Mobile Bay, moss draped oaks, and antebellum design is reminiscent of the Old South.

Its thirty-six holes of golf have earned the Silver Medal Award as one of *GOLF* magazine's "Top 50 Resort Courses in the U.S." Golfers can look forward to playing on challenging, scenic terrain with fairways lined and shaded by massive, 300-year-old oaks and towering pines. The resort is 50 minutes by car from Mobile Airport or 49 miles west of Pensacola, Florida.

THE WIGWAM RESORT
LITCHFIELD PARK, ARIZONA

Regarded as one of the finest and most exclusive of all desert resorts, The Wigwam resort offers a Mobil Five-Star rated oasis just west of Phoenix. There's only a handful of Five-Star golf resorts in the country. Interestingly, this one started as a corporate retreat for Goodyear, which needed staple cotton to make its early automobile tires. They found that after the boll weevil knocked out the cotton crops in the Southeast and German submarines in the World War knocked out shipments from Egypt, the southern Arizona desert could support a good cotton crop. Voila! The town of Litchfield Park was born, and the Wigwam opened as a guest lodge for company visitors.

They dubbed the place (originally called "Organizational House") "The Wigwam" and persuaded Goodyear to open it as a resort. An interesting competition built up over the years between Goodyear and Firestone in golf as well as in tires, with both Goodyear's The Wigwam and Firestone's Firestone Country Club hiring Trent Jones to design top-flight golf courses. Firestone got Firestone South—a perennial top-100 course, while the Wigwam got the Gold Course—a perennial top-seventy-five resort course. Both are parsimonious when it comes to yielding pars. For a good warm-up to the Gold Course, Jones' Blue Course is a short par-seventy appetizer and the Red Course designed by desert pioneer Red Lawrence is a visually appealing and stimulating 6,805-yard course built around several lakes and a stream. It's an unusually strong combination of courses; but don't forget the food at The Wigwam. There are three stellar restaurants serving American and Southwestern fare. The resort also offers a cornucopia of additional activities, including tennis, croquet, swimming, fitness and spa facilities, trap and skeet shooting, bicycling, and horseback riding.

PAINTED MOUNTAIN GOLF CLUB/RODEWAY INN
MESA, ARIZONA

Red Mountain in Mesa is the backdrop for Painted Mountain Golf Club and the Jacobs' school. This place in the sun offers an eighteen-hole golf course, a nine-hole executive course, two practice areas, including the 270-degree Learning Center range, the largest on-course teaching facility in Arizona. An excellent restaurant and fully stocked golf shop

add to the amenities. The golf club is near Superstition Mall and offers good access to all Valley of the Sun attractions. The club is 30 minutes from Phoenix's Sky Harbor Airport. Please note that all five-day schools include a full seven nights accommodation.

The Rodeway Inn has recently completed an interior and exterior renovation. It now offers swimming, a jacuzzi, and a restaurant with an overall desert color design scheme.

MARRIOTT'S MOUNTAIN SHADOWS RESORT
SCOTTSDALE, ARIZONA

Set against the backdrop of Camelback Mountain in Scottsdale, perhaps the Valley of the Sun's best known physical landmark, Marriott's Mountain Shadows Resort is designed as a desert oasis and offers an array of restaurants and recreation activities. Its on-site 3,060-yard Executive Course is regarded as one of the finest of its type. All instruction is carried out at Camelback Golf Club about 3 minutes up the road. Camelback is not regarded in the same rank as the TPC of Scottsdale or The Wigwam, but as pure resort golf, it is certainly a lot more friendly to the mid-handicapper. Red Lawrence designed the 6,559-yard par-seventy-one Padre Course, which is more suited to the shorter hitter with a tight fairway framed by pine and eucalyptus trees. There are only two lakes—and not particularly daunting ones, either. There are no forced carries, and the greens are generally open in the front to allow for the desert version of the bump-and-run. The 7,014-yard, par-seventy-two Indian Bend Course opened seventeen years ago from a design by Arthur Jack Snyder. It's more suited to the big swatter with wide open landing areas and a links-style design (nine holes out and nine in). Not much tree cover here, and no place to lose golf balls. Perhaps the only weakness of the course is that the opening hole, a monstrous 432-yard par-four, is the most difficult. Not a particularly friendly start, but it sweetens considerably from there.

MARRIOTT'S FAIRFIELD INN
SCOTTSDALE, ARIZONA

The Fairfield nonresort option is considerably more economical (with the price dropping over $250 for a five-day school) than Mountain Shadows and yet offers instruction on the same courses at Camelback. It's a scaled-back offering, of course, particularly in the cuisine department, but there are plenty of restaurants and everything else up and down Lincoln Boulevard in Scottsdale. Those who opt for Fairfield won't starve. (If you're stuck for a really good, non-Southwestern restaurant in Scottsdale, try La Chaumiere for chic and cozy French dining.)

TUCSON NATIONAL RESORT & SPA
TUCSON, ARIZONA

Tucson National is one of the host sites of the PGA TOUR's Northern Telecom Open, and it's a great place for golf. From excellent American cuisine in the Fiesta Room to the twenty-seven-hole golf club to the sometimes overlooked but extremely impressive spa facilities, Tucson National may well be worth a very hard look in deciding where to do a Jacobs'

school. Those of us who like Arizona especially value Tucson. It is at almost the 3,000-foot level, which takes the sting out of the hottest of the summer weather and extends the comfortable golf season well into May.

The original course at Tucson National is the Orange/Gold rotation, designed by golf architecture pioneer Robert Bruce Harris in 1960 and remodeled extensively since to keep up with modern design practice. It's unusual because it was built before water restrictions were imposed; thus it has lush, wide open fairways and bentgrass greens. The new nine dates from the era of desert target golf and is shorter at 3,222 yards than the 7,108 tournament track. They've stuffed the holes in to get a full nine, but stuffed them with intelligence by keeping the par-threes short rather than having a series of mid-length par-fours.

Most of the 167 suites at Tucson National have fireplaces and kitchens. All of them are conveniently located near the spa facilities for convenient access to a massage and loofah scrub after a long day on the practice tee.

INN AT NAPA VALLEY/ CHARDONNAY CLUB
NAPA, CALIFORNIA

Founded by a group of wine growers, this delightful club meanders through Chardonnay grape vineyards and is noted for its elevated tees and incredible scenery. The eighth and ninth holes, both par-fours, are long, delightful, and terribly humbling. There's also a new private course, Club Shakespeare, which accepts reciprocal play.

The Inn combines all the amenities of a first-class hotel with the warm charm of country decor. Besides, the wine list is suitably long and distinguished, and the touring options are endless with San Francisco an hour to the South and the famed Napa Valley vineyards offering tours and tasting events. Besides, for what it's worth, the Napa Valley is where this author began to learn the game. Twenty-four years later I'm still playing and still cherishing the memories of golf in the Valley of the Moon.

MARRIOTT'S DESERT SPRINGS RESORT AND SPA
PALM DESERT, CALIFORNIA

Five years ago a Who's Who of Golf descended on Desert Springs for the biannual Golf Summit. Everyone left with great memories of a great resort. The Ted Robinson–designed thirty-six holes forms one of his finest exercises in the water-laden oasis style that he developed. The food, accommodations, and ambience are quite outstanding. This fits in the top three of all the Marriott golf resorts.

The four on-site restaurants, the Sea Grille, Mikado, Tuscany's, and Lake View, are all outstanding for dining, and Lake View has a great brunch. The resort is also home to a well-rounded spa, several pools, jogging and fitness trails, and a seemingly endless parade of staffers named Bernard who come by and spritz you with fine mists on hot days.

As for golf, Ted Robinson is the architect who commissioned a survey on memorable desert holes and found that golfers remember the water holes best. He then designed two extremely memorable and water-laden courses at Desert Springs in the Palms and Valley courses. Both come in at around 6,700 yards, but the Palms Course is far flatter and wide

open, while the Valley Course has pitches, rolls, uneven lies, blind shots, and reflects a little Scottish flair in the design. In turn, Palms is the wetter of the two; on the back nine there are several opportunities to make a splashdown on the finishing stretch. Did I say that Palms was the more open? Generally it is, but on everyone's list of the "Palm Springs Mean Eighteen" is Palms' par-four fifth hole, 432 yards, with a narrow landing area. The big, straight drive is a huge bonus here, so be sure to have your instructor go over that part of the game twice. A birdie at the fifth would be a fine memory to take back home.

MARRIOTT'S RANCHO LAS PALMAS
RANCHO LAS PALMAS, CALIFORNIA

Just a few miles as the crow flies from the Desert Springs is the Rancho Las Palmas Resort, which is by contrast to Desert Springs and just about everything else in the Coachella Valley, decidedly low-key. An early Mission-style architecture of textured stucco and barrel-tile roofs gives it a timeless look and a siesta-time aura. It's been extensively renovated recently to keep the amenities and decor modern, but they've preserved that hideaway ambience that made Rancho Las Palmas the first (and to date only) Palm Springs area resort to earn the Mobil Five-Star rating.

As with Desert Springs, Ted Robinson designed the course here, twenty-seven holes of not incredibly overwhelming golf when it comes to yardage. The longest combination is just 6,019 yards. So the bigger hitters may wish to try elsewhere, but Robinson knows how to make a good golf hole, and all three nines, North, South and West, have some merit. North is the most open and rolling. South and West have, in their finishing holes, probably the best two holes on the course. For the very big hitter, there are a few par-fours reachable off the tee with a good bounce.

In all, however, it's the laid-back ambience and its proximity to shopping that defines the resort more than the courses. This resort figures high on the recommendation list only if after-hours golf is not on the program or if your party is composed of shorter hitters.

SKYLAND MOUNTAIN GOLF RESORT
SKYLAND, COLORADO

Nestled against the southern slope of the towering Mount Crested Butte, Skyland Country Club rests in the heart of the majestic Colorado Rocky Mountains. Skyland is not exactly in an urban center; it's roughly equidistant from Grand Junction and Denver on the edge of the Gunnison National Forest near the Crested Butte National Landmark, on the south side of Castle Peak (Aspen is on the north side). So expect a lot of the conditions of Aspen without the crowds.

The centerpiece of the Skyland community is the eighteen-hole Robert Trent Jones Jr. golf course. The 7,200 yard, par-seventy-two course flows through an Alpine valley with Mount Crested Butte and Paradise Divide forming a backdrop. Designed with four tee boxes for every hole, it's well suited for tournament players to beginners. It's 30 minutes from Gunnison Airport. The accommodations come in the shape of an Alpine village-style club. The rooms are generously sized, and there is plenty of good food to tuck

into after a day in the thin air of the high Rockies.

BONAVENTURE RESORT & SPA
FORT LAUDERDALE, FLORIDA

A 1,250-acre reserve on the edge of Fort Lauderdale, Bonaventure is very well known as a spa and increasingly so of late as a golf resort, thanks to the dramatic course designed by Joe Lee known as the East Course, and ranked in Florida's top ten by *GOLF* magazine. The Charlie Mahanna–designed West Course is relatively speaking, a cakewalk, and thus Bonaventure can truly boast that it has courses for golfers of all abilities. The setting of both courses is lush, everglade with lakes, waterfalls, and manicured greens. The resort offers an outstanding spa, dining, tennis, swimming, and fitness and health-related activities.

MARRIOTT'S ORLANDO WORLD CENTER
ORLANDO, FLORIDA

Marriott's Orlando World Center stakes a claim as Florida's largest and most spectacular resort, which is a little of a stretch when one considers the gargantuan size of the Disney complex (which exceeds the size of the District of Columbia. But if you take the spirit instead of the letter of the claim you get the idea. An eighteen-hole beauty from the vastly underrated Joe Lee is the centerpiece of the golf offering. And the resort may well offer the most central access to the primary Orlando attractions such as Walt Disney World, Epcot Center, Universal Studios, Cypress Gardens, Sea World, and Busch Gardens.

MARCO ISLAND RESORT & GOLF CLUB
MARCO ISLAND, FLORIDA

Less than an hour from Fort Myers Airport is the offshore Marco Island, which with Sanibel and Captiva may be the prize jewels of Florida's West Coast. Marco is the last stop before the Everglades National Park. It is situated about 15 miles north on the edge of the Big Cypress National Preserve and approximately 100 miles due north of Key West. The resort offers airboat tours of the Everglades, seashells, sunsets, a 16-acre golf practice facility that's in the top shelf of such facilities and a short drive from the hotel. Tennis and a health club complete the resort's active vacation options. The Marco Island course at 6,925 yards is no pushover. Carved out of 240 acres of cypress and palms, it's one of the most attractive as well. It's another Joe Lee experience. Well done!

GRAND HARBOUR GOLF & BEACH CLUB
VERO BEACH, FLORIDA

Billed as the "Best Little Town in Florida," Vero Beach is home to Grand Harbour, an 877-acre subtropical island collection along the Intracoastal Waterway. Grand Harbour has two courses, one designed by Joe Lee and

the other by Pete Dye. They're both excellent, particularly the Dye course, which features all the undulating fairways, blind holes, pot bunkers, deep rough, and general Scottish interference that one expects from the famed designer and co-author of *Bury Me in a Pot Bunker.*

GRAND TRAVERSE RESORT
TRAVERSE CITY, MICHIGAN

Grand Traverse resort is located on 1,200 acres of forest and lake-front scenery on the shores of Lake Michigan's Grand Traverse Bay, 6 miles northeast of Traverse City, Michigan, and in the heart of the golf-rich resort country of northern Michigan.

This is the Midwest's largest resort. It abounds with amenities and two eighteen-hole courses, which have brought the resort recognition through numerous top-fifty resort course rankings. Grand Traverse is the home of The Bear, the notorious Jack Nicklaus–designed course that was given to Nicklaus with one edict: "Make the toughest course in the United States."

He succeeded.

Since The Bear was opened, courses such as PGA West and The Ocean Course have challenged The Bear for sheer resistance to scoring, but none can match it for its heather-covered mounding, cavernous pot bunkers, and tiered fairways. The course is half paradise, half hell; paradise ends, incidentally, at the edge of the fairway! The English language strains to capture The Bear's bestial beauty. It's a good deal tougher than anything else Nicklaus has cooked up, and he's cooked up some dandies. Also, in the area nestled among the unspoiled, hilly landscape of northwest Michigan, this *GOLF* magazine

Silver Medal–winning Boyne Mountain resort with the Donald Ross Memorial Course, recreates eighteen of Ross' most memorable holes, including several from Oakland Hills and Pinehurst No. 2.

MARRIOTT TAR-TAN-A RESORT
OSAGE BEACH, MISSOURI

For some reason the name Tar-Tan-A conjures up visions of a dude ranch, but this is in fact a pretty decent golf resort. It recently hosted the PGA Club Pro Championship, which fills the club pro slots for the PGA Championship. The resort rests serenely on 420 wooded acres in central Missouri on the eastern edge of the Lake of the Ozarks. Horseback riding and hiking along the scenic woodland trails is a featured amenity.

The eighteen-hole Oaks course was designed by Bruce Devlin and Robert von Hagge, yesterday's design wunderkind who still puts out some very intelligently designed courses. The resort is also home to a nine-hole full-length course offering demanding approaches, large and relatively flat greens, and a series of daunting water hazards.

ANGEL PARK GOLF CLUB
(COMMUTER ONLY)
LAS VEGAS, NEVADA

Angel Park has two eighteen-hole championship courses designed by Arnold Palmer and Ed Seay, the long-standing duo responsible for almost 100 courses nationwide. Opened in 1989, Angel Park is the sole

Palmer and Seay design in the Vegas area. It is well worth a look. Course strategy comes first for the pair, but they also have a flair for visually exciting courses. The Palm course offers rugged terrain with fast bentgrass greens, while Mountain has spectacular views of Vegas. There's also an eighteen-hole putting course, which is one of the best as such experiences go. Cloud Nine, a par-three course, replicates twelve of the most celebrated par-threes in golf.

MARRIOTT'S SEAVIEW RESORT
ATLANTIC CITY, NEW JERSEY

This is one of Marriott's best resorts and one of the few truly outstanding resorts in the Northeast—670 acres of resort and 100-year-old Jersey pines provide the backdrop.

For golfers, the main event is the presence of a Donald Ross–designed golf course—the Bay Course. But the Pines course by William Flynn and Howard Toomey is no slouch, either, and their design pedigree goes almost as far back as Ross'. They designed Shinnecock Hills, Merion, and Cherry Hills, among other courses. And of course, Atlantic City has the famed boardwalk, casinos, live shows, boxing, horse racing, Ice Capades, and once a year— the Miss America Pageant. Those who have found Atlantic City a bit depressing would do well to lock themselves within the Seaview's gates and play the courses here. There's not a depressing inch on either of them.

HANAH COUNTRY INN & GOLF RESORT

MARGARETVILLE, NEW YORK

This old-line resort holed up in the Catskills has a recently redesigned 7,000-yard golf course that offers a challenge that can't quite match the Concord Hotel's Monster for the toughest course in the Catskills, but it could well be a good second. Hanah showcases 900 acres of unspoiled Catskills and rural New York countryside.

WIND WATCH HOTEL & GOLF CLUB
(COMMUTER ONLY)

HAUPPAGE, LONG ISLAND, NEW YORK

Joe Lee did the course here, one of the many that he has designed for Marriott, but he added a 3-acre golf practice and Learning Center. The Wind Watch area features rolling farmland hills, rocky beaches, and ferry-port towns with antique stores and wineries. The hotel itself is situated atop 165-foot Colonie Hill and overlooks the course. The course is 10 minutes from MacArthur Airport in Islip and under an hour from LaGuardia Airport. The hotel is also within a half-hour of Bethpage State Park, home of one of the finest public courses in the country in the Black course.

LANGDON FARMS GOLF CLUB
(COMMUTER ONLY)

PORTLAND, OREGON

Bob Cupp and John Fought (a former U.S. amateur champion and PGA TOUR winner) were the architects here—the same pair that put Oregon on the national golf design map with Witch Hollow and Ghost Creek at Pumpkin Ridge. Depressed fairways give Langdon Farms its distinctive look. Large greens are the order of the day, with bentgrass thriving throughout the golf season here. Ground contours have been used to create chipping zones, adding another element of interest to the experience.

The practice area is state-of-the-art. It has a bentgrass putting course (an unusual touch), as well as several teaching stations situated around The Barn, which houses the golf shop, a full- service restaurant, and a picnic area.

Although this is only a commuter school, it's well worth a look no matter what you have to do for accommodations. Oregon has to be the up-and-coming golf state, along with perhaps Alabama, and most of the courses such as Salishan, Oregon Country Club, and Pumpkin Ridge, which have burnished the state's reputation are found within easy driving distance.

RANCHO VIEJO RESORT

SOUTH PADRE ISLAND, TEXAS

Right at the southern edge of Texas on the edge of the Padre Island National Seashore is Rancho Viejo Resort, where the most well-known attraction is a 6,000-square-foot landscaped pool large enough to earn its own name—Alberca Grande, featuring a cascading waterfall and a swim-up bar. But golf is a star, too.

Rancho Viejo features two eighteen-hole championship-length courses, El Diablo and El Angel, which offer striking contrast. El Diablo begins with a sleepy, parkland style before exploding into a melange of movement and roll via undulating fairways, steep bunkering, and enticing water hazards. El Angel is designed in the Scottish style, with flat elevations, wide open fairways, and large greens that encourage bold strokemaking and reward precision. Rancho Viejo is located 20 minutes from either Harlingen or Brownsville South Padre International Airport.

HOMESTEAD
HEBER VALLEY, UTAH

Twenty-five minutes from Park City, nestled in the pastoral Heber Valley, is Utah's most complete four-season resort, Homestead. It is known for a country charm and wide resort activity selection. Its eighteen-hole championship golf course presents a panoramic view on the front nine, meandering through Snake Creek Valley, while the back nine is set against the backdrop of the Utah Rockies and the Uinta National Forest. The course features a three- to five-tee system to extend the challenge from the tips, while preserving a fun course for resort golfers. Homestead is 60 minutes from Salt Lake International Airport.

LAKE LAWN LODGE
DELAVAN, WISCONSIN

The Lake Geneva area is Wisconsin's golf mecca, with the Americana Resort and Blackwolf Run on the eastern tip of the lake, Geneva National nearby, and Lake Lawn Lodge 10 miles northwest of the lake in nearby Delavan. A 90-minute connection from O'Hare, Lake Lawn is one of the established Wisconsin resorts and features a certain rustic simplicity that has become sort of a signature for golf resorts in the state. They dub it "heartland hospitality," and that's a fair assessment. Lake Lawn has a lake of its own in Lake Delavan, home to most of the resort activities, including fishing, sailing, and waterskiing. The eighteen-hole course is set in the forest that surrounds the lake and is best known for the premium it places on a straight game off the tee. It's narrow and quite extensively trapped.

JACKSON HOLE GOLF COURSE/WORT HOTEL
JACKSON HOLE, WYOMING

This is the part of the world where civilization ends and the wilderness still reigns. Jackson Hole is an island of resort development in the Wyoming Rockies surrounded by Grand Teton National Forest and 13,771-foot Grand Teton on the west, Bridgerton National Forest to the east and south, and Yellowstone National Park to the north. It's also on the edge of a national elk refuge. Serious wilderness!

Jackson Hole is best known for some of the best skiing in the country, but summers are dedicated to golf. The season picks up in late

May on an Arnold Palmer and Ed Seay course in the area. Plus, the local Big Kahuna, Jackson Hole Golf Course, remodeled by Robert Trent Jones Jr., rated in the top twenty-five public courses in the country by *GOLF Digest*. It's water, water everywhere, with the liquid stuff available on eleven of the eighteen holes. But why not? No point in going somewhere as remote as Jackson Hole for a roll-over golf experience.

The Wort Hotel is an elegant, small hotel with spacious, uniquely styled rooms and restaurants. The hotel started off like most old Wyoming hotels as a gambling palace. Wort's Silver Dollar Bar is named in tribute to the hotel's somewhat dangerous past. The Hotel is a few minutes from the course and under 20 minutes from Jackson Airport. You'd really miss one of life's great adventures if you didn't mosey an hour north into Yellowstone, too.

OVERSEAS SCHOOLS

GOLF CLUB MURHOF
GRAZ, AUSTRIA

The package includes four days of golf instruction, five nights accommodation, breakfast and dinner daily, a cocktail party, and all green fees and practice balls. Murhof is priced at $1850 per person based on double occupancy ($2010 for single occupancy). As a special bonus, the school is conducted personally by John Jacobs, the master himself.

SAN ROGUE GOLF CLUB
CADIZ-GIBRALTAR, SPAIN

The package includes five days of golf instruction, seven nights accommodations at the Suites Hotel on the golf course, breakfast and dinner daily, a Gala dinner, welcome cocktail party, a rental car shared by two golfers, greens fees, practice balls, and bag storage and cleaning. The price for the school is $2995 per person (double occupancy) or $3380 (single occupancy). Duty-free shopping in Gibraltar will take some of the sting out of the price, as will the weather in southern Spain in this February school. In addition, the school is personally conducted by John Jacobs.

MERITIM GOLF CLUB
HAMBURG, GERMANY

The package includes four days of golf instruction, five nights accommodations, breakfast and dinner daily, a cocktail party, green fees, and practice balls. The club is located 60 minutes from Hamburg and the cost for the school is $1875 per person (double occupancy) or $2150 (single occupancy). In addition, the school is personally conducted by John Jacobs.

LAND & GOLF CLUB
OESCHBERGHOL
(BLACK FOREST), GERMANY

The package includes four days of golf instruction, five nights accommodations, breakfast and dinner daily, a cocktail party, green fees, and practice balls. The club is located 50 minutes from Zurich, Switzerland. The cost for the school is $1995 per person (double occupancy) or $2180 (single occupancy). The school is personally conducted by John Jacobs.

CHUNG SHAN HOT SPRING GOLF CLUB

ZHONGSHAN CITY, CHINA

The package includes three days of golf instruction, three nights accommodations, all meals daily, green fees after 4 p.m., caddie services, take-home video, 45-minute massage, two nights accommodation at the Club Hotel, round-trip hydrofoil tickets from Hong Kong to Zhuhai, China, and transportation from Zhuhai to Chung Shan. The cost for the school is HK$9500 per person (double occupancy) or HK$10,300 (single occupancy) for a weekend school. Midweek schools are priced at HK$5500 (double occupancy) and HK$6300 (single occupancy).

Chung Shan, the Arnold Palmer/Ed Seay–designed course, has operated since 1984 in mainland China. It was the first course constructed in that country.

■ CONTACT ■

John Jacobs' Golf Schools
7825 East Redfield Road
Scottsdale, AZ 85260-6977
800-472-5007
In Arizona 602-991-8587

KEN BLANCHARD, THE GOLF UNIVERSITY OF SAN DIEGO

SAN DIEGO, CALIFORNIA

PROGRAMS Schools run every week, June–November. Four-day schools begin on Mondays; three-day schools begin each Friday.

ABOUT THE PROGRAM The Golf University was founded in 1988 by Ken Blanchard to reach out to golfers and bring them an easy-to-learn, individualized golf curriculum. Blanchard's innovative management ideas are applied to golf in a way that enhances performance and enjoyment of the game. Over 3,500 students have graduated from the schools, which begin with goal-setting and working out a curriculum with the Professional. The Golf University is the type of school that adapts itself to the student's needs, rather than imposing a training and swing regimen.

The typical four-day program includes an opening night dinner, four days of classroom and swing instruction work, on-course playing lessons, videotape swing evaluation with voice-over analysis, personal practice programs, personal club evaluation and fitting, physical evaluation and exercise program, instruction manual and notebook, take-home video cassette, unlimited green fees and carts, range balls, club storage and shoe service, and deluxe accommodations on-site at the Rancho Bernardo Inn. The club-fitting service and continuous video analysis receive special emphasis, as well as transferring the teaching role gradually from the instructor to the student. The goal of the program is to have the students correct their own mistakes, notice what went well, and where improvement can be made. Instruction ranges from the full swing right through the short game to putting. In addition, the Golf University provides a back-home practice program to continue the learning process beyond graduation.

COSTS Three-day school $1095 (double occupancy), $1275 (single occupancy), $895 (commuter); four-day school $1295 (double occupancy), $1535, (single occupancy), $1050 (commuter).

STUDENT/TEACHER RATIO 3:1.

HEAD INSTRUCTOR The head instructor is Ken Blanchard. "Do you want to know the secret about golf?" asks Ken Blanchard in his advertisements. Well, the big secret about this school is that . . . hmmn, Ken Blanchard isn't really much of a golfer compared to most of his colleagues in the golf school game. Blanchard is widely known as the co-author of *The One-Minute Manager* and *Situational Leadership*. One of his most recent books is *Playing the Great Game of Golf*, which is actually quite good and won his speaking engagements with the National Golf Foundation and a column in *Links* magazine. In the book, Blanchard applies his innovative management ideas to golf in a way that enhances performance and enjoyment of the game. The Golf University is designed as an extension of those ideas. To handle the actual instruction, Blanchard has smartly surrounded himself with a capable staff of actual golf instructors under Tom Wischmeyer, but Blanchard's lack of actual experience in the field and particularly in tournament play makes this school a question mark for serious low-handicappers and professionals, but excellent for beginners through mid-handicappers.

■ **ABOUT THE LOCATION** ■

RANCHO BERNARDO INN AND GOLF CLUB

SAN DIEGO, CALIFORNIA

The Rancho Bernardo Inn is situated 25 miles from San Diego in the San Pasqual Mountains. Blessed by the mild marine climate of San Diego, luxurious but laid-back Rancho Bernardo has forty-five holes of golf, including three nine-hole executive courses and the eighteen-hole West Course redesigned by Ted Robinson in 1991. Rancho Bernardo is also home to twelve tennis courts, a 5,000-square-foot Fitness Center, and a seasonal children's program. The West Course has had its moments in history, hosting the 1963 San Diego Open won by Art Wall and the LPGA Inamori Classic in the late 1970s. Robinson's remodeling added extra spice to the course, especially on the back nine with some lengthening. He added greatly to the beauty with an extensive tree-planting program to complement the eucalyptus, olive, sycamore, and pine trees that line the course. In all, it's a very worthy test of golf.

One of the highlights of the resort is actually indoors, however, in the elegant French cuisine served at E Bizcocho, a Mission-style dining room with commanding views of the golf course and the mountains. The resort also serves Continental cuisine and fresh seafood specialties in The Veranda Room, amidst an early California ranch atmosphere.

The resort's 287 rooms are tastefully secluded among the sycamores and eucalyptus. The staff are well trained and serve with a degree of attention rarely seen at larger resorts.

■ CONTACT ■

The Golf University of San Diego
17550 Bernardo Oaks Drive
San Diego, CA 92128
800-426-0966
In California 619-485-8880

KEN VENTURI GOLF LEARNING CENTERS

BLUFFTON, SOUTH CAROLINA;
RANCHO MIRAGE, CALIFORNIA

PROGRAMS Stroke Savers clinic, half-day sessions, full-day schools; year-round.

ABOUT THE PROGRAM Who could resist a lesson from the original "Stroke Saver" himself, Ken Venturi, who has graced the CBS golf telecasts for years with his insights and instructional tips? Venturi appears at both schools on selected dates, but throughout the year his hand-picked staff of instructors teach the "Venturi System"—a proven program of basic fundamentals designed to meet the individual needs and goals of each student.

The Stroke Saver Clinics are conducted by the Center's staff, focusing on chipping, pitching, putting, and bunker shots, just as in the CBS Sports "Stroke Saver" segments.

The half-day schools include 3 1/2 hours of instruction, take-home video analysis, and a special focus on the "Stroke Savers" short-game techniques.

The full-day schools offer the best value, as they stretch to a full 8 hours of instruction complete with a nine-hole playing lesson. Comprehensive full-swing and short-game instruction is provided, as well as the take-home videotaped swing analysis, a take-home audio cassette, lunch, and refreshments. Students are paired with others of similar abilities. The Venturi School is well grounded in the Venturi philosophy, so one needn't wait for the maestro to make an appearance.

But Kenny's worth waiting for if your calendar is flexible. He makes his appearance at Hilton Head to coincide with the MCI Classic (April 10–16 in 1995), typically between Tuesday and Thursday.

COSTS Stroke Savers clinic (1 hour) $25; half-day sessions $149; full-day sessions $299.

STUDENT/TEACHER RATIO 4:1.

HEAD INSTRUCTOR Ken Venturi hardly needs an introduction as the CBS Sports golf analyst for the past twenty-eight years. But he's been so long in the broadcast booth that perhaps a few words of introduction to Ken Venturi the golfer would be appropriate. Venturi was one of the leading young amateurs of the early 1950s and turned professional in 1956 after finishing runner-up at The Masters. He won fourteen PGA TOUR events in his storied career, including a dramatic victory in the 1964 U.S. Open at Congressional, when the mercury passed 100° in the final round, and Venturi overcame heat exhaustion in the final holes to score one of the most dramatic Open victories ever. *Sports Illustrated* named Venturi its Sportsman of the Year for 1964. Venturi went on to play on the 1965 Ryder Cup team and, after joining CBS Sports in the late 1960s, began to build a considerable reputation as a golf analyst and teacher. He was named one of the Ten Living Legends of Golf Instruction by the PGA of America in 1992.

■ ABOUT THE LOCATIONS ■

OLD SOUTH GOLF LINKS
BLUFFTON, SOUTH CAROLINA

Old South Golf Links is one of the most exciting premium daily-fee courses constructed in the entire Southeast during the 1990s and was nominated by *GOLF Digest* for its Best New Resort Course award in 1992. Old South has an absolutely breathtaking setting overlooking the marshlands and Hilton Head Island, which is directly across the Intracoastal Waterway from Old South's Bluffton locale. Old South's front nine roll through densely wooded forests with some intriguing marshside holes, but the back nine ranks as one of the best nines in South Carolina. Several holes skirt the coast and offer an excellent test of golf as well as commanding views. Architect Clyde Johnston was also responsible for Heather Glen in the Myrtle Beach area of South Carolina, voted Best New Resort Course by *GOLF Digest* in the late 1980s.

Since Old South does not have on-site accommodations, vacationers are encouraged to try the Westin Resort on Hilton Head Island at 800-681-4000, a perennial Five-Diamond winner right on the beach with three good golf courses on-site in Hilton Head's Port Royal Plantation.

THE WESTIN MISSION HILLS RESORT
RANCHO MIRAGE, CALIFORNIA

The Westin Mission Hills comes at you like a mirage out of the desert. The sprawling 360-acre Moroccan village is bedecked in waterfalls, archways, swaying palms, and lush gardens with peach-colored buildings that blend effortlessly into the desert floor. Opened in 1987, the Resort features a 7,000-square-foot swimming pool and waterslide and the art deco Bella Vista restaurant (one of three on the property). The Mission Hills Resort course, which opened with the resort in 1987, is a kinder, gentler Pete Dye design. While the fairways are tight, many of the greens allow for bump-and-run shots as opposed to full carries over water hazards. Where there is water there is danger, however, particularly on the long par-four finishing hole, with water all the way to contend with and into the prevailing winds. The resort added a Gary Player course in 1991, which is one of the most intimidating that Player has ever come up with, and sports a mammoth 75.0 rating from the tips. Don't play from there! Opt for the regular tees and enjoy the man-made waterfalls and rock formations that enhance the stunning backdrop of the San Jacinto Mountains. The greens are without undulation, as is Player's penchant, and the fairway is wide open, so if you can manage the approach shots well you will be fine.

■ CONTACT ■

Ken Venturi Golf Training Centers
The Market Place
7600 Drive Phillips Boulevard, Suite 72
Orlando, FL 32819
800-735-3357
In Florida 407-352-9669

LA COSTA SCHOOL OF GOLF

CARLSBAD, CALIFORNIA

PROGRAMS Instruction is offered year-round at the resort in full- and half-day programs.

ABOUT THE PROGRAM A "must-consider" golf school, under the direction of Carl Welty, who teaches Tom Kite, Curtis Strange, Davis Love III, and Sandy Lyle and who also was Jim McLean's teacher (see Doral). His specialty is videotape swing analysis, and La Costa is considered by most authorities to offer the best video facilities in the world. Tom Kite once came in during the Tournament of Champions to check on his putting stroke by comparing putts from 1988 and putts from 1993 and fired a record-tying 64 the next day, including four 10-foot or longer birdie putts. Welty is a featured instructor in the Tommy Armour PGA Teaching & Coaching Summit. Welty ignores most of the truisms of golf instruction for a simple "First we determine where the ball went. Second, we figure out where the club went. Then we can start to fix the problem." Fix it he will. At fairly low rates, too!

Welty-World is high-tech, to say the least, and if you think at some stage that you've dropped into the twenty-fourth century, don't worry. You're not the first person to have these thoughts.

The program offers Lebelon tape for sweet-spot analysis, cybernetic repetition, laser-beam alignment, swing analyzers to measure swing and accuracy, high-speed video cameras with super slow motion VCR playback, indoor driving in the indoor studio, and large full-length mirrors for swing analysis. Among the many unique teaching techniques Welty

■ La Costa Resort and Spa.

employs is to have students describe their feelings and the ball's action during the video recording. Welty realized that golfers forget which ball felt good when they review video playbacks of their swings. Almost all instruction and certainly all videotaping is conducted on-source rather than on a range.

COSTS $85 per hour for individual instruction; $100 per hour for 2 students.

STUDENT/TEACHER RATIO 1:1.

HEAD INSTRUCTOR Carl Welty is a "mad scientist" when it comes to golf instruction. He has assembled the world's largest collection of videotapes of the world's great golf swings. When he founded the La Costa Golf School in 1964 he had already been working with video golf instruction for over twenty years. As of this writing, Welty now has 160 miles of tape on players' golf swings dating back fifteen years. A favorite Welty story is his analysis of touring pro Peter Jacobsen. He freeze-framed Jake's five-iron swing at impact, placed a protractor on the screen, and measured the angle formed by the five-iron and the ground. The angle was 61°, while Welty's notes show that the angle for tournament winners falls between 53° and 55°. He makes notes for Jacobsen's improvement. Now, that's swing analysis.

■ ABOUT THE LOCATION ■

LA COSTA RESORT AND SPA
··
CARLSBAD, CALIFORNIA

There are two famous spas in the United States that boast excellent Dick Wilson-Joe Lee golf courses and host prestigious PGA TOUR events. In the east there's Doral, where Carl Welty's student, Jim McLean, reigns supreme

as resident golf guru. In the west there's La Costa, where one finds Carl Welty himself and the Mercedes Championships. This famous resort was voted the favorite place to stay of all the stops on the tour by the PGA TOUR players and families.

Dick Wilson crafted the South Course in 1965, and the Tournament of Champions arrived in 1969. The more forgiving North Course, a Joe Lee project opened in 1985, is a little easier on the high-handicapper, but neither course is a pussycat. In fact, the four-hole finish on the tournament course, at 1,671 yards directly into the Pacific breezes, is known as "the longest mile in golf."

For all the fame of the resort as a golfing mecca, it is still probably best known as a spa. It is a frequent haunt of Hollywood stars and is currently home to luxurious, Mediterranean-style accommodations, eight restaurants, twenty-three tennis courts, four lounges, five pools, a theater showing first-run movies, and a Lifestyle Center with all the massages, saunas, rock steam baths, Swiss showers, Roman pools, whirlpools, skin analysis, manicures, facials, herbal wraps, and loofah scrubs anyone could ask for. The cuisine is excellent, by the way, even if it is good for you. And there is a Gaucho Steakhouse at the resort should you tire of spa living.

■ CONTACT ■

La Costa Golf School
La Costa Resort
Costa del Mar Road
Carlsbad, CA 92009
800-653-7888
In California 619-438-9111

MARLENE FLOYD'S FOR WOMEN ONLY GOLF SCHOOL

HILTON HEAD ISLAND,
SOUTH CAROLINA

PROGRAMS Three two-day schools in October and two in April.

ABOUT THE PROGRAM The Marlene Floyd program is taught by women and is for women—even the program assistants are female. It all stems from Floyd's observation that women, particularly those new to the game of golf, become intimidated less easily if instructed by other women.

The program begins with Basic Fundamentals, concentrating on grip, alignment, stance, and posture. Floyd's instruction even can go all the way back to as simple a device as teaching students how to toss a ball and how to achieve the power positions for throwing or swinging. The school progresses to the full swing with irons and woods, emphasizing increased distance, which, of course, is a particularly important subject in women's golf. The final phase of the two-day program concentrates on chipping, pitching, sand play, and putting. The emphasis throughout the program is on a relaxed, natural swinging of the club like that taught by Floyd's renowned father, golf instructor L.B. Floyd, and by legendary instructor Johnny Revolta. All instructors are PGA and LPGA certified, and Marlene leads each school in person.

The school is affiliated with the Executive Women's Golf Leagues.

COSTS Two-day school $399.

STUDENT/TEACHER RATIO 3:1.

HEAD INSTRUCTOR Marlene Floyd is the younger sister of PGA TOUR star Raymond Floyd, the daughter of influential instructor L.B. Floyd, and an LPGA veteran in her own right who led the LPGA in lowest putting average in 1980 and 1981. Floyd is best known to golfers as a seventeen-year veteran of golf broadcasts, most recently with NBC. Marlene teaches and plays golf with Fortune 500 executives in numerous corporate outings and gives many clinics for charity organizations. Aside from her professional credentials, Marlene Floyd is also one of the nicest people in the game.

■ ABOUT THE LOCATIONS ■

PALMETTO DUNES RESORT

HILTON HEAD ISLAND,
SOUTH CAROLINA

Palmetto Dunes offers the most consistent and challenging collection of courses on Hilton Head Island, and the resort was recognized by *Links* magazine with a "Best of the South" award for combination of courses as well as a Silver Medal from *GOLF* magazine for the resort as a whole.

The Robert Trent Jones Course is the oldest of Palmetto Dunes' trio opened in 1969. It winds through parts of an 11-mile network of navigable lagoons, and four holes run alongside the main thoroughfare, which, when celebrities such as President Clinton are on the course, has created some Hilton Head–style traffic tie-ups. The Jones course is typical Trent Jones with landing strip–like tees, long, and flowing lines, and mammoth greens. The Fazio Course was added in 1974 and was rated for many years in the nation's top-100. The par-seventy layout is long, difficult, and beset with yawning waste bunkers that seem to surpass the Sahara desert for sheer size. The terrain is rolling, and the course is very highly recommended for lower-handicappers. The Arthur Hills Course was added in 1986 and has hosted the Golf World Collegiate since then. It's kinder than the Fazio Course and, built on a secondary dune line, features dramatically rolling terrain. The Hills course also hosted the 1990 NCAA Women's Championship.

Palmetto Dunes has myriad choices in accommodations, including more than 500 rental homes and villas in all sizes and settings. The resort is also home to two outstanding hotels: the 505-room Hyatt Regency (which plays host to the elite Renaissance Weekend each year that attracts the Washington political heavyweights) and the Caribbean-style 325-room Hilton Resort, which is set amidst lush gardens and fountains and features oversized guest rooms. Both are directly on the ocean.

■ CONTACT ■

Marlene Floyd's For Women Only Golf
   School
5350 Club House Lane
Hope Mills, NC 28348
800-637-2694
In North Carolina 919-323-9606

NICKLAUS/FLICK GOLF SCHOOLS

PALM BEACH, FLORIDA;
SCOTTSDALE, ARIZONA;
PEBBLE BEACH, CALIFORNIA;
HARBOR SPRINGS, MICHIGAN

PROGRAMS Master golf I: three days full instruction; master golf II: five days full instruction; master golf III: three half-days instruction plus three eighteen-hole rounds;

master golf IV: three half-days instruction plus two playing rounds with instructors; master golf V: two half-days short game instruction plus two nine-hole rounds.

Desert Mountain
   Master golf I: three schools in February, four in March, one in April, three in May, two in October, and two in November; master golf II: one in March and one in May; master golf V: one in February.

Ibis
   Master golf I: two in January, one in February, one in March, two in April, one in May, one in October, two in November, and three in December; master golf II: one in March; master golf III: one in January, one in April, and one in December; master golf IV: one in January, one in February, one in March, one in April, two in November, and one in December; master golf V: one in January, one in April, two in November, and one in December. Ibis also hosts a ladies-only program (three days) in February.

Boyne Highlands
   Master golf I: two in August; master golf II: one in August; Boyne Highlands also hosts an Alumni program (three days) in June and a Parent/Child program (three days) in July.

Pebble Beach
   Master golf I: one in February; master golf III: one in April, one in July, and one in August. Pebble Beach also hosts a Couples program (three days) in February around Valentine's Day.
ABOUT THE PROGRAMS All Nicklaus/Flick instructors are handpicked by Jack Nicklaus and Jim Flick and are under the direct supervision of Flick, who is based at Nicklaus/Flick headquarters in Palm Beach. Their operation is part of the Golden Bear colossus in West Palm Beach, but they fan out to several sites throughout the country.

The program includes a seminar by a sports psychologist; one-on-one instruction on the full swing; short game; and course management; video swing analysis; take-home video with computer graphic enhancement; golf equipment fitting and evaluation, a nine-hole daily round; and the popular eighteen-hole Tournament with prizes.

COSTS Rates are also available for non-golfing guests.

Desert Mountain

Master golf I (double occupancy) $2995, (single occupancy) $3695, (commuter) $2250; master golf II (double occupancy) $4250, (single occupancy) $4995, (commuter) $3395; master golf V (double occupancy) $2395, (single occupancy) $2895, (commuter) $1895.

Ibis

Master golf I (double occupancy) $2695, (single occupancy) $3320, (commuter) $2995; master golf II (double occupancy) $3895, (single occupancy) $4695, (commuter) $2995; master golf III (double occupancy) $2550, (single occupancy) $3195, (commuter) $1895; master golf IV (double occupancy) $2395, (single occupancy) $2850, (commuter) $1850; master golf V (double occupancy) $2295, (single occupancy) $2795, (commuter) $1795.

Boyne Highlands

Master golf I (double occupancy) $2550, (single occupancy) $3095, (commuter) $2050; master golf II (double occupancy) $3750, (single occupancy) $4395, (commuter) $2995.

Pebble Beach

Master golf I (double occupancy) $3350, (single occupancy) $4095, (commuter) $2595; master golf III (double occupancy) $3250, (single occupancy) $3995, (commuter) $2450.

STUDENT/TEACHER RATIO 1:1.

HEAD INSTRUCTOR Jim Flick has been one of the nation's top instructors for many years, and Jack Nicklaus needs little introduction either as a player or communicator within the game; but they teamed up late in their careers after Flick's advice had resulted in some noticeable improvements in the Nicklaus game. Flick has trained probably more PGA TOUR pros than any contemporary instructor except perhaps Jimmy Ballard and has written scores of articles for magazines over the years.

Jack Nicklaus needs no introduction as a player, but he has also had significant impact on the game in the field of instruction through his series of books with Ken Bowden, most notably, *Play Better Golf*. Interestingly, Jack Nicklaus was the first prominent professional player to publicly acknowledge his teachers (and he's had many, beginning with Jack Grout at Scioto). As other professionals followed his lead, the great "golf guru" phenomenon was begun, with prominent teachers vying to have top professionals among their students. (It also has led to the unfortunate policy of several instructors to claim they had "worked with" certain top professionals when the work in question was more along the lines of making a suggestion on the driving range.)

■ ABOUT THE LOCATIONS ■

IBIS GOLF & COUNTRY CLUB
PGA NATIONAL RESORT AND SPA
PALM BEACH GARDENS, FLORIDA

Ibis, a distinguished private club in Palm Beach County, Florida, opened in 1990, features two courses (one designed by Jack Nicklaus and the other designed by his son

Jack Nicklaus II). PGA National Resort and Spa was founded some fifteen years ago as the PGA of America's headquarters and as its statement in golf resort excellence. The amenity base is, to say the least, sumptuous. There are five golf courses, a European-style spa, nineteen tennis courts, three swimming pools, croquet, health and racquet club, 335 rooms, and seven dining establishments. The resort has received a Four-Star rating from Mobil and Four Diamonds from AAA for ten consecutive years, no small achievement in itself.

There are two seasons in the Florida travel calendar. First there is the warm season, which runs from November to March and features crowded hotels and courses, high prices, and the best weather in the country. The hot season, from April through October, features empty courses and hotels, low rates, and the worst weather in the country. Use your best judgment. (Note: Palm Beach Gardens receives some temperature relief from the ocean breezes but is beset by thunderstorms in the summer afternoons.)

PGA National is home to three courses designed by George and Tom Fazio (Haig, Champion, and Squire), one by Karl Litten (Estate), and the fifth by Arnold Palmer and Ed Seay (The General). Each of the courses features water on at least thirteen holes, so accuracy and judgment will be at a premium.

If you have a free day at the beginning of your stay at PGA National, play Estate, Haig, or Squire. Haig gives more room off the tee for big hitters, while Estate and Squire are more friendly to short hitters—but all three are good "tune-up" courses, especially if you are coming off a sabbatical.

On your final day at the resort, try to get out to Champion or The General. They're great aesthetic rewards for all the hard work you've been through at golf school—and both

will test your new fount of golfing knowledge with a combination of tough landing areas, length, toughness, and emphasis on accuracy (the General more so off the tee; Champion on the approaches).

The course that receives the bulk of national attention is Champion, which hosted the Ryder Cup (1983) and the PGA Championship (1987) and is the annual site for the PGA Seniors Championship. Champion, which was remodeled by Jack Nicklaus in 1990, features a trio of difficult opening holes and is not the ideal first-day course. Thus it is hard to generalize about the sort of game that will succeed. Larry Nelson's precision game and Arnold Palmer's gambles have both netted major victories here.

The resort is built around a 26-acre lake, and features a Mediterranean Revival architectural theme. Vaulted ceilings and tiled floors abound throughout the resort. The spa is a late addition to the resort and inspired a 1992 renovation and remodeling effort. Several of the restaurants feature spa cuisine, but Explorers serves Continental cuisine in a formal setting for those seeking a more traditional resort experience.

PGA National is billed as a complete resort, and it certainly doesn't disappoint. Values are certainly excellent in the off-season, but be prepared for some sweating on the range if you try the budget route.

DESERT MOUNTAIN GOLF CLUB
SCOTTSDALE PRINCESS RESORT
SCOTTSDALE, ARIZONA

Nestled in the mountains of Carefree, just north of Scottsdale, this prestigious golf club hosts The Tradition, which is a major championship on the PGA Senior TOUR, features three world-class golf courses (including two ranked in the top 100 in the United States by *GOLF Digest*), and practice facilities designed by Jack Nicklaus. Students enjoy golf on the Renegade Course. The Four-Star Scottsdale Princess, which is the place the pros stay when they come to town for the Phoenix Open, offers students oversized rooms and a host of amenities, including four restaurants (one of which is the world-class Marquesa), three lounges, two eighteen-hole courses of its own designed by Weiskopf and Morrish, (including the TPC Stadium Course that hosts the Phoenix Open), ten tennis courts, swimming, a fitness center, a spa, racquetball, squash, and an equestrian center.

PEBBLE BEACH RESORT
INN AT SPANISH BAY
PEBBLE BEACH, CALIFORNIA

Pebble Beach, the world's most famous golf resort, offers outstanding golf on three distinctive courses, all of which have been ranked in the top 100 in the United States, as well as breathtaking views of the Pacific shoreline. The Inn at Spanish Bay at Pebble Beach was recently voted by *Conde Nast Traveler* as the "Best Mainland Resort." The Inn has four of the Monterey Peninsula's finest restaurants, not to mention a clubhouse complete with pro shop, fitness center, tennis facility, and heated outdoor pool. The Pebble Beach resort offers biking, shopping boutiques, and a fine equestrian facility.

But who would want to spend time in an equestrian facility when the Links at Spanish Bay, Spyglass Hill, and Pebble Beach Golf

Links beckon? The Links is the least known of the three, since it has too fragile an ecosystem to handle the crowds of a golf tournament. It was designed by Tom Watson, Robert Trent Jones Jr., and former USGA president Sandy Tatum. Spyglass Hill is of course the notorious Robert Trent Jones–designed course opened in 1966 that prompted Lee Trevino to suggest that Jones should be taken out and shot. It has the second-highest rating slope in the United States after the Ocean Course at Kiawah. Pebble is of course Pebble, host of the 1972, 1982, and 1992 U.S. Opens, as well as a regular tour stop (with Spyglass Hill) via the AT&T National Pro-Am. Typically rated among the top three courses in the world, Pebble Beach is also home to the Tap Room, routinely rated among the five best nineteenth holes in the world.

BOYNE HIGHLANDS RESORT
HEATHER HIGHLANDS INN
HARBOR SPRINGS, MICHIGAN

Nestled among the unspoiled, hilly landscape of northwest Michigan, this *GOLF* magazine Silver Medal–winning resort has five world-class golf courses, plus tennis, swimming, biking, hiking, trout fishing, waterskiing, and the famous Gaslight District with its 100 specialty shops located in nearby Petosky. Perhaps the most interesting of the courses is the Donald Ross Memorial Course, which recreates eighteen of Ross' most memorable holes, including several from Oakland Hills and Pinehurst No. 2.

■ CONTACT ■

Nicklaus/Flick Golf School
11780 U.S. Highway 1
North Palm Beach, FL 33408
800-642-5528
In Florida 407-626-3900

PARADISE GOLF SCHOOLS

MARCO ISLAND, FLORIDA;
NAPLES, FLORIDA

PROGRAMS Two-, three-, and five-day programs.

ABOUT THE PROGRAMS This is a "work with what you have" school, using videotape analysis at the commencement of the school to identify the golfer's natural abilities and plan out a program for the school and for after-school review. Following in the Ben Sutton tradition of on-course instruction, classes are limited to around 20 students and cover the entire range of instruction from rules and etiquette to full-swing instruction.

A masters program is available with instructor Jim Wright at the Apache Junction and Carmel locations. The format is essentially the same, but the instruction with Wright is one-on-one.

The three-day program features 18 hours of instruction, two playing lessons, tapes, instruction handbook, club cleaning and storage, green and cart fees, and club fitting. The five-day program adds 9 more hours of instruction, an extra playing lesson, and two cocktail receptions.

COSTS Marco Island summer and fall two-day school (double occupancy) $520, (single occupancy) $575, (nonstudent) $150, (commuter) $400; three-day-school (double occupancy) $720, (single occupancy) $820, (nonstudent) $200, (commuter) $595; five-day school (double occupancy) $1220, (single occupancy) $1420, (nonstudent) $345, (commuter) $975.

Marco Island winter and spring two-day school (double occupancy) $775, (single occupancy) $875, (nonstudent) $225, (commuter) $450; three-day-school (double occupancy) $1125, (single occupancy) $1275, (nonstudent) $275, (commuter) $650; five-day school (double occupancy) $2195, (single occupancy) $2275, (nonstudent) $470 (commuter) $1075.

Naples summer and fall two-day school (double occupancy) $420, (single occupancy) $475, (nonstudent) $100, (commuter) $350; three-day school (double occupancy) $620, (single occupancy) $720, (nonstudent) $150, (commuter) $520; five-day school (double occupancy) $1120, (single occupancy) $1320, (nonstudent) $295, (commuter) $875.

Naples winter and spring two-day school (double occupancy) $525, (single occupancy) $625, (nonstudent) $175, (commuter) $375; three-day school (double occupancy) $745, (single occupancy) $900, (nonstudent) $225, (commuter) $545; five-day school (double occupancy) $1300, (single occupancy) $1545, (nonstudent) $420, (commuter) $900.

STUDENT/TEACHER RATIO 3:1.

HEAD INSTRUCTOR The head instructor is Bill Beyer. All instructors are PGA professionals.

ACCOMMODATIONS Accommodations are included in the rates.

■ ABOUT THE LOCATION ■

MARCO ISLAND RESORT

MARCO ISLAND, FLORIDA

Less than an hour from Fort Myers airport is the offshore Marco Island, which with

Sanibel and Captiva may be the prize jewels of Florida's west coast. Marco is the last stop before the Everglades National Park and is situated about 15 miles north on the edge of the Big Cypress National Preserve and approximately 100 miles due north of Key West. The resort offers tours of the Everglades, seashells, sunsets, and golf at the Marco Shores Golf & Country Club.

NAPLES BEACH RESORT & HOTEL

NAPLES, FLORIDA

Strangely for a major resort destination, Naples isn't exactly overloaded with great places to stay once you get past the Regent and the Ritz-Carlton. The Naples Beach Hotel is practically alone in the middle rank, not a Five-Star destination, but certainly well above the run-of-the-mill. The 315-room resort is right on the water, and Naples is possessed of a fine stretch of beach. Just about everything is on tap here—tennis, swimming, fishing, sailing, and all the usual water sports of a beach resort. A good restaurant, too. The course is a championship-length affair that attracts a number of the better area pros for practice and play.

■ CONTACT ■

Paradise Golf Schools
975 Imperial Golf Course Boulevard
Naples, FL 33942
800-624-3543 or 813-592-0204

THE PHIL RITSON GOLF SCHOOL

OVERLAND PARK, KANSAS; MYRTLE BEACH, SOUTH CAROLINA; PAWLEY'S ISLAND, SOUTH CAROLINA

PROGRAMS Three- and five-day programs. All half-days. Overland Park, April–September. Myrtle Beach, Brunswick Plantation, Pawley's Island, year-round. Juniors welcome.

ABOUT THE PROGRAM This is one of the most respected programs in the country. Phil Ritson doesn't have the name recognition of, say, David Leadbetter or Jimmy Ballard, but he packs 'em in, the professionals that is, at his schools. It is hard to say if a heavy turnout by professionals is a sign of a good school for amateurs, but if it is, then this is a fine one.

What is the school about? Fundamentals, mostly. There is a smattering of fashionable sports psychology instruction, and Phil is perhaps the only major instructor with a major associate who is left-handed and teaches from the other side. It is great news for southpaws, but not bad for righties, either. Watching Andy O'Brien is like studying the golf swing in a mirror.

The basic three-day course involves 3 1/2 hours of instruction per day and includes high-speed, stop-action video analysis, a take-home video with audio comments from the instructors, a Phil Ritson video, and unlimited range balls.

COSTS Three-day schools (double occupancy) $530–$690, (single occupancy) $570–$770, (commuter) $425-$545; five-day schools (double occupancy) $970–$1245, (single occupancy) $1010–$1410, (commuter) $750–$950.

STUDENT/TEACHER RATIO 3:1.

HEAD INSTRUCTORS The head instructor is Phil Ritson. He achieved a small amount of fame through his "Encyclopedia of Golf" video series. It established for a lot of people who hadn't heard much of Ritson that he really knows his golf. One of his professional students is one of my own golf teachers, and I can tell you that the instruction is precise and fruitful. All instructors are PGA professionals.

ACCOMMODATIONS Not included in the package. The staff will advise on local hotels.

■ ABOUT THE LOCATIONS ■

DEER CREEK GOLF CLUB
OVERLAND PARK, KANSAS

A finalist in the *GOLF Digest* Best New Public Course ratings for 1990, welcome news in a market that is better known for its golf enthusiasm than its great courses. Robert Trent Jones Jr. was the designer, and the course is very much in the Jones tradition, which is to say that there is plenty of threading to be done between the bunkers.

BRUNSWICK PLANTATION
MYRTLE BEACH, SOUTH CAROLINA

A new Willard Byrd design set in the heart of a 600-acre residential plantation. Front nine mixes tree-lined fairways, strategic bunkering, and water hazards with three open, Scottish-style holes. Back nine is more demanding with thick woodlands and two difficult par-threes. Greens are quick Penncross bentgrass.

PAWLEY'S PLANTATION
PAWLEY'S ISLAND, SOUTH CAROLINA

Jack Nicklaus did the Signature course at Pawley's Plantation. It is situated near Pawley's Island, one of the oldest resort areas in the country and one of the most unspoiled. Locals can't decide if Long Bay or Pawley's is the better Nicklaus course along the Grand Strand, but this one is certainly the prettier of the two. It has plenty of natural wetlands to play through and a ton of water around the course. The course is somewhat intimidating to some. It was designed during a period when Nicklaus seemed to get hired only for jobs where the developers wanted monster courses, but it is mitigated by Nicklaus' characteristic insistence on bail-out areas and multiple options for the golfer.

■ CONTACT ■

Mel Sole/Rosemary Sole
The Phil Ritson Golf School
2710 Butler Bay Drive North
Windermere, FL 34786
800-624-4653 or 407-876-6487

PINE NEEDLES/ GOLFARI
SOUTHERN PINES, NORTH CAROLINA

PROGRAMS Three-day Learning Centers are held weekly between February and April, and then twice each month in May–June and September–November; four-day Learning Centers are held weekly January–April, then twice a month May–July and weekly again through November.

<u>ABOUT THE PROGRAMS</u> Pinehurst is loaded with top-flight instructors, but Peg Bell still shines head and shoulders above the rest. A legendary instructor for decades now, she still barks out her advice along with fellow instructors Dr. Jim Suttie and PGA TOUR professional Pat McGowan. Peggy Kirk Bell also offers highly regarded youth camps and the famed Golfari, the women-only five-day program that did much to land Ms. Bell the Richardson Award for Lifetime Achievement from the Golf Writers' Association of America last year.

The Learning Center programs employ a combination of sight-sound-feel "cues" and concentrate on high-speed video to film the swing from different angles, using a computer overlay to turn the taped swing into a three-dimensional model.

From there, basics of the short game and full swing are addressed, as are the psychology of the game, course management, physical preparedness, and equipment evaluation. In addition to range work, there is on-course instruction utilizing the Donald Ross–designed course. The combination of Peggy Bell, her staff of instructors, and a Ross course is bound to excite the golf traditionalist. The opportunity to study the short game on a Ross course should put this school on the short list, especially if short-game improvement is on your list.

<u>COSTS</u> Five-day Golfari $925; three-day Learning Center $995; four-day Learning Center $1495. The Golfari (ladies only) is held in September.

<u>STUDENT/TEACHER RATIO</u> 4:1

<u>HEAD INSTRUCTOR</u> Peggy Kirk Bell is one of the legends of twentieth-century golf, no question about it. Bell was one of the founders of the LPGA TOUR and has been recognized by *GOLF Digest* as one of the five most influential women in the game. She was recently honored with the Richardson Award for Distinguished Service, the highest award given by the Golf Writers' Association of America. Bell also received the LPGA Teacher of the Year award; was a two-time Curtis Cup member, the first LPGA Senior champion, and winner of many titles, including one professional major championship; and is author of *Women's Way to Better Golf* and many articles for national golf publications.

■ ABOUT THE LOCATION ■

PINE NEEDLES RESORT

SOUTHERN PINES, NORTH CAROLINA

Pine Needles may be as close to golf heaven as one gets, with a Donald Ross course good enough to host the 1995 U.S. Women's Open, no crowds, and terrific weather. Pine Needles Resort was constructed in 1928 by the owner of the Pinehurst Hotel. The resort was taken over by the government during World War II, but in 1953 was purchased by Warren "Bullet" and Peggy Kirk Bell. The original hotel became what is now Saint Joseph's Hospital located on the second tee, and ten rustic swiss-like lodges were designed and built by "Bullet" Bell who wanted to create a unique resort for a select number of golfers. The atmosphere is casual with uncrowded golf; the resort caters to guests only. The accommodations are on the American plan, and meals are served in the main dining room, where many a group over the years has stayed late, arguing golf and scorecard controversies and playing liar's poker late into the night. Pine Needles has always been among my all-time top-five golf resorts. I recommend it without hesitation whether or not instruction is in your plans for the coming year.

■ CONTACT ■

Pine Needles Lodges and Country Club
600 Midland Road
Southern Pines, NC 28388
910-692-7111

PINEHURST ADVANTAGE GOLF SCHOOL

PINEHURST, NORTH CAROLINA

PROGRAMS Four-day and three-day schools weekly March–October (two weeks off in June and two in August); junior schools weekly June–July, one advanced junior school in August.

ABOUT THE PROGRAM The Pinehurst Advantage Golf School has become one of the most respected programs in the country and is based on state-of-the-art video analysis and on-course and in-classroom instruction. The classroom area is a 4,500-square-foot facility with a covered hitting area, video room, and classrooms.

The basic program includes lodging at the Pinehurst Hotel, three meals daily, daily green fees on the Pinehurst resort courses, cart rental, club storage and cleaning, unlimited range balls, personalized video analysis and a taped record of schoolwork, personalized club fitting, access to all Pinehurst amenities, and a graduation cocktail party and awards ceremony.

The daily schedule includes a morning clinic, full-swing practice, and videotaping, followed by a short game around the lunch hour and the all clear to play golf after 2:30 p.m. on the Pinehurst courses.

The Junior program accepts boys and girls ages 11 to 17 with no handicap restrictions. These weeklong schools are held in the summer and include adult supervision. Rules, etiquette, and fundamentals are stressed, the last via supervised instruction, drills, exercises, and playing lessons. There is also an Ad-vanced Junior Golf Advantage School restricted to golfers with fifteen handicaps or less.

Juniors and adults take weekends or week long programs of instruction. One would be hard pressed to name any better course for learning than the famed Pinehurst No. 2, which is a golf school all in itself.

COSTS Four-day schools (double occupancy) $1750, (single occupancy) $2195, (nonparticipating resort guest) $950; three-day schools (double occupancy) $1295, (single occupancy) $1595, (nonparticipating resort guest) $605; summer three-day schools (double occupancy) $1075; (single occupancy) $1250, (nonparticipating resort guest) $495; junior golf advantage $860; advanced junior golf advantage $925. Premiums are added to package costs for play on Pinehurst No. 2 and No. 7.

STUDENT/TEACHER RATIO 5:1.

HEAD INSTRUCTOR The head instructor is Don Padgett, former President of the PGA of America.

■ ABOUT THE LOCATION ■

PINEHURST RESORT & COUNTRY CLUB

PINEHURST, NORTH CAROLINA

No one ever wrote up Pinehurst or summed up the similarities between the North Carolina Sandhills and St. Andrews better than Dick Taylor in an article several years ago for *Links* magazine:

"When a pilgrim arrives in St. Andrews, Scotland, he or she is immediately accepted because they are a golfer. They will find a wonderful walking town, four quite wonderful golf courses with dozens more nearby, will breathe history back to the 14th century, and will see school children on bikes carrying golf clubs for an after-school round. Sacks of golf clubs will be lined up against the wall in a pub as the locals munch on those doughy 'filled rolls' and discuss anything pertaining to golf, the separation from England that must come, and the peculiar clothes of the American visitors.

"Fade out from the Kingdom of Fife, fade into a kingdom of golf in the pine forests of North Carolina in a geologically peculiar area known as the Sandhills. A pilgrim to Pinehurst is immediately accepted because he or she is a golfer. They will discover a wonderful walking village lifted right out of England, and seven quite wonderful golf courses with several dozen more nearby. They will discover not kids on bikes, but an adult population whizzing around in golf cars to the club, to the post office, and these same residents munching on corned beef on rye at the Village Deli, or humongous hamburgers at the Donald Ross Grill at the Country Club. The townspeople will be discussing anything relating to golf, the strange politics of this state, and the peculiar clothes of the European tourists."

Let me just add two pieces of advice. One, don't miss the opportunity to play No. 2 while you are at Pinehurst. There often is an extra tariff, and there is often a wait. But if all the courses said to be worth the wait and worth the money were to fall into the ocean tomorrow and only one course spared, it would be good fortune indeed if this were the one.

Second, take a side trip to the Pine Crest Inn. There's lots of golf history and not a few golfing celebrities and near-celebrities mulling around.

■ CONTACT ■

Pinehurst Advantage Golf School
Pinehurst Resort & Country Club
P.O. Box 4000
Pinehurst, NC 28374
800-795-GOLF

PROFESSIONAL GOLF SCHOOLS OF AMERICA

MESA, ARIZONA;
HOLLYWOOD, FLORIDA;
MAGGIE VALLEY, NORTH
CAROLINA; MOUNT AIRY,
PENNSYLVANIA

PROGRAMS Arizona Golf Resort, Mesa: three- and five-day schools, January–May, November–December; Diplomat Country Club/Hollywood Beach Resort, Hollywood: three- and five-day schools, January–May, November–December; Maggie Valley Resort, Maggie Valley: three- and five-day schools, year-round; Mount Airy Lodge, Mt. Pocono: three- and five-day schools, April–October.

ABOUT THE PROGRAM One of the oldest acronyms around has to be KISS, for Keep it Simple, Stupid. This gentlemanly group has subtracted the "Stupid" from the equation and present their teaching philosophy simply as

"Keep it Simple" or KIS. No student is stupid in their eyes.

The KIS program aims to expose misconceptions and teach clarity with respect to the golf swing. Mike Lucas says, "I'd venture that every golfer can get a lot better by grasping the simplicity of the swing rather than the complexities."

The five-day program features 25 hours of course or range instruction broken into 1-hour intervals, with sessions on video analysis and mental conditioning in between. In a departure from typical golf school protocol, on-course instruction is included in each day's teaching routine. But the unique aspect of the school is the emphasis on teaching swing mechanics through extensive short-game and short-iron instruction before moving on to long irons and woods. It isn't until the afternoon of the third day that students work with the driver and repeated emphasis is given throughout the program to drilling in up-and-down situations. This is also the only school with a scheduled session on the crucial area of lag putting . . . and PGSA adds another session on reading greens. Bravo!

Video analysis is given perhaps less emphasis here than high-tech schools. The key here is personal instruction and a well-structured program. Mike Lucas abhors "paralysis through analysis," so students should expect to spend more time grooving their swings than looking at them or discussing the latest in kinesthetic philosophy.

Each school includes all range balls, daily green fees, video analysis, bag storage and club cleaning, and the PGSA instruction manual.

COSTS Five-day schools, Arizona: April–May, November–December (double occupancy) $1230, (single occupancy) $1490, (nonparticipating resort guest) $580, (commuter) $825; January–March (double occupancy) $1410, (single occupancy) $1805, (nonparticipating resort guest) $745.

Three-day schools, Arizona: April–May, November–December (double occupancy) $750, (single occupancy) $905, (nonparticipating resort guest) $360, (commuter) $499; January–March (double occupancy) $855, (single occupancy) $1090, (nonparticipating resort guest) $446.

Five-day schools, Florida: April–May, November–December (double occupancy) $1250, (single occupancy) $1425, (nonparticipating resort guest) $450, (commuter) $820; January–March (double occupancy) $1325, (single occupancy) $1595, (nonparticipating resort guest) $530, (commuter) $825.

Three-day schools, Florida: April–May, November–December (double occupancy) $750, (single occupancy) $960; (nonparticipating resort guest) $320, (commuter) $495; January–March (double occupancy) $790, (single occupancy) $960, (nonparticipating resort guest) $320, (commuter) $495.

Five-day schools, North Carolina: March–October (double occupancy) $1130, (single occupancy) $1318, (nonparticipating resort guest) $425, (commuter) $755; November–February (double occupancy) $825, (single occupancy) $920, (nonparticipating resort guest) $216, (commuter) $745.

Three-day schools, North Carolina: March–October (double occupancy) $680, (single occupancy) $795, (nonparticipating resort guest) $260, (commuter) $457; November–February (double occupancy) $499, (single occupancy) $560, (nonparticipating resort guest) $120, (commuter) $445.

Five-day schools, Pennsylvania: (double occupancy) $1185, (single occupancy) $1436, (nonparticipating resort guest) $500, (commuter) $850.

Three-day schools, Pennsylvania: (double occupancy) $716, (single occupancy) $825, (nonparticipating resort guest) $300, (commuter) $510.

STUDENT/TEACHER RATIO 4:1.

HEAD INSTRUCTOR The head instructor is Mike Lucas. All instructors are PGA professionals.

ACCOMMODATIONS Accommodations are included in package prices, as are the meals.

■ ABOUT THE LOCATIONS ■

ARIZONA GOLF RESORT
MESA, ARIZONA

One of the best values in the desert, Arizona Golf Resort is somewhat off the beaten tourist path, but it has a solid setup for a golfing vacation. The property itself is small (162 acres in total) but it is well groomed and priced for the bargain hunter. The prime rib at Annabell's, the on-site restaurant, is locally renowned.

The course is of modest length at 6,574 yards. It is accordingly narrow off the tee and offers some rather enormous greens, and three-putts come aplenty when the approach shots wander off line.

HOLLYWOOD BEACH RESORT
HOLLYWOOD, FLORIDA

Here's an interesting option: an art deco–style main building with a hi-rise condo complex attached. Thus there's plenty to please the eye and all modern conveniences and relatively affordable prices. Unfortunately, the resort does not have its own golf course; schools are conducted at the nearby Diplomat

Country Club. But there is seemingly endless stretch of beach right outside the doors and plenty of exciting local events, attractions, and shopping opportunities.

MAGGIE VALLEY RESORT
MAGGIE VALLEY, NORTH CAROLINA

Located 325 miles west of Asheville in the North Carolina mountains, Maggie Valley offers a collection of lodge rooms and one- or two-bedroom villas and a variety of amenities ranging from swimming and tennis to nightly lounge entertainment. The course has long been regarded as one of the best in the mountains, hosting several North Carolina Opens over the years. One of the most memorable Carolina mountain golf experiences comes on the back nine at Maggie Valley, where golfers climb 900 feet in altitude between the tenth and thirteenth tees. Plunging is a word that comes to mind in describing the two-hole finale, which includes a reachable and very tempting 293-yard par-four seventeenth.

MOUNT AIRY RESORT
MOUNT AIRY, PENNSYLVANIA

■ CONTACT ■

Professional Golf Schools of America
Winter
    4105 Luff Street #1
    Panama City Beach, FL 32408
    800-447-2744 or 904-233-9200
Summer
    P.O. Box 1543
    Maggie Valley, NC 28751
    800-447-2744 or 704-926-0132

RICK SMITH GOLF ACADEMY

G AYLORD, M ICHIGAN;
P ALM B EACH, F LORIDA

PROGRAMS

Treetops

The Rick Smith Signature series runs three times a week (Saturday, Sunday, and Monday afternoons) from May 20–October 1. The Henry Young Masters Session runs four times a week (Monday, Tuesday, and Wednesday mornings, plus Tuesday afternoons) May 8–October 1. The Weekend workshop runs each weekend May 5–October 1.

The Breakers

The Rick Smith Signature series runs once in January, three times in February, and eight times in March. The Henry Young Masters Session runs seven times in January, twelve times in February, eight times in March, and eight times in April.

ABOUT THE PROGRAM

"Rick's not a method teacher, and that is what I like about him." That's one of the recent testimonials to Rick Smith and his Academy. From a fellow by the name of Jack Nicklaus.

For several years now the Rick Smith Academy has been one of the hottest around. It attracts "pilgrims" from the amateur and professional ranks, including several stars of the PGA TOUR, to the Treetops Sylvan Resort in Northern Michigan or Smith's winter headquarters at The Breakers.

The Rick Smith Golf Academy has three programs. The Rick Smith Signature Session is a three-day-a-week half-day workshop for 4 students. His Director of Instruction, Henry Young, conducts a half-day workshop four times a week and an occasional weekend school.

■ Treetops Sylvan Resort.

The Rick Smith Signature session includes two videotapes, unlimited range balls, and a personally autographed photo of Rick Smith. The Henry Young Masters Session is broken into a full-swing session thrice weekly and a session on the short game each Tuesday. The session includes unlimited range balls and a personal videotape with audio analysis. The weekend session includes both full-swing and short-game instruction, unlimited range balls, and a personal take-home video with audio analysis.

COSTS

Treetops

Rick Smith Signature Session (double occupancy) $687, (single occupancy) $721, (commuter) $550; Henry Young Masters Session (double occupancy) $437, (single occupancy) $571, (commuter) $300; weekend workshop (double occupancy) $839, (single occupancy) $905, (commuter) $565; commuter rates do not include golf.

The Breakers

Day session only: Rick Smith Signature Session $675; one-night package: Rick Smith Signature Session (double occupancy) $850, (single occupancy) $1000; Henry Young Masters Session (double occupancy) $600, (single occupancy) $750; three-day package: Rick Smith Signature Session (double occupancy) $1398, (single occupancy) $1848; Henry Young Masters Session (double occupancy) $1148, (single occupancy) $1598.

STUDENT/TEACHER RATIO 4:1. All instructors are PGA certified.

HEAD INSTRUCTOR One of the newest of the golf gurus, Smith is a three-time Michigan PGA Teacher of the Year who doubles as the Director of Golf at the Treetops resort and triples as a golf course architect with the third (Rick Smith Signature) course at Treetops to his credit. Smith's students run the gamut from beginners to over 100 tour players, including Lee Janzen, Rocco Mediate, and Billy Andrade.

Smith was recognized as one of *GOLF Magazine's* 50 best golf instructors and is a former Spalding National Teacher of the Year.

ACCOMMODATIONS Accommodations are included in the package price. Accommodations at Treetops include room, green fees, club cleaning and storage, unlimited use of the range and practice facilities, and access to all resort facilities. The Breakers package includes room, green fees and cart, unlimited use of range and practice facilities, club storage and cleaning, daily lunch, and transportation to and from Breakers West.

■ ABOUT THE LOCATIONS ■

TREETOPS SYLVAN RESORT
GAYLORD, MICHIGAN

Treetops, in Gaylord, Michigan, was literally made for golf. Lake Michigan covered the area in ages past. The resulting sub-soil is the sandy sort known to the Scots as "links-perfect" for golf. A designer can be very creative with shaping and still have turf drain.

Three championship courses plus a par-three course known as Threetops make up the rotation at the resort. The oldest of the courses was designed by Robert Trent Jones. Jones called his Treetops course "my masterpiece." This may surprise golfers at Mauna Kea, Spyglass, Firestone, Peachtree, Bellerive, and the like, but it is a nice sentiment, and Jones doesn't say it about all his courses—only a select few.

The Tom Fazio course is one of his most playable and is considered the premier course at Treetops. Fazio is generally considered the best of the current generation of American designers because of his ability to fashion courses that are both subtle and saucy, a delight to look at, and a puzzle to figure out. The Fazio course has plenty of movement and swirl on the fairways and some of his most interesting greens.

Rick Smith himself is the designer of the Rick Smith Signature Course. The golf world was somewhat astonished and generally delighted by the result. Tom Fazio himself said of the par-seventy course. "You can tell by his layout, from the types of shots required, and the design of the greens, that he is a player and that with all the lessons he has given he knows how other people play the game." It is a nice point and a nice compliment. And it is quite true that Rick Smith, as an accomplished golfer and a famous teacher, may well know better how to run that difficult gamut from "playable" to "challenging" better than anyone else.

The resort itself is built in a contemporary resort design. Skiing has been the primary business here over the years, and the resulting ambience is a little more Swiss than Klondike. But the Horizon restaurant goes the other way with an emphasis on steaks, seafood, and game. Other resort activities include tennis, outdoor pools, hot tubs, volleyball, hiking, and rivers for fishing and canoeing. The resort also has a smattering of on-site shopping, a sports bar, and lounge.

THE BREAKERS AND BREAKERS WEST
PALM BEACH, FLORIDA

Let's start here: The Breakers *is* Palm Beach. The Breakers had as much to do with the popularization of Southern Florida as anything else save the architecture of Addison Mizner, the Florida Railroad Company, and the winter sunshine. The hotel was described by golf and travel writer Brett Borton as "painstaking Palm Beach panache," and the result has been a Mobil Five-Star rating for many years now.

The Breakers, featured in the motion picture *Some Like it Hot* and other films, preceded the era of the modern golf resort by at least a generation. So, golf is carried out at Breakers West in West Palm, some 20 minutes away. It is a well-done Joe Lee course with his customary emphasis on water holes with accompanying doses of scenery and daunting carries.

When it comes to resort amenities and resort style, The Breakers is right up there with Mauna Kea and the La Quinta Hotel on the short list for best resort hotel in the country. The food is without peer, the rooms stately without toppling over into pretentiousness, and the setting is a model for resort planners.

■ CONTACT ■

Rick Smith Golf Academy
3962 Wilkinson Road
Gaylord, MI 49735
800-444-6711
In Michigan 517-732-6711

RILEY SCHOOL OF GOLF

••••••••••••••••••••••••••••••••••••••

SAN DIEGO, CALIFORNIA;
MYRTLE BEACH, SOUTH
CAROLINA

PROGRAMS Three-, four-, and five-day basic and premium schools. Premium programs feature on-course playing lessons.

ABOUT THE PROGRAM Riley emphasizes personally fitted clubs and instruction in student groups with similar levels of ability. Technical instruction is balanced with physical training regimens, leaving plenty of free time to apply lessons in unsupervised play or to enjoy the other resort amenities. A low student to instructor ratio is a decided bonus.

The overriding philosophy of the school is to "simplify your circle" in the full swing. This eliminates swing movements that golfers believe are essential but are actually superfluous or even harmful.

The program begins with morning clinics about work on improvements in mechanics and technique. After lunch, students opt for either continued technical work on the range or on-course playing instruction with the Riley instructors.

Personal evaluation is accomplished both through observation and high-speed, stop-action video. Students also receive an instructional video that can help in review of fundamental swing concepts. Classroom instruction covers golf fitness, course management, rules, and equipment selection.

The basic package includes daily instruction, accommodations, lunch, green fees and cart, club cleaning and storage, and a follow-up with the teacher after completing the school.

COSTS

Myrtle Beach, South Carolina

Fall/Winter season (January–February, September–December): Three-day basic (AM) school (double occupancy) $559, (single occupancy) $624, (commuter) $494; three-day premium school (double occupancy) $664, (single occupancy) $729, (commuter) $599; four-day basic (AM) school (double occupancy) $745, (single occupancy) $831, (commuter) $659; four-day premium school (double occupancy) $875, (single occupancy) $961, (commuter) $789; five-day basic (AM) school (double occupancy) $951, (single occupancy) $1058, (commuter) $844; five-day premium school (double occupancy) $1023, (single occupancy) $1130, (commuter) $916.

Spring season (March–May): Three-day basic (AM) school (double occupancy) $582, (single occupancy) $670, (commuter) $494; three-day premium school (double occupancy) $787, (single occupancy) $875, (commuter) $699; four-day basic (AM) school (double occupancy) $777, (single occupancy) $895, (commuter) $659; four-day premium school (double occupancy) $970, (single occupancy) $1088, (commuter) $852; five-day basic (AM) school (double occupancy) $991, (single occupancy) $1138, (commuter) $844; five-day premium school (double occupancy) $1125, (single occupancy) $1272, (commuter) $978.

Summer season (June–August): Three-day basic (AM) school (double occupancy) $639, (single occupancy) $784, (commuter) $494; three-day premium school (double occupancy) $744, (single occupancy) $889, (commuter) $599; four-day basic (AM) school (double occupancy) $852, (single occupancy) $1045, (commuter) $659; four-day premium school (double occupancy) $982, (single occupancy)

$1175, (commuter) $789; five-day basic (AM) school (double occupancy) $1085, (single occupancy) $1326, (commuter) $844; five-day premium school (double occupancy) $1157, (single occupancy) $1398, (commuter) $916.

Palm Springs, California

Add $12 for Friday and Saturday night accommodations.

Winter/Spring season (January–May): Three-day basic (AM) school (double occupancy) $727, (single occupancy) $868, (commuter) $585; three-day premium school (double occupancy) $922, (single occupancy) $1063, (commuter) $780; four-day basic (AM) school (double occupancy) $936, (single occupancy) $1124, (commuter) $747; four-day premium school (double occupancy) $1172, (single occupancy) $1360, (commuter) $983; five-day basic (AM) school (double occupancy) $1134, (single occupancy) $1370, (commuter) $898; five-day premium school (double occupancy) $1427, (single occupancy) $1663, (commuter) $1191.

Summer season (June–September): Three-day basic (AM) school (double occupancy) $610, (single occupancy) $685, (commuter) $535; three-day premium school (double occupancy) $805, (single occupancy) $873, (commuter) $730; four-day basic (AM) school (double occupancy) $797, (single occupancy) $897, (commuter) $697; four-day premium school (double occupancy) $1033, (single occupancy) $1133, (commuter) $933; five-day basic (AM) school (double occupancy) $973, (single occupancy) $1098, (commuter) $848; five-day Premium school (double occupancy) $1266, (single occupancy) $1391, (commuter) $1141.

Fall season (October–December): Three-day basic (AM) school (double occupancy) $693, (single occupancy) $801, (commuter)

$585; three-day Premium school (double occupancy) $888, (single occupancy) $996, (commuter) $780; four-day basic (AM) school (double occupancy) $891, (single occupancy) $1036, (commuter) $747; four-day Premium school (double occupancy) $1127, (single occupancy) $1272, (commuter) $983; five-day basic (AM) school (double occupancy) $1078, (single occupancy) $1259, (commuter) $898; five-day Premium school (double occupancy) $1371, (single occupancy) $1552, (commuter) $1191.

Warner Springs Ranch

Add $12 for Friday and Saturday night accommodations.

May-October: Three-day Premium school (double occupancy) $995, (single occupancy) $1118, (commuter) $871; four-day premium school (double occupancy) $1204, (single occupancy) $1369, (commuter) $1039; five-day premium school (double occupancy) $1413, (single occupancy) $1619, (commuter) $1207.

STUDENT/TEACHER RATIO 3/1.

HEAD INSTRUCTOR Director of Instruction, Mike Schroeder, is a former PGA TOUR professional with over 20 years of teaching experience. Prior to joining the Riley School of Golf, he spent twelve years at his own Strand Golf Academy in Myrtle Beach. Schroeder played golf at LSU and competed in the 1981 U.S. Open.

■ ABOUT THE LOCATIONS ■

WARNER SPRINGS RANCH

SAN DIEGO, CALIFORNIA

Ninety minutes northeast of San Diego, Warner Springs Ranch is situated at the 3,000-foot level. The ranch itself encompasses

2,552 rolling acres in the foothills of Palomar Mountain. The eighteen-hole course has immaculately maintained bentgrass greens, while tree-lined fairways and challenging landing areas add bite on the drives. The ranch features guest cottages with fireplaces, and a spa and health center offering facials, sauna, exercise equipment, and natural hot springs. Fifteen tennis courts, three restaurants, and an equestrian center with riding trails top off the amenity package.

RIVER HILLS PLANTATION

MYRTLE BEACH,
SOUTH CAROLINA

River Hills is a Tom Jackson–designed course that is heavily wooded with dogwoods, oaks, maples, and pines, as well as frequent elevation changes of up to 40 feet. The layout of the course evokes Scottish design elements; the course was nominated for *Golf Digest's* Best New Public Course in 1989.

ACCOMMODATIONS Riley recommends the Ocean Creek resort, a 57-acre oceanfront plantation with moss-draped oaks and ponds with swans and ducks. The plantation has swimming, jacuzzis, tennis courts, and restaurants in its amenity package.

■ CONTACT ■

Riley School of Golf
P.O. Box 3695
Palm Desert, CA 92261
800-847-4539

ROLAND STAFFORD GOLF SCHOOLS

PEMBROKE PINES, FLORIDA;
PENSACOLA, FLORIDA;
FRANCESTOWN, NEW
HAMPSHIRE; CLYMER, NEW
YORK; WYNDHAM, NEW YORK,
QUEBEC, CANADA

PROGRAMS The programs include two- and three-day weekends; two-, three-, and five-day midweek schools.

ABOUT THE PROGRAM Roland Stafford Golf Schools are one of the most successful golf school operators in the country. They attribute their success to their PGA-trained staff, the custom club-fitting program, the instructional tapes and books of the Stafford method, the large student practice areas, small classes, and video analysis.

The Stafford Method avoids over-analysis of the swing. He emphasizes a good grip, understanding how connection between the arms and the body generates power, keeping a level swing plane, and maintaining a steady tempo for a smooth, rhythmic swing.

School begins with a presentation of the Roland Stafford Golf School Method and continues for morning work each day on assigned practice areas such as full swing, pitching, chipping, and putting. Groups rotate through the various practice areas and participate in video analysis. School is complete by mid-afternoon, allowing for time to play on course, practicing, or enjoying resort amenities. In addition, golf etiquette and rules clinics are conducted, along with golf equipment presentations and demonstrations.

One unique feature of the Stafford program is the Frequent Golfer Reward Program. Second-time attendees receive a $15-per-day discount, and the discount grows by $5 per day per visit (e.g., $20 discount for three-time attendees, $25 for four-time attendees.)

COSTS All rates are based on double occupancy. Additional rates for groups, single occupancy, commuters, and nonstudents are quoted on request by the Roland Stafford main office.

Grand Palms Resort
Three-day weekend (October–April only) $575; five-day midweek (October–April) $973; two-day weekend (April–September only) $367; five-day midweek (April–September) $933.

Perdido Bay Resort
Three-day weekend (October–April only) $379; five-day midweek (October–April) $941; two-day weekend (April-September only) $373; five-day midweek (April-September) $924.

Tory Pines Resort (all schools May-October only)
Two-day weekend $443; three-day weekend (holidays only) $665; two-day midweek $398; five-day midweek $995.

Peek'N Peak Resort (all schools May-October only)
Two-day weekend $498; three-day weekend (holidays only) $705; three-day midweek $649; five-day midweek $998.

Christman's Windham Resort (all schools May-October only)
Two-day weekend $383; three-day weekend (holidays only) $575; two-day midweek $332; five-day midweek $833.

Hotel L'Esterel (May-October only)
Three-day weekend (April-June, September) $709; five-day midweek (April-June, September) $1181; three-day weekend (July-August only) $739; five-day midweek (April-June, September) $1232.

STUDENT/TEACHER RATIO 6:1

HEAD INSTRUCTOR Roland Stafford has been playing and teaching golf since 1959. A graduate of Northwestern University, he holds a masters in music education from the University of Arizona. He has had a successful playing career, including several top-ten finishes on the Senior PGA TOUR, plus victories in the Pennsylvania Open, the Grand Bahama Island Open, and three PGA section championships. Stafford has his own line of golf clubs, "The Stafford Legato," and is author of the instructional book and tape "Roland Stafford's Golf Course."

■ ABOUT THE LOCATIONS ■

GRAND PALMS RESORT
PEMBROKE PINES, FLORIDA

Twelve months of Florida sunshine, great golf, tennis, swimming, and sunning are the leading amenities at the Grand Palms Golf and Country Club Resort located in southeast Florida. Accommodations are suites or spacious rooms with poolside and golf course views. The golfside restaurant has a bright, scenic setting. In addition to the hotel facilities, the surrounding area abounds with opportunities for dining, shopping, entertainment, and sports action.

The golf school practice areas consist of an aqua driving range with floating targets, chipping and putting greens, bunkers, a video station, and a classroom. Grand Palms also is home to a twenty-seven-hole course.

PERDIDO BAY RESORT
PENSACOLA, FLORIDA

The Gulf of Mexico's alluring white sand beaches and Perdido Bay's 7,154-yard golf course are two added attractions here. The course was ranked as one of the most challenging on the PGA TOUR during the days of the old Pensacola Open. It offers a four-tee system for play at all ability levels. Accommodations are golf villas located directly on the course, within walking distance of the first tee.

The Golf School consists of a private driving range, chipping and putting greens, bunkers, and a classroom for video analysis.

TORY PINES RESORT

FRANCESTOWN,
NEW HAMPSHIRE

Francestown is a full 90 minutes from Boston, but is worth a look because of its eighteen-hole Donald Ross–designed course, rated the third-most scenic in New Hampshire. History abounds not only in the golf, but in the Gibson Tavern, an eighteenth-century Georgian Colonial design, which houses the resort's restaurant.

The modern villas are complete with fireplaces and a kitchenette and are within walking distance of all the amenities of the resort— including the golf school practice areas. The school areas include a driving range with a covered tee area, chipping and putting greens, a video station, and classrooms.

PEEK'N PEAK RESORT

CLYMER, NEW YORK

Peek'N Peak is located in southwestern New York near the Pennsylvania and Ohio borders, and it is the leading resort in the area following a multimillion-dollar renovation effort. The Inn at the Peak is designed in an Edwardian style and includes three restaurants, twenty-seven holes of golf, indoor swimming, sauna, whirlpool, fitness center, and tennis courts.

The golf school practice areas consist of a driving range with covered tee area, chipping and putting greens, bunkers, a video station, and a schoolhouse building with classrooms.

CHRISTMAN'S WYNDHAM HOUSE

WYNDHAM, NEW YORK

The Wyndham House is located in the Catskills approximately 2 1/2 hours from Manhattan. The Green Revival-style Inn dates back to 1805 and is surrounded by five Colonial-style buildings to accommodate guests in modern facilities. Swimming and tennis are featured activities, along with the inn's attractive and historic dining room.

The golf school practice areas consist of a driving range with covered tee area, chipping and putting greens, bunkers, a video station, a classroom, and a regulation-length nine-hole course. The eighteen-hole Windham Golf Course is approximately 5 minutes away.

HOTEL L'ESTEREL

QUEBEC, CANADA

The Hotel L'Esterel is on 5,000 acres of lakes, forest, and mountains. Situated on the banks of Lake Depuis, the resort contains an eighteen-hole golf course, indoor swimming, whirlpool and sauna, and tennis courts in addition to the golf school. French and Continental cuisine is served on the premises.

The golf school practice areas consist of a driving range with covered tee area, chipping and putting greens, bunkers, and a video station.

■ Eagle Ridge Inn & Resort.

■ Sugarloaf/USA.

■ The Sheraton Steamboat Resort & Conference Center.

■ Treetops™ Sylvan Resort.

■ Golf Digest Schools.

■ La Costa Resort and Spa.

■ Dave Pelz Short Game School.

■ Jacobs' Golf Group.

■ Samoset Resort.

■ The Coeur d'Alene.

■ **CONTACT** ■

Roland Stafford Golf Schools
P.O. Box 81
Arkville, NY 12406
800-447-8894
In New York 914-386-3187

SEA PINES ACADEMY OF GOLF

HILTON HEAD ISLAND,
SOUTH CAROLINA

PROGRAMS Half-day school/half-day golf, one-day school, four-day school, individual lessons, private group clinics, and playing lessons.

ABOUT THE PROGRAMS This is the school that camps out in the shadow of the famed Harbour Town lighthouse at Harbour Town Golf Links. Don Trahan, "The Swing Surgeon," heads the school, which is based on the Trahan method as explained in his book *Golf Plain and Simple* and its successors *Golf Tips Plain and Simple* and *Golf, Plain and Simple: Straight Golf.*

There are three schools offered in the Sea Pines program. The half-day school/half-day golf includes 4 hours of morning instruction, including full-swing instruction, drills and exercises, written analysis, and video analysis. Following the lesson players may play a complimentary eighteen holes of golf (alas, Harbour Town is excluded from the offer).

The Sea Pines Academy of Beginner Golf is a four-day program offering 10 hours of instruction—including a complete introduction to rules, set-up fundamentals, full swing, pitching, bunker play, chipping, putting, equipment recommendations, and club fitting.

The Sea Pines Academy of Golf is taught by Don Trahan and Director of Instruction Rick Barry. It is a one-day school offering 7 hours of instruction, including full swing, short game, drills and exercises, video analysis, supervised practice, continental breakfast, and lunch.

Individual lessons, private group clinics, and playing lessons are also offered by the Sea Pines instructional staff.

Trahan has developed a number of unique training tools to amplify the instruction offered in his books and video. The Plane-Trainer intends to keep the student's arms on correct path and plane and in sync with the body, and the Alignment-Arrows teach correct body alignment for the full swing, short game, and especially putting. Trahan also developed Compu-Golf, a PC and Windows-based computer program that gives a personalized diagnosis of swing problems and prescriptions for cures and keeps track of the student's progress each time the program is used. The program contains color graphics and analyzes over 30,000 combinations of grip, stance, posture, alignment, weight distribution, and ball flight patterns.

COSTS One-half-day golf lessons with eighteen holes of golf $165; full day of golf Wednesday $165; lessons for beginners four days a week $200; daily clinics Monday to Saturday, one hour between 9 and 3:30, $18 per person.

STUDENT/TEACHER RATIO 4:1.

HEAD INSTRUCTOR The head instructor is Don Trahan. He is a PGA Master Professional and rated one of the top 50 instructors in the country by *GOLF* magazine. He became known as "The Swing Surgeon" for his ability to dissect swing problems and instantly offer prescriptions and cures. A PGA professional since 1972, Trahan is a *GOLF* magazine teaching editor as well as the author of several books, a video, and the computer program Compu-Golf. Don has worked with several touring professionals, but his most remarkable work may well be with his own son, D.J. Trahan, who in 1994 became the youngest player ever to qualify for the U.S. Junior Amateur (at the ripe old age of 13, ahead of the pace set by Jack Nicklaus, Phil Mickelson, and Tiger Woods, among others).

■ ABOUT THE LOCATION ■

SEA PINES RESORT

HILTON HEAD ISLAND,
SOUTH CAROLINA

Sea Pines is the granddaddy of all the modern Southeastern golf resorts, the original Hilton Head Island resort, and the home of Harbour Town as well as two other resort courses. Recently Sea Pines became the third development to receive the highest award given by the Urban Land Institute in tribute to its impact on the development of resorts nationwide. It was one of the first self-contained resort destinations in the United States, with a range of recreational amenities that twenty years ago was extraordinary. It is still matched by only a few resorts worldwide—with three public-access courses, the thirty-court Sea Pines Racquet Club (designed by host professional Stan Smith which hosts the Family Circle Cup and was recently named the finest resort tennis facility in the country by *Tennis* magazine), 5 miles of beaches, two marinas with adjacent shopping villages, miles of bike paths, a stable that hosts top equestrian events, more than 500 rental homes and condominiums, and a dozen restaurants offering everything from snacks to Continental cuisine. The resort facilities are hidden behind nature preserves and stands of oak, magnolia, and southern pine, making Sea Pines one of the most beautiful and natural resorts in the world.

The three public courses open to resort guests at Sea Pines include the Ocean and Sea Marsh courses designed by George Cobb. Sea Marsh is the friendliest of the three, with wide fairways that traverse several large lagoons and marshes. The Ocean course is a much sterner test with a superb and testy back nine. The fifteenth hole is one of the most photographed of all the Hilton Head Island golf holes, a 207-yarder directly into the wind and uphill to a green situated on an oceanside dune line.

Of course there is Harbour Town, the monumental course of Southeastern lowland golf, which has been voted the second-most favored course by PGA TOUR professionals (after Pebble Beach) and has been rated in the top ten in the United States by *GOLF Digest*. Veteran CBS Sports commentator Ben Wright, who's seen most of the great courses, rates it among the top five in the world. It was also the course that jump-started three design careers: Pete Dye, the previously unknown designer; Alice Dye, his wife and national amateur champion who leapt into design by working the infamous thirteenth hole while Pete was taking a day off; and Jack Nicklaus, who consulted with Pete Dye on the design. Harbour Town's secret (narrow fairways and small greens) was designed by having Nicklaus hit bag after bag of golf balls from the tees and landing areas after the course was cleared and designing the course around the results. The course has hosted the Senior Amateur and the Nabisco Championships (now the Tour Championship) and is the annual host of the MCI Classic—The Heritage of Golf. The finishing hole at Harbour Town, a monstrous 475-yard par-four that typically plays into the wind, is one of the most recognized holes in golf, with the Harbour Town lighthouse and marina as a backdrop. Winners at Harbour Town include Arnold Palmer, Jack Nicklaus, Tom Watson, Fuzzy Zoeller, Greg Norman, Nick Faldo, Davis Love III, Payne Stewart, Hale Irwin, Bernhard Langer, Johnny Miller, and Hubert Green—a who's who of golf if ever there was one.

■ CONTACT ■

Sea Pines Academy of Golf
P.O. Box 7000
Hilton Head Island, SC 29938
800-925-GOLF

STRATTON GOLF SCHOOL

SCOTTSDALE, ARIZONA;
STRATTON MOUNTAIN,
VERMONT

PROGRAM Two-day and five-day schools and an instruction program with a pro-am tournament. Schools are offered every week except October and the first two weeks of May. All rates are for each person based on the occupancy shown.

ABOUT THE PROGRAMS Each golfer fills out a questionnaire prior to attending the school to allow for complete tailoring of the program to each student's abilities. The objective is to work with student's strengths and weaknesses and improve one or two areas rather than rebuilding the entire swing.

The school features extensive high-speed, stop-action video analysis, teaching aids and drills, exclusive practice areas with target greens,

putting and chipping greens, wide fairways, practice bunkers, and teaching classrooms.

Two-day and five-day programs are offered in both locations. Each program includes an instruction booklet, welcome party, graduation banquet, greens fees, and continental breakfast and lunch daily. The five-day program includes four days on instruction and a fifth free day for golf. The instruction program includes 1 1/2 days of on-course instruction and a pro-am tournament.

COSTS

One-bedroom villa (2 students) two-day Monday–Tuesday school (regular) $473, (fall season) $418; two-day Wednesday–Thursday School (regular) $442, (fall season) $393; two-day weekend school (regular) $552, (fall season) $477; five-day midweek school (regular) $880, (fall season) $788.

Two-bedroom villa (4 students) two-day Monday–Tuesday school (regular) $448, (fall season) $393; two-day Wednesday–Thursday school (regular) $417, (fall season) $368; two-day weekend school (regular) $527, (fall season) $452; five-day midweek school (regular) $818, (fall season) $726.

Three-bedroom villa (6 students) two-day Monday–Tuesday school (regular) $440, (fall season) $385; two-day Wednesday–Thursday school (regular) $409, (fall season) $360; two-day weekend school (regular) $519, (fall season) $444; five-day midweek school (regular) $797, (fall season) $705.

Four-bedroom villa (8 students) two-day Monday–Tuesday school (regular) $436, (fall season) $381; two-day Wednesday–Thursday school (regular) $405, (fall season) $356; two-day weekend school (regular) $515, (fall season) $440; five-day midweek school (regular) $786, (fall season) $694.

STUDENT/TEACHER RATIO 5:1

HEAD INSTRUCTOR Keith Lyford is a three-time collegiate All-American, a former PGA TOUR player, and the 1987 New England PGA Champion. His instruction articles have appeared in *GOLF Digest* and *Golf Tips*. He also serves on the PGA of America's National Teaching Committee, has produced three instructional videos, and is the author of a soon-to-be-published book of golf articles.

■ ABOUT THE LOCATIONS ■

MCCORMICK RANCH GOLF CLUB
SCOTTSDALE, ARIZONA

Situated on the shore of Camelback Lake in the heart of Scottsdale, the Ranch is a Valley of the Sun sleeper. It has a 125-room, 50-villa inn, thirty-six holes of parkland-style golf (Pine and Palm courses), tennis, outdoor swimming pool, jacuzzi, private lake for sailing or fishing, one restaurant serving Southwestern specialties, and a lounge featuring nightly entertainment.

STRATTON MOUNTAIN RESORT
STRATTON MOUNTAIN, VERMONT

Stratton Mountain is a twenty-seven-hole facility designed by legendary architect Geoffrey Cornish (co-author of *The Architects of Golf*). The course is rated one of the top resort courses in the Northeast, a tree-lined delight winding amidst lake, mountain, and forest. The course hosts the annual *McCall's* LPGA Classic each August, as well as the Acura U.S. Women's Hardcourt Championships. The resort offers a tennis school, mountain biking, and summer concerts via an annual Arts Festival. Accommodations are fully equipped villas ranging from one to four bedrooms.

■ CONTACT ■

Stratton Golf School
Stratton Mountain Resort
Stratton Mountain, VT 05155
800-843-6867
In Vermont 802-297-2200

SWING'S THE THING GOLF SCHOOLS
LA QUINTA, CALIFORNIA; ORLANDO, FLORIDA; OCEAN CITY, MARYLAND; SHAWNEE, PENNSYLVANIA; MYRTLE BEACH, SOUTH CAROLINA

PROGRAMS
PGA West Stadium Course: two schools in February, seven in March; Orange Lake Resort & Country Club: three schools in January, eight in February, nine in March, eight in April, three in May, two each month June-November, one in December; Ocean Pines Golf and Country Club: six schools in April, nine in May, six in June, five in July, four in August; Shawnee Country Club: six schools in May, eight in June, seven in July, six in August; Colonial Charters Country Club: four schools in March, eight in April.

COSTS
PGA West Stadium Course (double occupancy) $780, (single occupancy) $860, (commuter) $695, (nonparticipating resort guest) $85; Orange Lake Resort & Country Club

(double occupancy) $765, (single occupancy) $875, (commuter) $645, (nonparticipating resort guest) $125; Ocean Pines Golf and Country Club (commuter) $645, resort rates not yet available; Shawnee Country Club (double occupancy) $780, (single occupancy) $850, (commuter) $645, (nonparticipating resort guest) $135; Colonial Charters Country Club (double occupancy) $760, (single occupancy) $875, (commuter) $645, (nonparticipating resort guest) $125.

ABOUT THE PROGRAM The Swing's The Thing teachers emphasize "Learning for a Lifetime" and the "Swing's The Thing Consistency System" in this low-cost, low-key instructional program. Swing's The Thing is a school that works with the student's individual swing rather than reconstruction—the goal is to achieve understanding of the swing and to achieve consistency of results from it. Ken Venturi, former Masters Champion Art Wall, and two-time U.S. Open winner Julius Boros are among the golf greats who have endorsed the school's methods.

The basic program is a three-day school that includes 18 hours of instruction; use of the school's patented swing training devices; high-speed, stop-motion video swing analysis; club cleaning and storage; textbook; and a Swing's The Thing videotape. Hotel accommodations are included in the price.

Swing's The Thing also offers a one-day refresher school eight times a year in three locations, featuring 7 hours of instruction, special attention to personal profiles and individual area of improvement, a new video analysis, a review of swing basics, and short-game drills.

STUDENT/TEACHER RATIO 4:1.

HEAD INSTRUCTORS The head instructors are Rick McCord and Dick Farley. While the school was founded by Harry Ovitz, one of the top 50 instructors in America, instruction today is jointly headed by Dick Farley and Rick McCord (maker of training videos with Orville Moody, Miller Barber, and Dale Douglas). They have recently created a 5-hour instruction series for NHK, the Japanese public television network. Both Farley and McCord were chosen for *GOLF* magazine's fifty Best Teachers in America list, lead PGA Teaching Workshops, and serve on the staff of *GOLF* magazine. Ovitz, McCord, and Farley have been responsible for over 100 instruction articles and six *GOLF* magazine covers.

■ ABOUT THE LOCATIONS ■

PGA WEST

LA QUINTA, CALIFORNIA

What serious golfer has not heard of The Stadium Course at PGA West, the infamous design by Pete Dye that serves as the hub of a golfing complex in La Quinta? It is just minutes from the famed La Quinta Hotel and within an hour's drive of over seventy courses that blanket the Palm Springs area. The Stadium Course is described by Tom Fazio as "the greatest triumph by an architect over a given piece of property," and it is rated in the top 100 in the world. So why all the controversy?

For starters, it's hard. Dye's design stretches to 7,261 yards and a 77.1 rating from the tips. But it is actually very playable from the forward tees and the regular men's box. For seconds, it is different. As in target golf, where relentless accuracy is the only road to birdie.

The trick at the Stadium Course is to get the ball in play and to keep it there. The fact that most golfers take foolish risks explains the high rating at PGA West. The course will mercilessly discipline you for overambitious play. The eleventh hole, dubbed "Eternity" by the local wags, is 618 yards from the tips and plays off the tee to a two-tiered fairway. Every shot on this hole (as with the course) requires perfect accuracy. Blind shots, water, and miles of sand are the penalties meted out for straying from the appointed line.

There is also the easier Jack Nicklaus Resort course at PGA West (in addition to two private courses, the Nicklaus Private and the Palmer course), although this is also target golf, with a high emphasis on accuracy off the tee.

Accommodations at PGA West include one- to three-bedroom condominiums; premium rates apply in the winter months, but they're well worth it. Also consider making a reservation around May, as the cactus will be in bloom, and there is nothing prettier than a flowering desert.

ORANGE LAKE RESORT & COUNTRY CLUB
ORLANDO, FLORIDA

Two-bedroom villa accommodations 4 to 12 miles west of Walt Disney World. The resort provides an eighteen-hole championship golf course, tennis, sauna, jacuzzis, pools, racquetball, basketball, an 80-acre lake for water sports and fishing, two restaurants and a lounge, a fitness center, a movie theater, and children's programs.

OCEAN PINES GOLF & COUNTRY CLUB
OCEAN CITY, MARYLAND

On the Maryland's Atlantic Coast, the city has its own Boardwalk with arcades, amusements, and white sand beaches.

SHAWNEE COUNTRY CLUB
SHAWNEE, PENNSYLVANIA

A classic course designed by A.W. Tillinghast at the dawn of his storied career (in 1906), Shawnee reached its peak of popularity as a championship course in 1938, when Paul Runyan walloped a young Sam Snead to win the PGA Championship. An additional nine was added in 1960. The Inn compares quite favorably to others in the Poconos/Delaware Water Gap region of eastern Pennsylvania, offering a variety of water-based sports, including boating, fishing, and swimming, as well as horseback riding and a small collection of restaurants and cafes in the American style.

COLONIAL CHARTERS COUNTRY CLUB
MYRTLE BEACH, SOUTH CAROLINA

Host site of numerous tournaments, the course is built on 185 acres of Carolina pine interlaced with dogwoods, holly, and native hardwoods. It hosted the 1993 NCAA Big South Championship. The par-seventy-two course is particularly testy for women, with a 72.0 course rating versus 69.8 for men. For accommodations, this is condo/villa world. Swing's The Thing will assist, but if you want you can procure your own lodgings. The best bets are Beach Colony Resort (800-222-2141) and the Water's Edge Resort (800-255-5554).

■ CONTACT ■
Swing's The Thing Golf Schools
Box 200, River Road
Shawnee-on-Delaware, PA 18356
800-221-6661
In Pennsylvania 717-421-6666

THE SCHOOL OF GOLF
(EXCLUSIVELY FOR WOMEN)

EL CAJON, CALIFORNIA

PROGRAMS Three- and five-day programs. Five-day schools are held March–July and October. A three-day school is held in September.

ABOUT THE PROGRAM While THE School of Golf is not for the rank beginner, it is one of the few programs available exclusively for the female golfer. High-handicappers to scratch players are welcomed to study golf at the school and develop confidence in a consistent swing, which leads to a positive mental attitude and success on the course. All instructors are women, and the crew is led by the indefatigable Master professional Shirley Spork, one of the founders of the LPGA (along with Peggy Kirk Bell) and a pioneer in instruction for women.

The program begins with morning range instruction, including full swing and pitching, chipping, putting, and bunker practice in specially designated practice areas. Afternoons are devoted to playing lessons and one Pro-Am scramble tournament. Evenings are taken up with a number of social events. High-speed, stop-action video analysis is provided, and a take-home videotape is provided for after-school follow-through.

The program fee covers all expenses— instruction, books, tapes, range balls, seminars, green and cart fees, social events, accommodations, and airport transfers.

COSTS Three-day school (double occupancy) $1100, (single occupancy) $1150, (commuter) $850; five-day school (double occu-

■ The School of Golf.

pancy) $1775, (single occupancy) $1875, (commuter) $1375.

HEAD INSTRUCTOR The head instructor is Shirley Spork, twice winner of the LPGA Teacher of the Year award, a founding member of the LPGA, and winner of the Joe Graffis Award from the National Golf Foundation for education in golf. All instructors are PGA and LPGA professionals.

STUDENT/TEACHER RATIO 5:1.

ACCOMMODATIONS Accommodations are included in the package cost.

■ **ABOUT THE LOCATION** ■

SINGING HILLS COUNTRY CLUB & LODGE

EL CAJON, CALIFORNIA

Singing Hills, just east of San Diego, is a thirty-six-hole golf facility with a small and well-appointed lodge. Oak Glen and Willow Glen are the two courses. Oak Glen is a fairly straightforward, average-difficulty track. Willow Glen is one of the best ten public courses in the San Diego area, as rated in *The Endless Fairway*. It is not hard to see why, with it's 71.4 rating and 122 slope from the forward tees on a tree-lined course featuring rolling terrain.

■ **CONTACT** ■

THE School of Golf
2252 Caminito Preciosa Sur
La Jolla, CA 92037
619-270-6230

UNITED STATES GOLF SCHOOLS

CLEARWATER, FORT LAUDERDALE, PALM CITY, SEBRING, FLORIDA; FRENCH LICK, INDIANA; BILOXI, MISSISSIPPI; ROSCOE, NEW YORK; LIBERTY, NEW YORK; BRAINERD LAKE, MINNESOTA; FREEPORT, GRAND BAHAMA ISLAND

PROGRAMS Two-, three-, and five-day programs.

ABOUT THE PROGRAMS In an unusual and pleasing approach to golf instruction, the United States Golf Schools devote half of the instruction program to the short game, which gets short shrift elsewhere, and places emphasis on on-course instruction. There are schools more devoted to the on-course teaching style and a few even more focused on the short game, but this one has perhaps the best balance. Each student works with the same instructor throughout the program—another relatively unusual feature. High-speed, stop-action videotape analysis is utilized throughout the school.

The basic curriculum includes 5 hours of instruction each day, 2 hours of on-course instruction, unlimited golf after school, club cleaning and storage, daily breakfast and dinner, and unlimited range balls.

COSTS

Belleview Mido

Two-day school (double occupancy) $500, (single occupancy) $640, (nonstudent) $235, (commuter) $330; three-day school (double occupancy) $725, (single occupancy) $910, (nonstudent) $337, (commuter) $550; five-day school (double occupancy) $1199, (single occupancy) $1500, (nonstudent) $550 (commuter) $775.

French Lick Springs

Two-day school (double occupancy) $490, (single occupancy) $555, (nonstudent) $175, (commuter) $340; three-day school (double occupancy) $695, (single occupancy) $825, (nonstudent) $265, (commuter) $475; five-day school (double occupancy) $1075, (single occupancy) $1250, (nonstudent) $400, (commuter) $725; seven-day school (double occupancy) $1400, (single occupancy) $1700, (nonstudent) $550, (commuter) $925.

Huff House

Two-day school (double occupancy) $485, (single occupancy) $530, (nonstudent) $250, (commuter) $375; three-day school (double occupancy) $650, (single occupancy) $760, (nonstudent) $340, (commuter) $560; five-day school (double occupancy) $995, (single occupancy) $1100, (nonstudent) $480, (commuter) $850.

Grossinger Resort

Two-day school (double occupancy) $475, (single occupancy) $500, (nonstudent) $170, (commuter) $350; three-day-school (double occupancy) $699, (single occupancy) $750, (nonstudent) $255, (commuter) $525; four-day school (double occupancy) $925, (single occupancy) $999, (nonstudent) $340, (commuter) $700; five-day school (double occupancy) $1100, (single occupancy) $1250, (nonstudent) $425, (commuter) $875.

Breezy Point

Two-day school (double occupancy) $475, (single occupancy) $575, (nonstudent) $200, (commuter) $325; three-day-school (double occupancy) $710, (single occupancy) $890, (nonstudent) $300, (commuter) $475; five-day school (double occupancy) $1050, (single

occupancy) $1400, (nonstudent) $500, (commuter) $700.

The Broadwater Beach

Two-day school (double occupancy) $450; (single occupancy) $520, (nonstudent) $160, (commuter) $320; three-day-school (double occupancy) $675, (single occupancy) $780, (nonstudent) $240, (commuter) $480; five-day school (double occupancy) $1099, (single occupancy) $1300, (nonstudent) $400, (commuter) $750.

Spring Lake

Two-day school (double occupancy) $375, (single occupancy) $450, (nonstudent) $129, (commuter) $340; four-day school (double occupancy) $725, (single occupancy) $875, (nonstudent) $258, (commuter) $680; seven-day school (double occupancy) $1150, (single occupancy) $1400, (nonstudent) $450, (commuter) $1100.

The Inverrary

Two-day school (double occupancy) $540, (single occupancy) $600, (nonstudent) $160, (commuter) $350; three-day school (double occupancy) $750, (single occupancy) $840, (nonstudent) $224, (commuter) $475; five-day school (double occupancy) $1200, (single occupancy) $1350, (nonstudent) $400, (commuter) $850; seven-day school (double occupancy) $1540, (single occupancy) $1750, (nonstudent) $553, (commuter) $1199.

Bahamas Princess

Three-day school (double occupancy) $675, (single occupancy) $875, (nonstudent) $225; four-day school (double occupancy) $875, (single occupancy) $1166, (nonstudent) $300; five-day school (double occupancy) $1075, (single occupancy) $1400, (nonstudent) $375; seven-day school (double occupancy) $1500, (single occupancy) $1850, (nonstudent) $500.

STUDENT/TEACHER RATIO 4:1.

HEAD INSTRUCTORS The head instructors are Mitchell Crum and Mike Mallon. All instructors are PGA professionals.

ACCOMMODATIONS Accommodations are included in the package price (with daily breakfast and dinner).

■ ABOUT THE LOCATIONS ■

BELLEVIEW MIDO RESORT HOTEL
CLEARWATER, FLORIDA

Based in the oceanside town of Clearwater on the west side of Tampa Bay north of St. Petersburg. Belleview Mido is its signature resort dating from the roaring twenties. The course was routed by Donald Ross—although the identity of the actual on-site architect is not known.

Nevertheless, it is a well-maintained course, representative of the Ross style of the period. It is somewhat short by today's standards at under 6,600 yards, but eminently playable and a worthy addition to anyone's Ross portfolio.

The hotel has a shade under 300 rooms, and tennis, swimming, a spa, and fitness options. Dining options are varied—seafood is the best bet.

THE INVERRARY RESORT
FORT LAUDERDALE, FLORIDA

The Inverrary is located in the heart of Fort Lauderdale, one of the major tourist hubs in Southern Florida and near some outstanding beaches to the east and first-class golf to the north and south. The Inverrary offers a 209-room hotel that anchors the private Inverrary community, which for years hosted the Jackie Gleason Inverrary Classic and the LPGA's Phar-Mor Classic. Golfers in this school play at nearby Sunrise Country Club, which isn't quite Inverrary, but has proved a quite popular addition to the local line-up of courses.

CUTTER SOUND GOLF & YACHT CLUB/HOLIDAY INN
PALM CITY, FLORIDA

Across a small bay from the better-known resort town of Stuart, Palm City is at the northern edge of south Florida. It has escaped the overbuilding of south Florida. Cutter Sound is home to a Gary Player signature course. It offers most of the usual Player design traits smallish but flat greens, short length, particularly from the forward and regular tees, and an emphasis on precision and course conditioning).

The Holiday Inn is right on the ocean. It offers a large selection of rooms (181 in all), plus tennis and swimming.

SPRING LAKE GOLF & TENNIS RESORT
SEBRING, FLORIDA

The lake in question is a small one in something of an underpublicized part of Florida, the lower central part of the state roughly halfway between Tampa on the west coast and Stuart. Accommodations are in the form of two-bedroom villas. The resort has the usual range of outdoor and water-based activities, including tennis, a fitness center, boating, fishing, and waterskiing on the lake.

FRENCH LICK SPRINGS GOLF & TENNIS RESORT
FRENCH LICK, INDIANA

Despite a rather curious name, French Lick is actually one of the more prestigious old-time resorts of the Midwest. It hosted, for instance, two LPGA Championships on the Donald Ross-designed Country Club course. In addition to the Ross course, the resort now has a 6,000-yard, par-seventy Valley course, which is eminently playable. I heartily recommended it as a tune-up or for new golfers.

The resort has 485 rooms in a seven-storey brick structure and was built at the turn of the century as a health spa. Italian marble fills the entrance. The resort hosts up to 2,000 guests for dinner. French and American-style dining in the main dining room are options for families and vacationing golfers.

BROADWATER BEACH RESORT & PRESIDENT CASINO
BILOXI, MISSISSIPPI

Gambling has brought an infusion of investment into the old-line resorts of the Mississippi coast, which were quite popular a generation or two ago. The Broadwater is the leading golf resort of the area. It is just east of Biloxi.

Two courses are available. The Sea course plays right up to the Gulf and is long, tight, and tough. The far friendlier Sun course plays away from the ocean, although several lakes and ponds were scooped out to provide the dirt for mounding and elevation changes, resulting in water hazards on almost every hole!

The resort offers a large array of outdoor activities, including swimming and tennis, as well as fishing in and around the Gulf. The best part of the resort, however, is the regionally influenced cuisine served in five dining rooms, and in the casino itself, which bustles with all the usual suspects of a gambling palace—crowded roulette tables and rows of one-armed bandits.

HUFF HOUSE
ROSCOE, NEW YORK

The country's first specially designed practice facility for high handicappers and beginners is the main event in Roscoe, New York, in the heart of the golf-rich Catskills. The Main House is a graciously restored Victorian farmhouse with 45 guest rooms. The facility includes the practice facility, a par-three course, and the eighteen-hole championship course. Tennis, volleyball, croquet, and bocce ball are also offered.

GROSSINGER RESORT
LIBERTY, NEW YORK

Along with the Concord Monster, Grossinger's is considered the elite course of the Catskills resorts. This Joe Finger-designed beauty has received many accolades from magazines and guests. The facility as a whole features twenty-seven holes of golf, the newly renovated hotel, tennis, an Olympic-size indoor pool, Karaoke, and a spanking new bistro. Grossinger's has a "Mom-and-Pop" name, but certainly it is top-drawer for quality and is only about 2 hours out of New York City at a leisurely pace. The surrounding countryside is quite spectacular!

BREEZY POINT RESORT

BRAINERD LAKES, MINNESOTA

In the heart of Minnesota is the Brainerd Lakes region, home to a fairly astonishing array of top-quality golf courses and resorts. Breezy Point has received a fair amount of attention for its two courses, The Traditional and The Championship, which offer two divergent golfing experiences. Indoor swimming, a sauna, and whirlpools are also offered. Condos and chalets provide accommodations (the latter feature private jacuzzis).

THE BAHAMAS PRINCESS

FREEPORT, GRAND BAHAMA ISLAND

The only golf school option around that offers a beach and a casino in addition to golf, the Bahamas Princess is typical of the best of the Bahamas. It is mondo tennis (ten courts, six lit for night play), mondo golf (two courses), and a mondo private beach, mon. The hotel's cuisine is also highly touted, and don't forget to try the shopping arcade with duty-free buys. There are plenty of great hotel-style accommodations, and traditional gambling games are the favored nighttime activity.

■ CONTACT ■

United States Golf Schools
1631 S.W. Angelico Lane
Port Saint Lucie, FL 34984
800-354-7415

LOCAL SCHOOLS

ALABAMA

ALABAMA-AUBURN
TIGER-TIDE ACADEMY

TUSCALOOSA

PROGRAMS Junior golfers only (beginners to advanced).

ABOUT THE PROGRAM The Tuscaloosa facility includes a driving range, putting green, and chipping and bunker practice areas. High-speed, stop-action videotaping is available.

COSTS $525.

INSTRUCTORS Dick Spybey and Mike Griffin.

ACCOMMODATIONS College dormitories. Swimming available.

■ **CONTACT** ■

Alabama-Auburn Tiger-Tide
P.O. Box 40405
Tuscaloosa, AL 35404
205-348-3692

National Golf Schools offering Alabama Programs:
  GOLF Digest Schools
  John Jacobs' Practical Golf Schools

ALASKA

ELMENDORF JUNIOR GOLF CLINIC

ELMENDORF AFB

PROGRAMS Eight days, one day per week over an eight-week period. Juniors only (ages 7 to 17). The program begins in June and runs through August.

ABOUT THE PROGRAMS As a rule, military courses are among the finest in the world. For proof, one need look no further than Eagle Glen, designed by Robert Trent Jones in 1971. Incidentally, Jones got his start designing courses in central Alberta for Stanley Thompson, so permafrost is home turf to him. A modest golf instruction program has been developed for young Alaskans interested in enhancing their skills.

COSTS $55.

INSTRUCTORS The head instructor is Ernie Hamby. All instructors are PGA professionals.

ACCOMMODATIONS No accommodations, commuter only.

■ **CONTACT** ■

Eagle Glen Golf Course
Elmendorf AFB, AK 99506
907-552-3821

ARIZONA

GOLF SCHOOLS OF SCOTTSDALE

SCOTTSDALE

PROGRAMS Commuter, two-, three-, four-, and five-day schools, October–May.

ABOUT THE PROGRAMS Mornings feature instruction in preshot fundamentals, full-swing plus all aspects of the short game. High-speed, stop-action video analysis is employed to track student progress throughout. Green fees for after-school play plus club cleaning and storage are included.

COSTS Commuter from $190 per day.

January–April

Hampton Inn two-day schools (double occupancy) $475, (single occupancy) $645; three-day schools (double occupancy) $695, (single occupancy) $995; four-day schools (double occupancy) $895, (single occupancy) $1295; five-day schools (double occupancy) $1095, (single occupancy) $1595.

Red Lion's La Posada two-day schools (double occupancy) $595, (single occupancy) $845; three-day schools (double occupancy) $995, (single occupancy) $1345; four-day schools (double occupancy) $1245, (single occupancy) $1695; five-day schools (double occupancy) $1495, (single occupancy), 1995.

Stouffer's Cottonwood two-day schools (double occupancy) $745, (single occupancy) $995; three-day schools (double occupancy) $1095, (single occupancy) $1595; four-day schools (double occupancy) $1395, (single occupancy) $1995; five-day schools (double occupancy) $1745, (single occupancy) $2295.

The Scottsdale Princess two-day schools (double occupancy) $795, (single occupancy) $1195; three-day schools (double occupancy) $1295, (single occupancy) $1895; four-day schools (double occupancy) $1695, (single occupancy) $2395; five-day schools (double occupancy) $2095, (single occupancy) $2895.

October–December

Hampton Inn two-day schools (double occupancy) $395, (single occupancy) $595; three-day schools (double occupancy) $695, (single occupancy) $895; four-day schools (double occupancy) $795, (single occupancy) $1195; five-day schools (double occupancy) $895, (single occupancy) $1495.

Red Lion's La Posada two-day schools (double occupancy) $495, (single occupancy) $695; three-day schools (double occupancy) $795, (single occupancy) $1095; four-day schools (double occupancy) $995, (single occupancy) $1395. Five day schools (double occupancy) $1195, (single occupancy) $1695.

Stouffer's Cottonwood two-day schools (double occupancy) $595, (single occupancy) $795; three-day schools (double occupancy) $895, (single occupancy) $1295; four-day schools (double occupancy) $1195, (single occupancy) $1645; five-day schools (double occupancy) $1395, (single occupancy) $1845.

The Scottsdale Princess two-day schools (double occupancy) $695, (single occupancy) $995; three-day schools (double occupancy) $1095, (single occupancy) $1495; four-day schools (double occupancy) $1395, (single occupancy) $1995; five-day schools (double occupancy) $1695, (single occupancy) $2395.

ACCOMMODATIONS Accommodations are included in package price with daily breakfast, lunch, and a welcome reception. Four hotels are offered as accommodations, ranging from the budget-orientd Red Lion's La Posada and the Hampton Inn to the midscale Stouffer's Cottonwood and the upscale Scottsdale Princess. All are located in the heart of Scottsdale within sight of Camelback Mountain and a host of the finest daily-fee golf alternatives in the country. An excellent range of choices make this a school to carefully consider regardless of your budget.

STUDENT/TEACHER RATIO 5:1.

INSTRUCTORS The Director of Instruction is Andy Prosowski. All instructors are PGA professionals.

■ **CONTACT** ■

Golf Schools of Scottsdale
4949 East Lincoln Drive
Scottsdale, AZ 85253
800-356-6678 or 602-808-9146

SWING MASTERS

PHOENIX

PROGRAM Two-day programs, September–May.

ABOUT THE PROGRAM Ah . . . Ernest Jones. That one-legged pioneer of golf instruction and the author of *Swing the Clubhead*. The immortal Charles Price described him as "the pro from Fifth Avenue." His spirit lives on at Swing Masters, where natural rhythm and swing are emphasized. They begin with proper set-up to allow maximum freedom for the body and proceed from there. One thing they've got that Jones never did is high-speed, stop-action video to reinforce the lessons and provide a take-home reference for personal use or in work with one's local professional. One thing that Jones had that they don't is a portable record player to play Viennese waltzes to teach the idea of rhythm, flow, and poise in the swing. But they have their own devices! Like

Jones, and a few of the better teachers around, they emphasize the upper body's role in the swing.

COSTS Two-day school, $355.

ACCOMMODATIONS Not included in package price. Orange Tree was built next to the Orange Tree Golf Club, which has anchored north Scottsdale, not far from the TPC of Scottsdale, since the mid-1950s. Johnny Bulla designed the course in the old, flat, parkland style. Three reachable par-fives and little water to contend with make this a delightful course to play; a collection of long par-fours and some heavy trapping schemes put enough bite so that success feels well earned. The Resort is dominated by an imposing racquet and fitness center and one of the better equipped spas in the Valley of the Sun. Huge suites and three dining rooms complete the offering.

STUDENT/TEACHER RATIO 4:1.

INSTRUCTORS The school President is Kieran Dunlavy. All instructors are PGA professionals.

■ **CONTACT** ■

Swing Masters
5110 North 44th Street
Suite L210
Phoenix, AZ 85018
800-752-9162 or 602-952-8484

National Golf Schools offering Arizona Programs:

Bill Skelley School of Golf
Chuck Hogan Golf Schools
Craft-Zavichas Golf Schools
Gillette LPGA Golf Clinics
GOLF Digest Schools
John Jacobs' Practical Golf Schools
Nicklaus/Flick Golf Schools
Paradise Golf Schools
Professional Golf Schools of America
Stratton Golf Schools
Swing's The Thing Golf Schools

ARKANSAS

JACK FLECK COLLEGE OF GOLF KNOWLEDGE

Magazine

PROGRAMS Hourly sessions and full-day instruction, including both range work and on-course play. Programs are offered May through October. There is a limit of 5 students per class.

ABOUT THE PROGRAM Any program taught by a man who beat Ben Hogan in a play-off for the U.S. Open is one that *everyone* should consider carefully. This year marks the fortieth anniversary of Fleck's astonishing play-off victory at Olympic. The fact that he is still teaching at all is a marvel that makes this school well worth considering, especially with its one-on-one instruction style and affordable rates. Jack teaches full-time out of Lil' Bit A Heaven, but he winters in the Palm Springs area, so West Coast residents may enjoy his talents as well.

COSTS $100 per hour.

STUDENT/TEACHER RATIO 1:1.

HEAD INSTRUCTORS The head instructor is Jack Fleck.

ACCOMMODATIONS No accommodations, commuter program only. Call the Chamber of Commerce for local hotel rates, availabilities, and facilities.

■ CONTACT ■

Jack Fleck College of Golf Knowledge
Lil' Bit A Heaven Golf Club
Route 1 Box 140
Magazine, AR 72943
501-969-2203

CALIFORNIA

STANFORD GOLF SCHOOL

Palo Alto

PROGRAMS Six-day camps for juniors, June–August.

ABOUT THE PROGRAM When Goodwin and Baldwin take a summer break from coaching Tiger Woods, they can be found here. The schools feature intensive morning training and afternoon on-course instruction. Juniors work all day on the range and hit the course in the evenings. High-speed, stop-action video is employed throughout to monitor progress, and a final-day tournament is scheduled as an incentive for training.

Juniors also receive instruction in rules, history, practice routines, mental conditioning, etiquette, and advice on college-level play.

Daily lunches are included (juniors receive all meals).

COSTS From $795.

STUDENT/TEACHER RATIO 5:1.

INSTRUCTORS The head instructors are Wally Goodwin and Tim Baldwin. All instructors are PGA professionals.

ACCOMMODATIONS Stanford dorm rooms.

■ **CONTACT** ■

Stanford Golf Camp
919 Sir Francis Drake Boulevard
Kentfield, CA 94904
800-433-6060

INDIAN WELLS GOLF SCHOOL

INDIAN WELLS

PROGRAMS Day clinics throughout the year.

ABOUT THE PROGRAM Small classes and instruction in all phases of the game from full swing to putting are featured in this under-publicized entry. High-speed, stop-action video is employed.

COSTS $95 (Monday–Thursday), $105 (Friday–Sunday); $35 after 2 p.m.

STUDENT/TEACHER RATIO 4:1.

INSTRUCTORS All instructors are PGA professionals.

ACCOMMODATIONS Accommodations are not included in the package price. Golfers may stay at either one of two imposing and neighboring resorts, the Hyatt Grand Champions or the Stouffer Esmerelda. The Hyatt is California, in a European style, or Europe in a California style. All rooms are suites, and bougainvillaea, citrus trees, palms, flower gardens, lagoons, fountains, and waterfalls

are everywhere one looks. The three restaurants have views of the San Jacinto Mountains, and Wolfgang Puck was here. The Stouffer Esmerelda begins at the door with an eight-story atrium with dual staircases and a fountain. Handcrafted poster beds and 80,000 square feet of Adoquin stone suggest an ambience of complete elegance. And, just like the Regent Beverly Wilshire and other "grand hotels," there is an attendant always ready to spritz down guests sunbathing by the pool.

■ **CONTACT** ■

Indian Wells Golf School
44-500 Indian Wells Lane
Indian Wells, CA 92210
619-346-4653

OJAI GOLF ACADEMY

OJAI

PROGRAMS One-day schools.

COSTS Weekday (double occupancy) $154, (single occupancy) $234; weekend (double occupancy) $191, (single occupancy) $311.

STUDENT/TEACHER RATIO 4:1.

INSTRUCTORS All instructors are PGA professionals.

ACCOMMODATIONS Included in the package price. Guests stay at the Ojai Valley Inn and Country Club. Ojai Valley was the inspiration for Shangri-La in Frank Capra's *Lost Horizon*. It is a surprisingly remote and secluded resort given its proximity to Los Angeles (slightly over 2 hours) and Santa Barbara (40 minutes). Ojai was a retreat founded in the 1920s for Easterners who had read journalist Charles Nordhoff's sky-high praise of the Ojai Valley's beauty. Ultimately, Wallace Neff, who became the leading architect of the Spanish Revival period, designed a clubhouse, and George Thomas Jr., famed for Los Angeles Country Club, Bel-Air, and Riviera, co-designed the course. Jay Morrish recently rebuilt all the greens and restored the course. A par-seventy minor classic, it currently hosts the GTE West Classic on the PGA Senior TOUR. The Inn's over 200 rooms could be mistaken for small country estates.

■ CONTACT ■

Ojai Golf Academy
Ojai Valley Inn & Country Club
Ojai, CA 93023
805-646-5511

NORTHERN CALIFORNIA PGA JUNIOR SCHOOL

SACRAMENTO

PROGRAM One six-day program in June, Juniors ages 13–17.

ABOUT THE PROGRAM Morning instruction and afternoon playing lessons are the story here. This is one of the best-established junior programs in the country, now in its thirteenth year. Instruction covers full swing to short game, plus rules, etiquette, course management skills, and strategy.

COSTS $695.

STUDENT/TEACHER RATIO 12:1.

INSTRUCTORS The head instructor is Richard McShane. All instructors are PGA professionals.

ACCOMMODATIONS Dorm rooms at California State University at Sacramento with full adult supervision and all meals. Evening recreation program on campus. Haggin Oaks is a thirty-six-hole facility with a South course designed by Alister Mackenzie during his California period. This was the third of his great trio of courses (with Pasatiempo and Cypress Point), and it's a change of pace from both with narrow fairways and plenty of bunkers. The front is distinctly shorter, but it is actually the tougher of the nines. The North course is, in general, wider, longer, and more forgiving. The Blue Nine has an absolutely first class par-five finishing hole.

■ CONTACT ■

Northern California PGA
Haggin Oaks Golf Shop
3645 Fulton Avenue
Sacramento, CA 95821
916-481-4507

National Golf Schools Offering California Programs:

America's Favorite Golf Schools
Gillette LPGA Golf Clinics
The Golf Academy of Aviara
The Golf Clinic
GOLF Digest Schools
The Golf University of San Diego
Heritage Golf Schools
John Jacobs' Golf Schools
La Costa School of Golf
Nicklaus/Flick Golf Schools
Paradise Golf Schools
Riley School of Golf
Swing's The Thing Golf Schools

COLORADO

ROCKY MOUNTAIN FAMILY GOLF SCHOOL

LITTLETON

PROGRAMS Three-, four-, and five-day programs, June-August.

ABOUT THE PROGRAMS Heavy experience plus an emphasis on a simple, repetitive stroke (from full swing to putting) are the hallmarks of the Rocky Mountain program. "We teach the game to be simple and natural," is the outfit's credo. By relying on tried and true techniques (the one-swing and the Dave Pelz putting method) students can rest assured that instruction will be relatively painless and credible.

The program includes 4 hours of instruction daily, high-speed, stop-action video swing analysis, computer-enhanced picture printouts, daily golf, and evening sessions on mental conditioning (four- and five-day programs only).

COSTS $185-$395.

STUDENT/TEACHER RATIO 8:1.

INSTRUCTORS The head instructor is Ollie Woods. Staffer Hugh Wimberly is in the Golf Coaches Hall of Fame. All instructors are PGA professionals.

ACCOMMODATIONS Accommodations are not included in the package. The school will recommend area motels and campgrounds. A new program has just been launched offering

a youth camp experience for junior golfers. Students stay at Western State College dorms, and the program costs include meals and accommodations.

■ CONTACT ■

Rocky Mountain Family Golf School
40 West Littleton Boulevard
Littleton, CO 80120
303-932-2664

BOBBY ELDRIDGE GOLF SCHOOL

MOSCA

PROGRAMS Three-day programs, July-September.

ABOUT THE PROGRAMS The Eldridge program is one of several nationally that focus on making the student into his or her own best critic. The program includes not only swing fundamentals but swing diagnosis, not only putting stroke mechanics but practice in reading greens, not only short game technique but how to choose which technique where, and when.

COSTS Three-day schools (double occupancy) $1070, (single occupancy) $1430.

STUDENT/TEACHER RATIO 6:1.

INSTRUCTORS The head instructor is Bobby Eldridge. All instructors are PGA professionals.

ACCOMMODATIONS Included in package price. Students stay at the Great Sand Dunes Country Club and Inn. It is located within 5 miles of the entrance to the Great Sand Dunes National

Monument, surrounded by the Sangre de Cristo Mountains near Alamosa, Colorado.

One of the most remote resorts in the Southwest, Great Sand Dunes is of course on perfect terrain for golf. It is situated near some pristine frontier landscapes, from the mountains to nearby San Luis Lake. A bunk house, ranch house, and the inn contain fifteen rooms. The food is continental, the ambience Ponderosa.

■ CONTACT ■

Bobby Eldridge Golf School
Great Sand Dunes Country Club and Inn
5303 Highway 150
Mosca, CO 81146
800-284-9213 or 719-378-2356

SHERATON STEAMBOAT RESORT AND CONFERENCE CENTER

STEAMBOAT SPRINGS

PROGRAM One-day schools, May–October.
ABOUT THE PROGRAM This school finds the middle road between range and on-course instruction. Its 8-hour program includes full-swing and short-game instruction that segues into a nine-hole pro-am. High-speed, stop-action video analysis is also provided. It is a somewhat ambitious program for a one-day

■ Sheraton Steamboat Resort.

school, but well worth one of your days on a Steamboat getaway.

COSTS One-hour lessons from $45.

STUDENT/TEACHER RATIO 4:1.

INSTRUCTORS All instructors are PGA professionals.

ACCOMMODATIONS Accommodations are not included in package price. This is somewhat surprising because Steamboat is truly too far from any major center for day-trippers and is so beautiful and remote an area that a stay of several days is highly recommended. One of these days they'll put together an accommodations package. For the time being, it is a la carte at the resort, which is one of Sheraton's best. There are three hundred rooms, restaurants, a spa, tennis, and swimming. The Steamboat Springs course is by Robert Trent Jones Jr. It provides spectacular views on practically every hole.

■ **CONTACT** ■

Sheraton Steamboat Resort
and Conference Center
2200 Village Inn Court
Steamboat Springs, CO 80477
800-848-8878 or 303-879-2220

VAIL GOLF CLUB SCHOOLS

VAIL

PROGRAMS Three-day schools, May-August

ABOUT THE PROGRAM The advantage of Vail over Aspen is that it is infinitely easier to reach. Aspen is accessible only via plane, while Vail is not too taxing a car ride out of Denver. But this program is another good reason to choose Vail. It is a low-budget alternative to the *GOLF Digest* school offered at Vail's Singletree throughout the summer, and it is quite laid-back. The three-day program features full-swing instruction on the range and short-game instruction on the course. Five hours of daily instruction and high-speed stop-action video analysis is also provided.

COSTS Three-day school, $300.

STUDENT/TEACHER RATIO 4:1.

INSTRUCTORS All instructors are PGA professionals.

ACCOMMODATIONS Accommodations are not included in the package. The school recommends the Black Bear Inn, a twelve-room bed and breakfast, at 303-476-1304.

■ **CONTACT** ■

Vail Golf Club Schools
Vail Golf Club
1778 Vail Valley Drive
Vail, CO 81657
303-479-2260

CONNECTICUT

National Golf Schools offering Connecticut Programs:
  America's Favorite Golf Schools (See pages 20 and 23)

FLORIDA

AMELIA ISLAND PLANTATION GOLF SCHOOL
AMELIA ISLAND

PROGRAMS Three- and four-day schools plus a one-day mini-school available weekly (except December and January).
ABOUT THE PROGRAM Ron Philo combines video analysis, numerous visual aids, and an outstanding resort location into an impressive golf school offering. Philo concentrates on "Big Muscle Leadership" and "The Inside Moves The Outside" in guiding his students through classes limited to a maximum of twenty participants.
COSTS Three-day school $395; four-day schools $695; mini-schools $195.
ACCOMMODATIONS Accommodations are separate from the school price. Guests may stay at the villa program at Amelia Island Plantation (800-874-6878, one- to three-bedroom villas, kitchen, restaurant, bar, game room, lounge, pool, sauna, tennis, child activities, child care) or at the Ritz-Carlton Amelia Island (800-241-

3333), a Four-Star, Five-Diamond hotel offering what even the most demanding resort guest can dream up. Many restaurants, pools, a sauna, lounges, tennis, and the eighteen-hole Mark McCumber-designed Golf Club of Amelia Island are adjacent to the hotel.
STUDENT/TEACHER RATIO 5:1.
INSTRUCTORS The head instructor is Ron Philo. All instructors are PGA certified.

■ **CONTACT** ■

Amelia Island Plantation Golf School
Amelia Island Plantation
P.O. Box 3000
Amelia Island, FL 32035
800-874-6878

CAPE CORAL GOLF SCHOOL
CAPE CORAL

PROGRAMS Four-day schools, year-round.
ABOUT THE PROGRAM An amiable program for an amiable resort, featuring a not overly taxing 3 hours of morning instruction with unlimited use of the range and the golf course

in the afternoon. High-speed, stop-action video is provided, and playing lessons are part of the curriculum.

COSTS In-season (double occupancy) $510, (single occupancy) $630; off-peak (double occupancy) $740, (single occupancy) $840.

STUDENT/TEACHER RATIO 4:1.

INSTRUCTORS The head instructor is Todd Starane. All instructors are PGA certified.

ACCOMMODATIONS All accommodations are included in package price, along with breakfasts and dinners. Cape Coral is a small, somewhat overlooked hotel with an eighteen-hole resort course, which, at a maximum of 6,649 yards, is not overly taxing. The par-seventy-two course was designed in the traditional style by Dick Wilson (of Doral and Cog Hill fame) and complements the traditional design and service emphasis of the resort. Tennis, swimming, and an excellent array of restaurants also grace the 100-room property.

■ **CONTACT** ■

Cape Coral Golf School
Cape Coral Golf & Tennis Resort
4003 Palm Tree Boulevard
Cape Coral, FL 33915
800-648-1475 or 813-542-3191

THE FLORIDA GOLF SCHOOL

PALM COAST

PROGRAMS Three- and five-day schools, year-round.

ABOUT THE PROGRAMS The Florida Golf School is jointly administered with America's Favorite Golf Schools.

America's Favorite represents one of the most successful national instruction programs in the country. Their success is all the more remarkable because they have de-emphasized the role of the celebrity instructor. Instead, like John Jacob's program, America's Favorite is centered on fundamental, practical instruction from highly trained yet low-profile instructors, with low student to teacher ratios, and the aid of straightforward devices such as videotape replays.

Each of the staff instructors teaches golf full-time on a year-round basis. There are no moonlighting club pros picking up a few quick bucks here—they are all certified by the PGA or the United States Golf Teachers' Association. The programs are run at a variety of lengths in attractive locations throughout the country.

The typical program at America's Favorite includes 5 hours of lessons on the range and in the form of playing lessons. Video analysis for analyzing swing faults and monitoring of progress is used. There are classroom sessions on theory and course management skills, as well as on-course play with the instructing professional. All golfers are grouped by ability, and class size is limited to 4 golfers per professional.

Frankly, one of the prime advantages of the America's Favorite approach to golf school is the affordability. Considering the locations (which include Hilton Head, Palm Springs, Las Vegas, Tempe, Orlando, and The Bahamas), the rates are excellent. One note, however—rates do not include meals, so make allowances.

In addition to the regular programs, America's Favorite Golf Schools acts as a clearinghouse for the International Junior Golf Association (IJGA), a division of the USGTA, which offers a series of one-week summer golf camps in four locations (Fort Myers in southwest Florida and Hilton Head Island, plus a spring break camp in Orlando). Both options are definitely worth a look, as junior golf instruction has been somewhat overlooked by the major national golf schools.

The philosophy of America's Favorite Golf Schools is extremely low-key. There isn't much advanced swing theory here. Analysis, instruction, and plenty of practice under close supervision is the whole program. The locations are excellent, the rates very favorable, and as a basic golf instruction and vacation package, this one is a winner!

All schools offer three or five nights accommodations; 5 hours of daily instruction, including on-course play; daily videotape and critique; green fees and carts both during and after class; unlimited range balls; all taxes; and full use of resort facilities.

COSTS Three-day school (single) $595, (double) $495.

STUDENT/TEACHER RATIO 4:1.

INSTRUCTORS The head instructor is Geoff Bryant. All instructors are PGA certified.

ACCOMMODATIONS Accommodations are included in the school price. Guests stay at the Sheraton Palm Coast Resort, a 154-room resort right on the Intracoastal Waterway, offering golf, tennis, and boating activities as well as a private beach and swimming. Palm Coast is the resort centerpiece of one of the most ambitious developments ever undertaken, a 100-square mile residential city of the same name, planned by ITT Development Corporation. As with most Floridian communities, the emphasis is on outdoor activities—most of which are either located at or connected with the resort. The Sheraton could use a refurbishing. The design style is getting out of date—but it is home to one of the best marinas on the entire Intracoastal, a truly well-designed facility right next to a generous selection of tennis courts.

The golf at the resort is first-rate and more than plentiful. There are four courses in all. Two are designed by Arnold Palmer and Ed Seay, including the delightful Matanzas Woods (nominated for *GOLF Digest's* Best Resort Course of the Year in 1986), and perhaps the most difficult course ever designed by Gary Player is Cypress Knoll, a ball-eating monster from the back tees in an attractive marshland setting. First prize at Palm Coast, however, goes to the astonishing Hammock Dunes, which certainly is a contender for "Best Course Never to Reach the Top-100 Rankings." Set right against the beach, Hammock Dunes is Fazio golf from the late 1980s, when budgets were expanding and no expense spared to make courses right. This particular layout captures some of the characteristics of a Scottish links course, in particular its large greens and closely cropped aprons around the green, which encourage the bump-and-run as well as creative chipping skills. Wind is a huge factor here, giving a distinct advantage to players who can keep the ball low.

■ CONTACT ■

The Florida Golf School
P.O. Box 3225
Fort Pierce, FL 34948
800-365-6727 or 407-464-3706

UNITED STATES SENIOR GOLF ACADEMY

MELBOURNE

PROGRAMS Five-day programs, January–June, September–December.

ABOUT THE PROGRAM It's important to note that the seniors here are the instructors; the students come from all age groups. The specialty here is mental conditioning and its importance in establishing a repeatable swing. Small classes and plenty of on-course situational instruction (one third of all instruction time) also distinguish this hands-on program from the competition. High-speed, stop-action video analysis is included in the program.

COSTS Five days $1395; does not include accommodations.

STUDENT/TEACHER RATIO 3:1.

INSTRUCTORS The head instructor is Roy Smith. All instructors are PGA certified.

ACCOMMODATIONS Accommodations are included in the school price. Accommodations are located 15 minutes from the school, at the Melbourne Holiday Inn. The hotel is right on the beach and features tennis, swimming, and a health and fitness center with spa. The full five-day program includes eight days lodging to allow for enjoyment of Florida's many resort attractions.

Indian River Colony Club is the par-seventy-two course associated with the school. At 6,647 yards from the tips it doesn't overawe with length; rather it emphasizes precision and expert greenside play.

CONTACT

United States Senior Golf Academy
P.O. Box 410339
Melbourne, FL 32941
800-654-5752 or 407-253-5663

HOWIE BARROW SCHOOL OF GOLF

GRENELEFE

PROGRAM Three-day schools, year-round.

ABOUT THE PROGRAM Howie Barrow has been teaching at Grenelefe for more than a few years. The program is something of a free-form affair, reflecting Barrow's belief that since no two golfers are alike, no two programs should be alike, either. Programs are designed to groove a repeatable full swing.

Daily instruction includes 3 hours in the morning and a nine-hole playing lesson each afternoon. High-speed, stop-action video analysis is utilized throughout the program. Students have unlimited access to the range and Grenelefe courses during their visit.

COSTS Costs range from $525 to $860.

STUDENT/TEACHER RATIO 4:1.

INSTRUCTORS The head instructor is Howie Barrow. All instructors are PGA certified.

ACCOMMODATIONS Accommodations are included in the school price. One thousand wooded acres are home to the Grenelefe resort, less than an hour from downtown Orlando on the south side of the city. Grenelefe is quite convenient to Orlando's south-side attractions, including Sea World, MGM Studios, and Disney World.

The resort itself is one of the largest in the state, offering a twenty-court tennis complex, five swimming pools, a full-service marina, and three excellent golf courses. Guests stay in one- or two-bedroom villas with full kitchens.

The South Course at Grenelefe is a Ron Garl design, which means traditional Florida design with some links elements—extensive mounding and bunkering reflect the Scottish influence—plenty of water reflects the Floridian locale. At 6,869 yards from the tips, there's plenty of length to contend with. The East Course comes from Ed Seay, a rare solo course from Arnold Palmer's design partner. It comes from an earlier time in his career and is somewhat more flashy, with a lot of earth-moving done to create elevation changes. The first tee is situated on the second floor of the Conference Center. The showpiece course at Grenelefe, however, is the West Course by Robert Trent Jones, a massive 7,325 yards from the tips. To be truthful, Jones didn't build the course; he did the routing in 1965, and David Wallace completed the construction. It's been ranked the best course in Florida on more than one occasion and typically is included in top-ten Florida course rankings.

■ CONTACT ■

Howie Barrow School of Golf at Grenelefe
Grenelefe Golf and Tennis Resort
3200 State Road 546
Haines City, FL 33844
800-422-5333 ext. 6800 or
813-422-7511

CLUB MED
PORT SAINT LUCIE

PROGRAM Five-day schools, year-round.

ABOUT THE PROGRAM A straightforward instruction program featuring 20 hours of range instruction and two days of situation instruction on course, including development of course management skills. Perhaps the most distinctive feature of the Club Med school, in keeping with its emphasis on vacation fun, is the plethora of contests, awards, and prizes that are an integral part of the program. The school features two golf tournaments as well as an assortment of skill contests. Videotape analysis is conducted throughout the school's duration. After-school golf is both encouraged and complimentary.

COSTS Please call 800-874-6878 to obtain current cost information.

ACCOMMODATIONS Guests stay at Club Med's Sandpiper facility, a full-service resort.

STUDENT/TEACHER RATIO 5:1.

INSTRUCTORS The head instructor is Ron Philo. All instructors are PGA certified.

■ CONTACT ■

Amelia Island Plantation Golf School
Amelia Island Plantation
P.O. Box 3000
Amelia Island, FL 32035
800-874-6878

National Golf Schools offering Florida Programs:

Al Frazzini's Golf Course
 America's Favorite Golf Schools
 Arnold Palmer Golf Academy
 Ben Sutton Golf School
 Bill Skelley School of Golf
 Chuck Hogan Golf Schools
 Dave Pelz Short Game School

David Leadbetter Golf Academy
Doral Golf Learning Center
Galvano International Golf Academy
GOLF Digest Instruction Schools
Grand Cypress Academy of Golf
Heritage Golf Schools
Innisbrook Golf Institute
Jimmy Ballard Golf Workshops
John Jacobs' Practical Golf Schools

Ken Venturi Golf Training Centers
Marlene Floyd's For Women Only Golf
   Schools
Nicklaus/Flick Golf School
Paradise Golf School
Professional Golf Schools of America
Roland Stafford Golf School
Swing's The Thing Golf School

GEORGIA

National Golf Schools offering Georgia Programs:
   Gillette LPGA Golf Clinics *(See page 49)*
   GOLF Digest Instruction Schools *(See pages 51 and 56)*

HAWAII

KAPALUA GOLF CLUB

KAPALUA, MAUI

PROGRAMS Year-round one-day schools.

ABOUT THE PROGRAM This "hurry-up" program covers the gamut of golf instruction from full swing to putting game, and a nine-hole Pro-Am scramble is thrown in for the late afternoon. Try to get out on the Plantation Course. It will truly test a student's new-found short game skills. High-speed, stop-action video is on hand, plus an array of training drills for the range or home practice. This is not the king of golf instruction programs, but, then,

how many people voyage to Hawaii to spend three days in a golf school? This is a very solid one-day program. It is designed to make the rest of a golfing week far more rewarding and enjoyable.

COSTS $225.

STUDENT/TEACHER RATIO 4:1.

INSTRUCTORS The head instructor is Gary Planos. All instructors are PGA certified.

ACCOMMODATIONS Accommodations are separate from the school price. Kapalua is either the resort that put Mark Rohlfing on the map, or the resort that Mark Rohlfing put on the map. This is the home of the PGA TOUR's Kapalua Invitational, one of the best of the late-season events, with a strong Pro-Am tradition. This is, incidentally, the course where

John Daly earned his first suspension for leaving the course in the middle of a round.

There are three courses at Kapalua—and there's hardly a weak hole amongst them, but Crenshaw and Coore's Plantation Course is quite awe-inspiring and hosts the Invitational. The two courses by Arnold Palmer and Ed Seay are top-notch resort offerings; Village is friendly and Bay is memorable.

There are innumerable accommodations options at Kapalua—ranging from villas to hotels. For hotels, the Kapalua Bay Hotel has more than 300 rooms, the open-air lobby is as striking as ever, and the grounds (overlooking Molokai) are impeccably maintained. The newer Ritz-Carlton goes for splash and dash. It succeeds admirably in each of the 500 rooms. But the best dining is probably in the old Kapalua Bay with the French-influenced Plantation Verandah. Five hundred villas complete the accommodations package, with maid and room service included.

The Kapalua tennis is outstanding, the pro shop is close to the best in the country, and the Plantation General Store is well worth a visit. It's been a Maui institution since the 1940s, and it also stocks all the small necessities of the Hawaiian lifestyle, from sunscreen to surfboard wax.

■ CONTACT ■

Kapalua Golf Club
300 Kapalua Drive
Kapalua, Maui, HI 96761
808-669-8044

National Golf Schools offering Hawaii Programs:
The Golf Clinic
John Jacobs' Practical Golf Schools
Nicklaus/Flick Golf School

IDAHO

FLOATING GREEN GOLF SCHOOL

COEUR D'ALENE

PROGRAMS Two-, three-, and four-day programs, April–September; three- and four-day programs limited to beginners and mid-handicappers.

ABOUT THE PROGRAMS This is a specialty school with small classes, personalized instruction, and novice golfers. To paraphrase a recruitment ad, it's a great place to start. Four hours of daily instruction, club fitting, on-course instruction, and high-speed, stop-action video are the basic tools. The two-day school is completely devoted to short game instruction.

COSTS (All quoted costs are per night, per person) Economy April (double occupancy) $99, (single occupancy) $133; May (double occupancy) $119, (single occupancy) $158; June (double occupancy) $129, (single occupancy) $173; July–September (double occupancy) $163, (single occupancy) $218.

Regular April (double occupancy) $114, (single occupancy) $163; May (double occupancy) $134, (single occupancy) $188; June (double occupancy) $139, (single occupancy)

$193; July–September (double occupancy) $189, (single occupancy) $268.

Deluxe April (double occupancy) $145, (single occupancy) $183; May (double occupancy) $149, (single occupancy) $218; June (double occupancy) $179, (single occupancy) $273; July–September (double occupancy) $239, (single occupancy) $368.

ACCOMMODATIONS Accommodations are included in the package price. One of the more delightful developments of the 1990s is the resurgence of interest in the delights of the northern Rocky Mountains. Established Idaho resorts such as Sun Valley have done well enough, but the upstart in all this is the Coeur d'Alene Resort, which is set on one of the best and most unknown lakes in the United States. Coeur d'Alene made a huge splash in the national golf press a few years ago when its course opened (from a design by Scott Miller) with a floating green for the par-three fourteenth. It is well done as gimmicks go, with a ferry boat ready to transport golfers to and from the green, which can stretch out over 150 yards into the lake based on a system of tow-cables. It is successfully drawing golfing attention to the resort, but a better reason to visit is the brilliant course conditioning—one of the very best of resort courses in this regard.

The course is actually quite friendly and a little short, but is first-rate for newcomers.

The resort itself is based in the hotel towers situated by the lake. The suites are well designed, and the food is excellent. A Conde Nast *Traveler* poll rated this the number-one mainland resort in the country, which probably overstates the matter by a degree or two. Nevertheless, that is the level at which discussion of this resort begins.

Just about every resort activity imaginable is offered, including tennis, racquetball, bowling, horseback riding, and a fitness program, including a health spa.

STUDENT/TEACHER RATIO 5:1.

INSTRUCTORS The head instructor is Mary DeLong-Nuttelman. All instructors are PGA and LPGA professionals.

■ CONTACT ■

Floating Green Golf School
Coeur d'Alene Resort
900 Floating Green
Coeur d'Alene, ID 83814
800-688-5253 or 208-667-4653

National Golf Schools offering Idaho Programs:
GOLF *Digest* Instruction Schools

■ Eagle Ridge Inn & Resort.

ILLINOIS

EAGLE RIDGE GOLF ACADEMY

GALENA

PROGRAMS Two- and three-day schools. Special programs are offered for on-course instruction (playing academies), women only, juniors, low-handicappers, and alumni, April–September.

ABOUT THE PROGRAMS The beauty of the Eagle Ridge program isn't so much in the way of innovative instruction, but the rather impressive array of programs. Most schools pair golfers of like abilities, but Eagle Ridge really goes the extra step with complete programs given over to groups with special needs. It is something one expects with a large national outfit, but it is a welcome surprise here. Five hours of daily instruction is offered, ranging from full swing to short game. High-speed, stop-action video is a regular part of the program with a take-home tape offered to graduates. Daily green fees and carts are offered for after-hours golf.

In alternative programs, the Playing Academy and the Advanced Academy offer eighteen-hole playing lessons daily. The mini (weekend) academy offers 8 hours of instruction and course play daily. The alumni academy is a one-day refresher with 5 hours of instruction and a nine-hole playing lesson.

COSTS Spring/Fall Standard (double occupancy) $785, (single occupancy) $1030, (commuter weekday) $425, (commuter weekend) $525; Summer Standard (double occu-

pancy) $840, (single occupancy) $1080, (commuter-weekday) $475, (commuter weekend) $575; Mini (double occupancy) $615; (single occupancy) $775, (commuter weekend) $440; Alumni (double occupancy) $315, (single occupancy) $395, (commuter weekday) $190.

STUDENT/TEACHER RATIO 4:1.

INSTRUCTORS The head instructor is Laura Schlaman. All instructors are PGA or LPGA professionals.

ACCOMMODATIONS Accommodations are included in the package price, as are all meals. Eagle Ridge is one of the more unusual success stories among contemporary resorts. It is a full-scale first-rank golf resort . . . in the Midwest. The property's 6,800 acres offer a delight of outdoor activities, including tennis, swimming, bicycling, fishing, horseback riding, and a fitness center. The resort is family oriented and has a good children's program year-round. The lodge itself has a Scandinavian design and overlooks 7 miles of uninterrupted shoreline on Lake Galena. For history buffs, the town of Galena is the birthplace of Ulysses S. Grant. The resort has been cited by *Better Homes & Gardens* and Citibank's America's Greatest Resorts as one of the best family resorts in the country.

Eagle Ridge is home to three courses, the oldest of which, the North Course, dates back to a 1977 Roger Packard design. But it is the South Course by Larry Packard that drew crowds to the resort and won the Best New Resort Course Award from *GOLF Digest* in 1984 (a rare win for a Midwestern property).

■ **CONTACT** ■

Eagle Ridge Golf Academy
Eagle Ridge Inn and Resort
U.S. Route 20, Box 777
Galena, IL 61036
800-892-2269 or 815-777-2444

National Golf Schools offering Illinois Programs:
　Gillette LPGA Golf Clinics
　GOLF Digest Schools

INDIANA

INDIANA GOLF ACADEMY

MONTICELLO

PROGRAM Three-day programs, April–June, August–September.

ABOUT THE PROGRAM This is a by-the-book program presented in straightforward language for the golfer who wants the facts without the mush. Emphasis is placed on grooving a repeatable full swing, but all phases of the game are covered, as is on-course situational training. High-speed, stop-action video analysis is provided. This is not a fancy program by any means, but it is solid.

COSTS $405 to $445 per person.

STUDENT/TEACHER RATIO 4:1.

INSTRUCTORS The school president is Steve Bonnell. All instructors are PGA professionals.

ACCOMMODATIONS Accommodations are included in the package price. Pine View Golf Resort is situated near the popular Indiana resort area of Indiana Beach, alongside Lake Shafer and Lake Freeman. The resort offers fairly straightforward motel-style accommodations. Fishing and boating are the primary activities here, but there are forty-five holes in

total between two full-length courses and a nine-hole par-three course (lighted for night play). The motel offers a restaurant and lounge; all meals are included in the package price.

■ **CONTACT** ■

Indiana Golf Academy
Pine View Golf Resort
905 West Norway Road
Monticello, IN 47960
800-972-9636 or 219-583-7733

UNITED STATES GOLF ACADEMY

PLYMOUTH

PROGRAMS Three-day schools, April–September.

ABOUT THE PROGRAM This is one of the stronger on-course programs in the Midwest, with 3 hours of daily range work balanced by 3 hours of on-course situational instruction. Extensive videotaping and analysis is offered, as well as the unusual evening screening instructional videos and films. It is one of the only schools to attempt constructive use of the

■ The Indiana Golf Academy—Pine View Golf Resort.

after-hours (although, as at many other resort-based schools, there is unlimited use of the course for after-school play). Students are grouped by ability level, and men and women are taught in different groups.

COSTS $552.

STUDENT/TEACHER RATIO 5:1.

INSTRUCTORS The head instructor is Roger Swanson. All instructors are PGA professionals.

ACCOMMODATIONS Accommodations are included in the package price. Swan Lake is a lesser-known but solid golf resort. It has two full-length courses and is the closest golf school offering to the Chicago metro market, less than 2 hours from the Miracle Mile in northwest Indiana. The Academy Motel is set beside the course, offering standard rooms.

■ **CONTACT** ■

United States Golf Academy
Swan Lake Golf Resort
5203 Plymouth-LaPorte Trail
Plymouth, IN 46563
800-582-7539 or 219-935-5680

National Golf Schools offering Indiana Programs:
  United States Golf Schools

KANSAS

National Golf Schools offering Kansas Programs:
  The Phil Ritson Golf School *(See pages 94 and 95)*

MAINE

GUARANTEED PERFORMANCE SCHOOL OF GOLF

BETHEL

PROGRAMS Three- and five-day schools, May–September.

ABOUT THE PROGRAMS "Guaranteed" is a strong word for a golf school, but the program is intelligently designed and should come close to living up to the billing. Instruction is split equally between the range and the course, and high-speed, stop-action video is liberally employed throughout the course to identify areas of improvement and to monitor progress. The three-day program includes 10 hours of instruction while the five-day program offers 20 hours, leaving plenty of time for after-school golf (green fees and carts are included in the package price).

COSTS Three-day midweek (double occupancy) $480, (single occupancy) $420; three-day weekend (double occupancy) $450, (single occupancy) $510; seven-day week (double occupancy) $720, (single occupancy) $840.

STUDENT/TEACHER RATIO 4:1.

INSTRUCTORS The head instructor is Allen Connors. All instructors are PGA professionals.

ACCOMMODATIONS Accommodations are included in the package price. The Bethel Inn and the central Maine region as a whole is probably best known as a skiing destination, but the colonial-style resort is well worth a look for golf. It offers an excellent halfway point between the splash of a major resort and the intimacy of a country inn. Sailing and canoeing are the non-golf sports of choice, with lake or pool swimming next on the list. The setting for dining is suitably intimate, and all meals are included in the basic tariff.

The eighteen-hole course is by Geoffrey Cornish, one of the old China hands of golf design. It is designed to maximize the benefits of a mountain setting.

■ **CONTACT** ■

Guaranteed Performance School of Golf
Bethel Inn and Country Club
Bethel, ME 04217
800-654-0125 or 207-824-2175

SAMOSET GOLF SCHOOL
ROCKPORT

PROGRAM Three-day schools, May–June.

ABOUT THE PROGRAM The school works on a philosophy of high-quality instruction as opposed to quantity instruction. Sessions are only 2 hours per day (with a playing lesson offered on day three) and focus the student on one or two key areas of improvement. High-speed, stop-action video is employed as well as a video golf simulator on rain days.

The program is less than a full meal. Samoset's minimalist approach is doubtless better for those who genuinely need focus in a few areas rather than a boatload of instruction in all phases of the game.

COSTS (Double occupancy) $366, (single occupancy) $484.

STUDENT/TEACHER RATIO 5:1.

INSTRUCTORS The head instructor is Bob O'Brian. All instructors are PGA professionals.

ACCOMMODATIONS This town is more famous for its shoes than its resorts, but the Samoset has carved out a rather solid reputation and is usually included in top-ten rankings for New England resorts. The views of Penobscot Bay are the main drawing card, and a series of wine tastings, Monte Carlo nights, tours of historical homes, and golf are the hidden delights. Swimming, a health club, racquetball, and a children's program are also featured.

The eighteen-hole Samoset course runs along the bay and offers ocean views on more than half the holes. *GOLF Digest* rated it the fifth most beautiful United States Resort Course in 1992.

■ **CONTACT** ■

Samoset Golf School
Samoset Resort
Rockport, ME 04856
800-341-1650 or 207-594-2511

■ Samoset Resort.

SUGARLOAF GOLF CLUB AND SCHOOL

CARRABASSETT VALLEY

PROGRAMS Two- and five-day schools, June–September.

ABOUT THE PROGRAMS Likely the premier local program in New England, Sugarloaf offers many options for students. Each grouping offers high-speed, stop-action video analysis and instruction in all phases of the game and concentrates on working with what the student already has rather than rebuilding the swing. The two- and five-day schools also feature on-course instruction. Green fees and cart are included in the price for after-school play.

COSTS Two-day $439; three-day $579; four-day $699; five-day $799. All prices are for double occupancy.

STUDENT/TEACHER RATIO 4:1.

INSTRUCTORS The head instructor is Scott Hoisington. All instructors are PGA professionals.

ACCOMMODATIONS Accommodations are included in the package price. Sugarloaf was one of the most successful transitions by a New England resort from skiing to skiing/golf. They did it by hiring Robert Trent Jones Jr. to design the course. They gave him the land to make a crafty, beautiful, and secluded golfing experience. It's been rated the number-one course in the state by *GOLF Digest* for several years. The resort as a whole is routinely rated in Maine's top ten. The Sugarloaf Inn itself is fairly cozy at 105 rooms. All the villas have full access to the resort as well as full kitchens. Beware, the Sugarloaf area is condominium heaven.

■ **CONTACT** ■

Sugarloaf Golf Club & School
The Sugarloaf Inn
Route 27 Box 5000
Carrabassett Valley, ME 04947
800-843-5623

MARYLAND

National Golf Schools offering Maryland Programs:
Gillette LPGA Golf Clinics *(See page 49)*
The Golf School *(See pages 59 and 60)*
Swing's The Thing Golf Schools *(See pages 112 and 114)*

MASSACHUSETTS

BOB DIPADUA GOLF SCHOOL AT FIREFLY

SEEKONK

PROGRAMS Four-day schools, April–July.
ABOUT THE PROGRAM This is one of several smaller, independent schools in Massachusetts. This four-day, 6-hour program with appropriately limited aims works to identify areas of improvement and shows paths to better golf, especially in the full swing. It is possible to schedule four 1 1/2 hour sessions one day a week rather than a full-day school.
COSTS $99 per day for 6 hours.
STUDENT/TEACHER RATIO 6:1.
INSTRUCTORS The head instructor is Bob DiPadua. All instructors are PGA and USGTA professionals.
ACCOMMODATIONS Accommodations are not included in package price. Commuters only. The Firefly facility is based around an eighteen-hole precision course.

■ CONTACT ■

Bob DiPadua Golf School
Firefly Golf Course
320 Fall River Avenue
Seekonk, MA 02771
508-336-6622

OCEAN EDGE GOLF SCHOOL

SOUTH YARMOUTH

PROGRAMS Three-day schools, April–June.
ABOUT THE PROGRAM Five hours of daily instruction are standard. The school is very traditional. It emphasizes that fundamentals of the fluid golf swing are based in the pre-shot routine. Posture, grip, and alignment are thus given the most careful attention, and high-speed, stop-action video analysis tracks the results.
COSTS April–June (double occupancy) $599, (single occupancy) $699, (commuter) $399; July–August (double occupancy) $689, (single occupancy) $789, (commuter) $425.
STUDENT/TEACHER RATIO 6:1.
INSTRUCTORS The head instructor is Ron Hallett. All instructors are PGA professionals.
ACCOMMODATIONS The accommodations are included in the package price, and the Ocean Edge Resort is one of the more impressive in New England, with world-class golf and tennis facilities and a seaside inn right on Cape Cod Bay. Citibank's "America's Greatest Resorts" rated this among New England's best last year, and the course itself has hosted the New England PGA among other tournaments. An excellent restaurant and a fully equipped fitness center round out the resort amenity package. One- to three-bedroom facilities right on the course are available at the school.

The eighteen-hole course was designed by Cornish and Silva, the architects of a large number of distinguished New England courses. It is scenic and provides some tough carries from the back tees.

■ **CONTACT** ■

Ocean Edge Golf School
Ocean Edge Golf Resort and Golf Club
Route 6A, Brewster, MA 02631
800-343-6074 or 508-896-9000

CRUMPIN-FOX ADULT GOLF INSTITUTE

BERNARDSTON

PROGRAMS Three-day schools, one in May and two in June.
ABOUT THE PROGRAM A real sleeper. "Crumpin-Fox" is sort of a calling card among true golfers. It has acquired a tremendous reputation in a short time, and the golf instructor program sure hasn't hurt. As the name states, this school is for adult golfers; the better you

are going in, the better you'll be going out. High-speed, stop-action video is utilized throughout the program, which is standard in most of its methods, but a cut above in reputation and results.
COSTS Commuter, member rate $350, nonmember rate $450.
STUDENT/TEACHER RATIO 4:1.
INSTRUCTORS All instructors are PGA professionals.
ACCOMMODATIONS Accommodations are not included in package price. Crumpin-Fox is the extremely well received course designed by Roger Rulewich near the Vermont border. The club has announced plans but has not yet completed its Fox Inn, so it's commuters only for the time being.

■ **CONTACT** ■

Crumpin-Fox Golf Institute
P.O. Box 215
Bernardston, MA 01337
413-648-9101

National Golf Schools offering Massachusetts Programs:
  Chuck Hogan Golf Schools
  Gillette LPGA Golf Clinics
  GOLF Digest Schools

MICHIGAN

BOYNE SUPER FIVE GOLF WEEK

BOYNE FALLS

PROGRAMS Five-day programs, June–August.

ABOUT THE PROGRAM As much a resort package as a golf school, the Super Five offers a quintet of outstanding course experiences tied together with optional morning or afternoon instruction sessions of 3 hours each daily. Students utilize as much or as little as is needed and work on problems of their own choosing. High-speed, stop-action video is utilized in this most relaxed of golf school programs.

COSTS Schools range from $645 to $845 per person.

INSTRUCTORS All instructors are PGA or LPGA professionals.

ACCOMMODATIONS Accommodations are included in the package price, with all meals. Nestled among the unspoiled, hilly landscape of northwest Michigan, this *GOLF* magazine silver medalist resort has five world-class golf courses, plus tennis, swimming, biking, hiking, trout fishing, waterskiing, and the famous Gaslight District with its 100 specialty shops located in nearby Petosky. Perhaps the most interesting of the courses is the Donald Ross Memorial Course, which recreates eighteen of Ross' most memorable holes, including several from Oakland Hills and Pinehurst No. 2.

■ CONTACT ■

Boyne Super Five Golf Week
Boyne Mountain Resort
Boyne Mountain Road
Boyne Falls, MI 49713
800-462-6963

National Golf Schools offering Michigan Programs:
John Jacobs' Practical Golf Schools
Nicklaus/Flick Golf Schools

MISSISSIPPI

National Golf Schools offering Mississippi Programs:
United States Golf Schools *See pages 116 and 119)*

MISSOURI

National Golf Schools offering Missouri Programs:
John Jacobs' Practical Golf Schools *(See pages 65 and 78)*

NEVADA

National Golf Schools offering Nevada Programs:
America's Favorite Golf Schools *(See pages 20 and 24)*

NEW HAMPSHIRE

WORLD CUP GOLF SCHOOL

HUDSON

PROGRAMS One, two-, and three-day schools, including Junior, Senior, and beginners programs, May–October.

ABOUT THE PROGRAMS This is the only national or local school with a New Hampshire location; as a commuter-only school, it is for locals only and offers 5 hours of daily instruction and a nine-hole playing lesson in the afternoon session. High-speed, stop-action video analysis is employed, and a take-home video is provided for each student. Club fitting is offered through the school; daily lunch and green fees plus cart included in the package prices. Instruction is at the World Cup driving range, but the nearby Green Meadow Golf Course is utilized for on-course instruction.

COSTS From $200.

INSTRUCTORS The head instructor is Bob Griswald. All instructors are PGA professionals.

ACCOMMODATIONS Accommodations are not available.

■ **CONTACT** ■

World Cup Golf School
9 River Road
Hudson, NH 03051
603-598-3838

NEW JERSEY

National Golf Schools offering New Jersey Programs:
   John Jacobs' Practical Golf Schools *(See pages 65 and 78)*

151

NEW YORK

CONCORD GOLF SCHOOL

KIAMESHA LAKE

PROGRAMS Two-day programs, May–September.

ABOUT THE PROGRAM Considering that a number of national schools are operating in New York State, this is a tempting program. The driving range isn't much to look at, but the program emphasizes on course instruction. Concord has a particularly fine set-up in one straightforward and short resort course paired with the infamous Concord Monster, which is still one of the five toughest resort courses in the country. It's on anyone's short list of monster courses, public or private. Bill Burke is an accomplished senior golfer and runs an 18-hour instruction program based on *One Move to Better Golf*, the influential book by Carl Lohren. Burke teaches students to go beyond swing keys and to groove an athletic, flowing swing. Thus it's one of the few schools with a definitive philosophy and significant time on-course for situational instruction. High-speed, stop-action video analysis is provided, with a take-home video, a copy of *One Move to Better Golf*, club fitting, and all green and cart fees included in the package.

COSTS Two-day school $355.

STUDENT/TEACHER RATIO 5:1.

INSTRUCTORS The head instructor is Bill Burke. All instructors are PGA professionals.

ACCOMMODATIONS Accommodations and all meals are included with all meals in the package price. The Concord is the best of a string of good resorts in the Western Catskills in New York State. The resort is large, traditional, and highly rated by AAA and Mobil. The golf is just sublime! Summer entertainment is top-notch, and the convenience of a 2-hour drive to New York City can't be overestimated.

■ CONTACT ■

Concord Golf School
The Concord Resort Hotel
Route 17
Kiamesha Lake, NY 12751
800-431-3850

National Golf Schools offering New York Programs:

Gillette LPGA Golf Clinics
John Jacobs' Practical Golf Schools
Roland Stafford Golf School

NORTH CAROLINA

BONNIE RANDOLPH, MASON RUDOLPH GOLF INSTRUCTION

CASHIERS

PROGRAMS Four-day Bonnie Randolph mini-schools, April-September; five-day Mason Rudolph house party, May.

ABOUT THE PROGRAMS Daily eighteen-hole playing lessons follow morning range work in a routine, which sounds like Ben Sutton's routine. Not surprising, because Bonnie Randolph does double up as a Sutton instructor. This school has the advantage of a better location.

COSTS Program costs range from $335 to $582.

INSTRUCTORS Head instructors are Bonnie Randolph and Mason Rudolph. All instructors are PGA professionals.

ACCOMMODATIONS Accommodations are included in the package price with all meals. Intimate, historic High Hampton Inn has exquisite Smoky Mountain views and an outstanding eighteen-hole course by George Cobb. Rated the best resort in the Carolina mountains.

■ **CONTACT** ■

Bonnie Randolph
Mason Rudolph Golf Instruction
262 Hampton Road
Cashiers, NC 28717
800-334-2551 or 704-743-2411

MID PINES, SOUTHERN PINES

PROGRAMS One-day programs, March–September.

ABOUT THE PROGRAM The Mid Pines program is the shortest in this volume: just 1-hour tune-up sessions over two days, covering fundamentals and course management. The package is really an introduction to the splendid Donald Ross course, one of the few in the country to be constructed by Ross in person and never subsequently remodeled. The practice putting green is one of the most demanding in the country.

COSTS Program costs range from $55 per person for a group session to $150 for a golf clinic of 4 or more people. Instruction packages are available from $133 and up.

INSTRUCTORS The head instructor is Chip King. All instructors are PGA professionals.

ACCOMMODATIONS Accommodations are included in package price, with all meals.

■ **CONTACT** ■

Mid Pines Golf School
Mid Pines
1010 Midland Road
Southern Pines, NC 28387
800-323-2114 or 919-692-2114

CARL TYNER SCHOOL OF GOLF

SUNSET BEACH

PROGRAMS Three-day schools, May–September.

ABOUT THE PROGRAM Tyner used to work for Jimmy Ballard and thus with several of the best-known golfers in the country, notably Curtis Strange during Strange's years at the top. Tyner has added slight variations on the Ballard philosophy, but the elusive "feel" of the good golf swing is still the objective of his schools. High-speed, stop-action video is employed, and on-course playing lessons are given a particularly strong emphasis.

COSTS Please call Carl Tyner School of Golf at 800-334-1126 to obtain current cost information.

STUDENT/TEACHER RATIO 4:1.

INSTRUCTORS The head instructor is Carl Tyner. All instructors are PGA professionals.

ACCOMMODATIONS Accommodations are included in the package price. Students stay at the Colony at Oyster Bay, just across the border from the Myrtle Beach Grand Strand region. The Colony is a villa complex with one- and two-bedroom villas surrounding a common swimming and Jacuzzi (TM) facility.

The course in question, Oyster Bay, is one of a handful, including Tidewater, Heather Glen, and the Legends complex that have brought high-quality golf to one of the nation's busiest golfing meccas. Oyster Bay was voted *GOLF Digest's* Resort Course of the Year in 1983; it is a perennial in the top fifty United States public course rankings. It winds through old pines and marshlands, wrapping around several lakes. The greens are large, well trapped, and undulating. It is a must-play for the area.

■ CONTACT ■

Carl Tyner School of Golf
900 Shoreline Drive
Sunset Beach, NC 28468
800-222-1524

WOODLAKE TOTAL PERFORMANCE GOLF SCHOOLS

VASS

PROGRAMS Three-day programs, March–October.

ABOUT THE PROGRAM A complete health and fitness program for golf, involving everything from course strategy to mental toughness training to nutrition and exercise programs. The school also places emphasis on teaching the "feel" of the golf swing. The junior program also involves swimming and boating activities for a rounded camp experience. Playing lessons are offered as are additional Pinehurst play options at Southern Pines Country Club and Pinehurst 8 (Pinewild).

COSTS Three-day regular school $750; the Players School, $1052; Ladies Only $790 (May); Juniors (double occupancy) $595, (commuter) $452.

STUDENT/TEACHER RATIO 4:1 (except the Players School) .

INSTRUCTORS The head instructor is Tom Ream. All instructors are PGA professionals.

ACCOMMODATIONS Accommodations are included in the package price. The Woodlake Country Club has a number of residential villas utilized for the school; juniors receive adult supervision throughout their camp-style program. Woodlake is one of the Pinehurst area sleeper courses. The original eighteen is an Ellis Maples design with a 73 rating and 132 degree slope from the back tees, so look out. The new nine by Dan Maples is rather unusual—3,820 yards and par-forty from the back tees.

■ CONTACT ■

Woodlake Total Performance Golf Schools
Woodlake Country Club
150 Woodlake Boulevard
Vass, NC 28934
800-334-1126 or 910-245-4031

IMAGE GOLF

OCEAN ISLE BEACH

PROGRAMS Three- and five-day schools, year-round.

ABOUT THE PROGRAMS This school, conducted at Myrtle Beach West Golf Club in North Myrtle Beach, is a border straddler at the northern tip of the famous golfing mecca known as the Grand Strand. Veteran instructor Ben Hunt provides a full-service school with instruction ranging from posture to putting and all parts in between. Particular emphasis is placed on the full swing. The five-day program includes 17 1/2 hours of instruction plus a playing lesson. The three-day program drops down to 10 1/2 hours of instruction. Free green fees are included for after-school play. Videotaped swing analysis is included in the package.

COSTS One day (4 hours) $140; three days (12 hours) $395; five days (22 hours) $640.

STUDENT/TEACHER RATIO 4:1.

INSTRUCTORS The head instructor is Ben Hunt. All instructors are PGA professionals.

ACCOMMODATIONS No accommodations. Students are advised to stay at the neighboring Ocean Creek Resort (800-845-0353), which provides swimming, tennis facilities, and villa and hotel-style lodging.

■ CONTACT ■

Image Golf
Route 2
Box 142-B
Ocean Isle Beach, NC 28469
800-424-7947 or 919-579-1690

National Golf Schools offering North Carolina Programs:

Bertholy-Method Golf School
GOLF Digest Schools
John Jacobs' Practical Golf Schools
Marlene Floyd's For Women Only Golf School
Pinehurst Golf Advantage
Pine Needles/Golfari
Professional Golf Schools of America

OKLAHOMA

K.I.S.S. GOLF CLINICS

AFTON

PROGRAMS Three-day programs, May–July (juniors only, June–July).

ABOUT THE PROGRAMS Twenty hours of instruction, high-speed, stop-action video analysis, on-course afternoon sessions, and daily pro-am scramble events for situational instruction. Marshall Smith teaches essentially what is a Jimmy Ballard style, emphasizing an upper-body move, a baseball style, and fluid swinging.

COSTS From $750.

STUDENT/TEACHER RATIO 5:1.

INSTRUCTORS The head instructor is Marshall Smith. All instructors are PGA professionals.

ACCOMMODATIONS Accommodations are included in the package price. Shangri-La is a 650-acre resort on the Grand Lake o' the Cherokees. Four-hundred fifty guest rooms, tennis, swimming, racquetball, fishing, and a health spa are the primary attractions aside from golf. Golf is represented with thirty-six holes designed by Donald Sechrest. Neither the Blue nor the Gold course are killers, but Gold offers more room off the tee for stray hitters, while Blue has less water to contend with.

■ **CONTACT** ■

K.I.S.S. Golf Clinics
Shangri-La Resort
Route 3
Highway 125 South
Monkey Island, Afton, OK 74331

PENNSYLVANIA

SEVEN SPRINGS GOLF SCHOOL

CHAMPION

PROGRAMS Three-day schools, May–August.
ABOUT THE PROGRAM Five hours of daily instruction featuring high-speed, stop-action video analysis. Unlimited golf is available after conclusion of the afternoon session, plus a full eighteen-hole playing lesson with every school.
COSTS Three-day school $439, commuters $339; one-day programs available from $135.
STUDENT/TEACHER RATIO 4:1.
INSTRUCTORS The head instructor is Fred Haddick. All instructors are PGA professionals.
ACCOMMODATIONS Accommodations are included in the package price. This is a 300-room mountain retreat. Lodge rooms and condos are available. Tennis, bicycling, and swimming are featured non-golf activities. The resort has its own Seven Springs course, which is short and in the honorable tradition of the playable resort course.

■ CONTACT ■

Seven Springs Golf School
Rural Route 1
Champion, PA 15622
800-452-2223 or 814-352-7777

THE WOODLANDS GOLF ACADEMY

FARMINGTON

PROGRAMS One- and two-day programs, May-October.
ABOUT THE PROGRAMS A smorgasbord of programs makes this one of the choice Pennsylvania options. There are beginners, intermediate, expert, and one-day refresher school options. Instruction is fairly high-tech with both high-speed, stop-action video and computer-based swing analysis. Muscle memory teaching aids are also employed. The complete program includes a take-home video and club fitting.
COSTS Weekday (double occupancy) $195, (single occupancy) $252; weekend (double occupancy) $207, (single occupancy) $305.
STUDENT/TEACHER RATIO 4:1.
INSTRUCTORS The head instructor is Greg Ortman. All instructors are PGA professionals.
ACCOMMODATIONS The Nemacolin Woodlands Resort is a AAA Four-Diamond rated facility featuring tennis, swimming, equestrian events, and a variety of other outdoor activities. The centerpiece of the resort is the extremely well-appointed spa, where the loofah scrubs abound as well as all other typical European and American spa and fitness center activities. The eighteen-hole Woodlands course is in the mountain-course tradition of rolling fairways, uneven lies, and a generous helping of length (6,900 yards) from the back tees.

■ **CONTACT** ■

The Woodlands Golf Academy
Route 40 East
Farmington, PA 15437
800-422-2736 or 412-329-8555

National Golf Schools offering Pennsylvania Programs:

America's Favorite Golf Schools
Professional Golf Schools of America
Swing's The Thing Golf Schools

SOUTH CAROLINA

PALMETTO DUNES GOLF

HILTON HEAD ISLAND

PROGRAMS Three-day schools plus special clinics and private lessons.

ABOUT THE PROGRAM Half-days only at Palmetto Dunes, allowing plenty of time to enjoy the three courses and the many other resort activities. The school offers 6 hours of instruction and covers the entire game from posture to putting. Pay attention—the instruction goes at a fast clip.

COSTS Please call Palmetto Dunes at 803-785-1136 to obtain current cost information.

STUDENT/TEACHER RATIO 6:1.

INSTRUCTORS The head instructor is Chip Pellerin. All instructors are PGA professionals.

ACCOMMODATIONS Accommodations are not included in the package price. Palmetto Dunes is one of the resorts that has given Hilton Head Island its outstanding reputation. It is where President Clinton stays and golfs each New Year's Day with other celebrities at the annual Renaissance weekend. Students can elect to stay at any number of hotels throughout Hilton Head Island or make arrangements to stay within Palmetto Dunes Resort either in villa accommodations or in the Grand Hyatt or Hilton Resort hotels. Sand Dollar (803-785-1162) offers the best selection of villas and hotel rooms.

Palmetto Dunes is home to three outstanding golf courses and probably has the most balanced offering on Hilton Head Island. The Robert Trent Jones course is typical Jones runway-length tees, wide landing areas that are sharply bunkered, and huge putting surfaces that are quite undulating and offer a high premium to a crafty wedge player. The par-seventy Fazio course was a collaboration between George and Tom Fazio and was completed in 1974. For some time it was ranked second only to Harbour Town amongst Hilton Head Island courses and for years had a place in the top-100 rankings. Its yawning waste bunkers and undulating landing areas offer a mesmerizing challenge off the tee . . . and the course is long, long, long. The newest course, the Arthur Hills, is the gem of the three, now hosting the Golf World Collegiate Championship. Built partially on a secondary sand dune line, the Hills Course is also noted for its undulating fairways and tough approach shots.

■ **CONTACT** ■

Palmetto Dunes Golf
P.O. Box 5849
Hilton Head Island, SC 29938
803-785-1136

GOLF ACADEMY OF HILTON HEAD ISLAND

HILTON HEAD ISLAND

PROGRAMS One- and three-day programs.

ABOUT THE PROGRAMS One of the better programs on Hilton Head Island is the Golf Academy, which is conducted off the back of the range at Hilton Head's prestigious Port Royal Golf Club. Director Keith Marks favors the fundamental, diagnostic approach, teaching the basics of the golf swing and developing a customized program for each student depending on individual abilities and goals. Videotape analysis is utilized throughout the school, which features 5 hours of instruction daily as well as daily on-course play. Each student goes home with a personalized workbook.

COSTS Five days $1495; three days $995; weekend program $595; one day $299.

STUDENT/TEACHER RATIO 4:1.

INSTRUCTORS The head instructor is Keith Marks Jr. All instructors are PGA professionals.

ACCOMMODATIONS Accommodations are included in the package price. Guests can opt to stay at the Players' Club on the south end of the island or within Port Royal Resort (and within a minute of the teaching facility) at the Westin Resort. If at all possible, try the Westin. It is Hilton Head's only Five-Diamond rated hotel. It earned its rating not only because of a stunning beachside location but also due to first-rate service. A winner on every level!

Port Royal Plantation contains three golf courses. Planter's Row is quite narrow off the tee and rarely allows anything more adventurous than a three-wood. It played host to the Hilton Head Seniors Invitational when that event graced the Senior PGA TOUR calendar. Better courses for the average player are the Pete Dye-redesigned Robber's Row and the George Cobb-designed Barony courses. They're among the oldest on the island, but the Barony in particular plays well for families and groups of varied abilities.

■ CONTACT ■

Golf Academy of Hilton Head Island
95 Matthews Drive
Suite 306
Hilton Head Island, SC 29926
800-925-0467 or 803-686-8801

SKIP MALEK'S GOLF SCHOOL

HILTON HEAD ISLAND

PROGRAMS Three-day schools, year-round.

ABOUT THE PROGRAM Skip Malek is in a small group of highly successful instructors who continue to emphasize the highly personal instruction techniques over swing keys and cure-alls. Twelve hours of instruction cover the basics—teaching students a reliable, repeatable, personal swing. Although this school involves morning sessions only, the entire gamut of instruction is covered. Progress is monitored via consistent videotape analysis. This school is highly rated by long-time Hilton Head Island residents.

COSTS Three-day school, $995.

INSTRUCTORS The head instructor is Skip Malek. All instructors are PGA professionals.

ACCOMMODATIONS No accommodations are available through the Skip Malek School. Try

George Capuzello at Capuzello Vacations and Realty (800-627-6545) for recommendations and reservations.

■ CONTACT ■

Skip Malek's Golf School
79 Skull Creek Drive
Hilton Head Plantation
Hilton Head Island, SC 29926
803-689-2200 or 800-925-0467

KIAWAH ISLAND JUNIOR GOLF SCHOOL

KIAWAH ISLAND

PROGRAM Six-day sessions, June and July.

ABOUT THE PROGRAM Launching in the summer of 1995, this is already one of the most interesting junior programs in the country. The Kiawah school combines an enviable collection of golf coaches as instructors and the fabulous collection of Kiawah Island courses into a compelling school. Students between ages 13 and 17 are eligible to attend and will have a complete instruction program, including full swing, short game, putting, and a special emphasis on mature golfers' skills such as mental conditioning and course strategy. But the real bonus here is in the exposure junior golfers gain to some of the top college coaches in the country, including coaches at Clemson, College of Charleston, Virginia, and Florida State.

COSTS $895.

STUDENT/TEACHER RATIO 3:1.

INSTRUCTORS The Director of Golf is Tommy Cuthbert. All instructors are PGA professionals or coaches of top college golf programs.

ACCOMMODATIONS Students stay in college dormitories at the College of Charleston in historic downtown Charleston. The college is the thirteenth-oldest institute of higher education in the country, founded in 1770. Students have access to all college recreational and movie facilities and are supervised by school counselors and coaches throughout the program.

Students have access to all four of the Kiawah Island courses during the program: Marsh Point, a master's course in navigation and course management from Ron Kirby and Gary Player; Osprey Point, a thinking golfer's long course from Tom Fazio that is a perennial in the top seventy-five resort course rankings; Turtle Point, a heroic design by Jack Nicklaus, also appears in the top-seventy-five resort rankings and was Nicklaus' first use of the device of playing the first thirteen holes on the interior land before exploding out to the seashore to finish in a testing series of wind-beset links-style holes; finally, of course, the Ocean Course, the site of the 1991 Ryder Cup Matches, the most dramatic golf event ever staged—a seaside course very much in the links tradition. It was designed by Pete Dye and is one of the toughest and most dramatic experiences in the country—exceeded for sheer difficulty perhaps only by The Bear and PGA West.

■ CONTACT ■

Kiawah Island Junior Golf School
P.O. Box 1507
John's Island, SC 29457
803-768-2121 ext. 4050

GRAND STRAND GOLF INSTRUCTIONS

MYRTLE BEACH

PROGRAMS One-, two-, three-, and five-day programs, year-round.

ABOUT THE PROGRAMS A school without a stated style, Grand Strand is notable less for breakthroughs in swing philosophy than for a quite varied array of school options and for a quite low (3:1) student to teacher ratio. It is a standard-fare program of videotape analysis and 5 hours of daily instruction, but there is an optional on-course lesson opportunity that is recommended. Grand Strand is well worth a look, especially for golfers who thrive on more intimate instruction groups.

COSTS Please call Grand Strand at 800-453-6488 to obtain current cost information.

STUDENT/TEACHER RATIO 3:1.

INSTRUCTORS The school President is Glen Davis. All instructors are PGA professionals.

ACCOMMODATIONS No accommodations. Students are advised to contact the Holiday Inn Oceanfront (800-845-0313) or the Holiday Inn West (800-847-2707) for information and lodging reservations.

■ CONTACT ■

Grand Strand Golf Instructions
River Oaks Golf Plantation
831 River Oaks Drive
Myrtle Beach, SC 29577
800-453-6488

MYRTLE BEACH GOLF ACADEMY

MYRTLE BEACH

PROGRAMS Three- and five-day schools, year-round.

ABOUT THE PROGRAMS A highly personalized program utilizing high-speed, stop-action videotaped swing analysis for all aspects of the game. Another generally solid program in the Myrtle Beach area, distinguished primarily for a stronger emphasis on the short game. The five-day program includes 17 1/2 hours of instruction, while the three-day program provides 10 1/2 hours on the range.

COSTS Three days (commuter) $475; five days (commuter) $850.

INSTRUCTORS The head instructor is Matt Leslie. All instructors are PGA professionals.

ACCOMMODATIONS Included in the package price—several motel-style and villa lodging options are available.

Golf is at Arcadian Shores Golf Club, one of the finest in South Carolina and certainly one of the top five in the seventy plus course line-up in Myrtle Beach. It is a gorgeous track with an excellent early Rees Jones design. Bentgrass greens, sixty-four bunkers, and several natural lakes on site. Regularly recognized in national golf magazines as one of the finest public courses in the country.

■ CONTACT ■

Myrtle Beach Golf Academy
701 Hilton Road
Myrtle Beach, SC 29577
800-882-5121 or 803-449-5217

FAVORITE FIVE GOLF SCHOOL

MYRTLE BEACH

PROGRAMS Three-day schools, year-round.

ABOUT THE PROGRAM Another solid, highly personalized program well worth considering when traveling to Myrtle Beach. The striking feature of this school is the absence of assistant professionals; Dresser and Delk do the entire school by themselves, 8 students at a time. High-speed, stop-action videotaped swing analysis is available in this program with 2 hours of instruction daily.

COSTS Please call Favorite Five at 800-397-2678 to obtain current cost information.

STUDENT/TEACHER RATIO 4:1.

INSTRUCTORS The head instructors are Steve Dresser and Billy Delk. Both instructors are PGA professionals.

ACCOMMODATIONS Accommodations are not included in the package price. The school will recommend accommodations, or call Compass vacations at 800-624-6418 or Condotels 800-845-0631 for a good selection of villa accommodations.

■ CONTACT ■

Favorite 5 Golf School
9480 Indigo Club Drive
Murrells Inlet, SC 29576
800-397-2678 or 803-650-2678

National Golf Schools offering South Carolina Programs:

Ken Venturi Golf Training Centers
Marlene Floyd's For Women Only Golf Schools
The Phil Ritson Golf School
Riley School of Golf
Sea Pines Academy of Golf

TENNESSEE

National Golf Schools offering Tennessee Programs:
Bill Skelley School of Golf *(See pages 34 and 36)*

TEXAS

BARTON CREEK GOLF ADVANTAGE SCHOOL

AUSTIN

PROGRAM Three-day programs.

ABOUT THE PROGRAM This is one of the best programs in the country. It is headed by Chuck Cook, who has regularly worked with Payne Stewart. Cook was selected as one of America's Top 50 Instructors by *GOLF* magazine, largely on the strength of his Barton Creek program. The basic program includes 16 hours of instruction, including range, short-game, and on-course instruction. Video analysis is emphasized, and a special focus has been added on mental conditioning and course strategy.

COSTS (Double occupancy) $1465.

STUDENT/TEACHER RATIO 5:1.

INSTRUCTORS The head instructor is Chuck Cook. All instructors are PGA professionals.

ACCOMMODATIONS Accommodations are included in the package price. This is one of the finest resorts in the country, with an even finer selection of golf, including the top-100 ranked course by Tom Fazio. The two other courses (Palmer/Seay and Crenshaw/Coore) are also excellent. The resort is centered on the courses. The European spa facilities are generously done. Tennis, swimming, and health club activities round out the outdoor recreation program. The fairly intimate hotel is excellently staffed.

■ **CONTACT** ■

Barton Creek Golf Advantage School
Barton Creek Resort
8212 Barton Club Drive
Austin, TX 78735
800-336-6157 or 512-329-4000

TEXAS TECH UNIVERSITY GRADUATE GOLF WORKSHOP

JUNCTION

PROGRAMS Five-day program for juniors; three weeks for instructors.

ABOUT THE PROGRAM The prize for most unusual program in the country goes to this one, hands down. It's the only program where some of the enrollees do the teaching.

For the juniors it is a basic golf academy with emphasis on correct fundamentals, especially with the full swing via posture, grip, and alignment instruction. Short-game golf is also taught here.

The kicker is that the instructors are in fact students, too, who are learning the finer nuances of golf instruction. It is sort of like going down to the dentistry school to get one's teeth drilled, but it works well here in a closely monitored program. Teachers learn the newest teaching ideas and methods in a collegiate atmosphere. The program even provides college credit. The first two weeks focus on training; the final week allows actual work with juniors.

COSTS (Instructors) $500, (resident juniors) $249, (commuting juniors) $129.

INSTRUCTORS The head instructor is Danny Mason.

ACCOMMODATIONS Accommodations are not included in the package price for instructors. Juniors may stay in the Texas Tech dorms.

■ CONTACT ■

Texas Tech University Graduate Golf Workshop
Texas Tech University
Box 42191
Lubbock, TX 79409
806-742-2352 ext. 247

National Golf Schools offering Texas Programs:

Academy of Golf Dynamics
Chuck Hogan Golf Schools
Gillette LPGA Golf Clinics
Heritage Golf Schools
John Jacobs' Practical Golf Schools

UTAH

SUN DESERT GOLF ACADEMY

SAINT GEORGE

PROGRAMS Four- and six-day schools, November–June.

ABOUT THE PROGRAMS Thirteen hours of instruction in the four-day program; 20 hours in the six-day. This is a fairly high-tech school, with high-speed, stop-action video enhancing instruction in the full-swing sessions, but the instructors also use the person-to-person approach in teaching mental conditioning and course strategy skills.

COSTS Five days $579 (double-occupancy), $639 (single occupancy), $489 (commuter).

INSTRUCTORS The head instructor is Mike Smith. All instructors are PGA professionals.

ACCOMMODATIONS Accommodations are included in the package price, along with meals. Students have a choice between premium motel-based accommodations or the economy plan of Dixie College dormitories. Saint George is in the southwestern corner of the state quite close to Zion National Park (famous in John Ford westerns). Although Utah conjures up visions of Rocky Mountain-like cold, the weather here is more Arizonan than anything else, with mild winters and a dry climate.

■ **CONTACT** ■

Sun Desert Golf Academy
Dixie College
225 South 700 East
Saint George, UT 84770
800-545-4653

National Golf Schools offering Utah Programs:
  John Jacobs' Practical Golf Schools

VERMONT

NATURAL ASSET GOLF PROGRAM

STOWE

PROGRAMS Two-, three-, four-, and five-day programs, May–September.

ABOUT THE PROGRAMS A sleeper of a program offering a number of flexible program options and a highly developed philosophy of golf. It could eventually be considered a national school. The five-day program offers three days of on-course instruction, live situational golf that reflects Beckett's emphasis on working with real golfing assets, and real golfing situations. This is without question a "work with what you've got" school, but high-speed, stop-action video and teaching devices are utilized to drive home the lessons. Psychological instruction also receives a great deal of attention. An unusual emphasis on confidence and tempo and the connections between them make this a golf school option well worth considering.

COSTS Two-day school (double occupancy) $419–$459, (single occupancy) $479–$529; three-day school (double occupancy) $495–$539, (single occupancy) $556–$598; four-day school (double occupancy) $749–$795, (single occupancy) $871–$925; five-day school (double occupancy) $1025-$1075, (single occupancy) $1165-$1225; Play with the Pro program (double occupancy) $898–$948, (single occupancy) $1053–$1103.

STUDENT/TEACHER RATIO 5:1.

INSTRUCTORS The head instructor is Frank Plezia. All instructors are PGA professionals.

ACCOMMODATIONS AAA Four-Diamond rated resort known in winter for skiing, but summer brings tennis, swimming, and golf. A health and fitness center and copious fishing opportunities round out the offerings. Mount Snow Country Club, a few minutes away, is a rather pretty golf course that has hosted the New England Open in years past.

■ **CONTACT** ■

Natural Asset Golf Program
Stoweflake Inn and Resort
Box 369, Mountain Road
Stowe, VT 05672
802-253-7355

MOUNTAIN TOP GOLF SCHOOL

CHITTENDEN

PROGRAMS Two-, three-, and five-day schools.
ABOUT THE PROGRAMS Golfers may know DeCandia as a National Long Drive Champion in 1980 and 1989. DeCandia teaches a flatter and more comfortable swing plane. This is an unusual step, but reflects DeCandia's sense that swings are perceived to be much more upright than they really are. High-speed, stop-action video backs up his swing instruction. The program offers 6 hours of daily instruction. The five-day program adds a scramble tournament.
COSTS Program costs begin at $95 per person per day.
STUDENT/TEACHER RATIO 4:1.
INSTRUCTORS The head instructor is Scott DeCandia. All instructors are PGA professionals.

ACCOMMODATIONS Accommodations are included in the package price. Mountain Top is one of the many ski resorts in the Green Mountains that switch over to golf in the summer. The resort offers thirty-three guest rooms, and twenty-two cottages dot the grounds. Chief activities include tennis, water sports, horseback riding, and the Fitness Center. The resort lacks a course but has a 23-acre training facility, including a five-hole practice course.

■ CONTACT ■

Mountain Top Golf School
Mountain Top Inn and Resort
Mountain Top Road
Chittenden, VT 05737
800-445-2100

National Golf Schools offering Vermont Programs:
  The Golf School
  Stratton Golf Schools

VIRGINIA

THE KINGSMILL GOLF SCHOOL

WILLIAMSBURG

PROGRAMS Three-day schools, April–October.
ABOUT THE PROGRAM Tim Poland is a Jimmy Ballard disciple. He employs his swing connector and teaches the one-swing method and the upper-body moves one learns via Ballard or

Leadbetter at a significantly higher cost. The program covers set-up, grip, alignment, the full swing, sand shots, pitching, chipping and putting, course strategy, and the pre-shot routine. In short, soup to nuts golf instruction is offered, with the possible exception of mental toughness instruction.
COSTS Regular room $545, suite $605.
STUDENT/TEACHER RATIO 3:1.
INSTRUCTORS The head instructor is Tim Poland. All instructors are PGA professionals.

ACCOMMODATIONS Accommodations are included in the package price. The Kingsmill is home to the Anheuser-Busch PGA event and also Curtis Strange. It is an outstanding facility at an outstanding site near Colonial Williamsburg. This is either good news because of the historical recreations of colonial life or the proximity of Golden Horseshoe Golf Club, depending on your point of view.

■ **CONTACT** ■

The Kingsmill Golf School
Kingsmill Resort and Conference Center
1010 Kingsmill Road
Williamsburg, VA 23185
800-832-5665 or 804-253-1703

WINTERGREEN GOLF ACADEMY

WINTERGREEN

PROGRAMS One-, two-, and three-day schools, April–October.

ABOUT THE PROGRAMS Four hours of daily instruction as well as high-speed, stop-action video analysis, including a take-home video, are the highlights at this school. The program touts its low student to teacher ratio and the individualized approach to instruction as its key attraction. Students are grouped by ability for both range work and on-course instruction, which plays a key role in the school curriculum.

COSTS $250–$650.

STUDENT/TEACHER RATIO 4:1.

INSTRUCTORS The head instructor is Graeme Oliver. All instructors are PGA professionals.

ACCOMMODATIONS Accommodations are included in the package price. Wintergreen is better known as a ski resort, but was master-planned by the same team that built Harbour Town, so it has some authentic golf credentials. *GOLF* magazine has chimed in with a Silver Medal for the resort. Ellis Maples and Rees Jones are responsible for the two courses. Stoney Creek, by Jones, received a number of plaudits and best new course mentions when it opened several years ago. Students choose from studios to six-bedroom homes.

■ **CONTACT** ■

Wintergreen Golf Academy
Wintergreen Resort
P.O. Box 706
Wintergreen, VA 22958

WASHINGTON

DESTINATION GOLF SCHOOL

PORT LUDLOW

PROGRAMS Three-day school, April–September.

ABOUT THE PROGRAM Fundamentals are stressed in this program balancing range time with on-course situational instruction. One unusual feature is the rules seminar, which is common with junior instruction but often overlooked for adults. The on-course environment is ideal, particularly for bentgrass putting.

COSTS April (weekday) $40 per day, (weekend) $45; May–September (weekday) $50, (weekend) $55.

STUDENT/TEACHER RATIO 6:1.

INSTRUCTORS The head instructor is Lyndon Blackwell. All instructors are PGA professionals.

ACCOMMODATIONS Port Ludlow is scheduled to open a new marina and inn complex shortly.

This is good news for Washington's only golf school program, as the old resort facilities are a little dated. Nevertheless the course is outstanding and the setting exquisite, within 90 minutes of downtown Seattle. Skiing is available in the Olympic National Park, the Hoh Rainforest is nearby, and some of the best sailing conditions in the world are available. The twenty-seven-hole facility was designed by Robert Muir Graves and incorporates relics of the logging era, which led to Port Ludlow's establishment in the mid-nineteenth century. Boom chains and cedar stumps form hazards throughout the course, which is always in mint condition due to the unique bentgrass growing conditions offered by the cool, damp climate.

■ CONTACT ■

Destination Golf Schools
Port Ludlow Golf and Meeting Resort
9483 Oak Bay Road
Port Ludlow, WA 98365
800-732-1239 or 206-437-0272

WISCONSIN

SILVER SANDS GOLF SCHOOL OF WISCONSIN

DELAVAN

PROGRAMS Three- and five-day schools, April–August.

ABOUT THE PROGRAMS Wayne Rolfs reports: "One's golf swing involves body, mind, technique, and proper equipment." High-speed, stop-action video analysis, mental conditioning training, full-swing and short-game instruction, and a club fitting session are thus the highlights of the Silver Sands program. Wisconsin has one of the highest golf participation rates in the nation. This easy-to-utilize program could well be a part of the reason why.

COSTS (Double occupancy) $500.

STUDENT/TEACHER RATIO 4:1.

INSTRUCTORS The head instructor is Wayne Rolfs. All instructors are PGA professionals.

ACCOMMODATIONS Accommodations are included in the package price. Lake Geneva is a long-time getaway favored by Chicago and Milwaukee business executives. In recent years the former Playboy resort has been converted into one of the better resorts in the country. Blackwolf Run is nearby, but the resort has two outstanding courses of its own. They are routinely rated among the top resort courses in the country. The first is a Pete Dye/Jack Nicklaus course, designed in the Scottish style, while the Brute course designed by Robert Harris is in the American parkland style. The facility as a whole features 1,400 acres of rolling hills and countryside, skeet and trap shooting, indoor/outdoor tennis, horseback riding, and canoeing.

■ CONTACT ■

Silver Sands Golf School of Wisconsin
414-275-6122

National Golf Schools offering Wisconsin Programs:
Al Frazzini's Golf Course
Galvano Golf Academy
John Jacobs' Practical Golf Schools

WYOMING

National Golf School offering Wyoming Programs:
John Jacobs' Practical Golf Schools *(See pages 65 and 80)*

GOLF
ORGANIZATIONS

GOLF ORGANIZATIONS

UNITED STATES NATIONAL ASSOCIATIONS

AMATEUR GOLF ASSN. OF AMERICA
P.O. Box 3127
Cherry Hill, NJ 08034
609-354-9555

AMERICAN JUNIOR GOLF ASSN.
2415 Steeplechase Ln.
Roswell, GA 30076
404-998-4653

GOLF WRITERS ASSN. OF AMERICA
258820 Orchard Lake Rd.
Farmington Hills, MO 48336
810-442-1481

LADIES PROFESSIONAL GOLF ASSOC.
2570 W. International Speedway
Blvd., Ste. B
Daytona Beach, FL 32114
904-254-8800

NATIONAL AMPUTEE GOLF ASSN. (NAGA)
P.O. Box 1228
Amherst, NH 03031
800-633-6242 or 603-673-1135

NATIONAL GOLF FOUNDATION
1150 South U.S. Hwy. One, Ste 401
Jupiter, FL 33477
407-744-6006

PROFESSIONAL GOLFERS' ASSOC. OF AMERICA
100 Avenue of the Champions
Palm Beach Gardens, FL 33410
407-624-8400

PROFESSIONAL GOLFERS' ASSOC. TOUR
112 TPC Blvd.
Ponte Vedra Beach, FL 32082
904-285-3700

UNITED STATES GOLF ASSN.
Golf House
P.O. Box 708
Far Hills, NJ 07931
800-336-4446 or 908-234-2300

UNITED STATES REGIONAL ASSOCIATIONS

ALABAMA GOLF ASSN.
P.O. Box 660149
Birmingham, AL 35266
205-979-1234

BUFFALO DISTRICT GOLF ASSN.
P.O. Box 19
Cheektowaga, NY 14225
716-632-1936

CAROLINAS GOLF ASSN.
P.O. Box 428
West End, NC 27376
910-673-1000

CHICAGO DISTRICT GOLF ASSN.
619 Enterprise Dr., Ste. #204
Oak Brook, IL 60521
708-954-2180

COLORADO GOLF ASSN.
5655 S. Yosemite, Ste. #101
Englewood, CO 80111
303-779-4653

COLUMBUS DISTRICT GOLF ASSN.
5300 McKitrick Blvd.
Columbus, OH 43235
614-457-8169

CONNECTICUT STATE GOLF ASSN.
35 Cold Spring Rd.
Rocky Hill, CT 06067
203-257-4171

DELAWARE STATE GOLF ASSN.
7234 Lancaster Pike, Ste. 302 B
Hockessin, DE 19707
302-234-3365

FLORIDA STATE GOLF ASSN.
P.O. Box 21177
Sarasota, FL 34276
813-921-5695

GEORGIA STATE GOLF ASSN.
121 Village Pkwy., Bldg. 3
Marietta, GA 30067
404-955-4272

GOLF ASSN. OF MICHIGAN
37935 Twelve Mile Rd., Ste. #200
Farmington Hills, MI 48331
810-553-4200

HAWAII GOLF ASSN.
3599 Waialae Ave.
Honolulu, HI 96816
808-732-9785

IDAHO GOLF ASSN.
P.O. Box 3025
Boise, ID 83703
208-342-4442

ILLINOIS JUNIOR GOLF ASSN.
1 Pete Dye Drive
Lemon, IL 60439
708-724-1906

INDIANA GOLF ASSN.
P.O. Box 516
Franklin, IN 46131
317-738-9696

IOWA GOLF ASSN.
1930 St. Andrews Ct., NE
Cedar Rapids, IA 52402
319-378-9142

KANSAS GOLF ASSN.
3301 Clinton Parkway Ct., #4
Lawrence, KS 66047
913-842-4833

KENTUCKY GOLF ASSN.
P.O. Box 18396
Louisville, KY 40261
502-499-7255

MAINE STATE GOLF ASSN., INC.
P.O. Box 419
Auburn, ME 04212
207-795-6742

MARYLAND STATE GOLF ASSN.
P.O. Box 16289
Baltimore, MD 21210
410-467-8899

MASSACHUSETTS GOLF ASSN.
175 Highland Ave.
Needham, MA 02192
617-449-3000

METROPOLITAN GOLF ASSN.
49 Knollwood Rd.
Elmsford, NY 10523
914-347-4653

MICHIGAN ASSN. OF PUBLIC GOLF COURSES
225 W. Washtenaw
Lansing, MI 48933
517-482-4312

MINNESOTA GOLF ASSN.
6550 York Ave. So., Ste. #211
Edina, MN 55435
612-927-4643

MISSISSIPPI GOLF ASSN.
1019 N. 12th Ave., Apt. A3
P.O. Box 684
Laurel, MS 39441
601-649-0570

MISSOURI GOLF ASSN.
P.O. Box 104164
Jefferson City, MO 65110
314-636-8994

MONTANA STATE GOLF ASSN.
P.O. Box 3389
Butte, MT 59701
406-782-9208

NEBRASKA GOLF ASSN.
5625 "O" St., Ste. "FORE"
Lincoln, NE 68510
402-486-1440

NEVADA STATE GOLF ASSN.
P.O. Box 5630
Sparks, NV 89432
702-673-4653

NEW HAMPSHIRE GOLF ASSN.
45 Kearney St.
Manchester, NH 03104
603-623-0396

NEW JERSEY STATE GOLF ASSN.
1000 Broad St.
Bloomfield, NJ 07003
201-338-8334

NEW YORK STATE GOLF ASSN.
P.O. Box 3459
Elmira, NY 14905-0007
607-733-0007

NORTH DAKOTA GOLF ASSN.
P.O. Box 452
Bismarck, ND 58502
701-223-2770

NORTHERN CALIFORNIA GOLF ASSN.
P.O. Box NCGA
Pebble Beach, CA 93953
408-625-4653

OREGON GOLF ASSN.
8364 S.W. Nimbus Ave.
Beaverton, OR 97008
503-643-2610

PACIFIC NORTHWEST GOLF ASSN.
155 NE 100 St., #302
Seattle, WA 98125
206-526-1238

RHODE ISLAND GOLF ASSN.
10 Orms St., #326
Providence, RI 02904
401-272-1350

ROCHESTER DISTRICT GOLF ASSN.
333 Metro Park, Ste. M110
Rochester, NY 14623
716-292-5950

SAN DIEGO COUNTY WOMEN'S GOLF ASSN.
3102 Levante St.
Carlsbad, CA 92009
619-436-0266

SOUTH CAROLINA GOLF ASSN.
145 Birdsong Tr.
Chapin, SC 29036
803-781-6992

SPOKANE JR. GOLF
P.O. Box 3740
Spokane, WA 99220
509-536-1800

SYRACUSE DISTRICT GOLF ASSN.
129 Shady Ln.
Fayetteville, NY 13066
315-637-8200

TENNESSEE GOLF ASSN.
400 Franklin Rd.
Franklin, TN 37064
615-790-7600

TEXAS GOLF ASSN.
Sunday House Sq.
1000 Westbank Dr., #2B
Austin, TX 78746
512-328-4653

VERMONT GOLF ASSN.
P.O. Box 1612, Sta. A
Rutland, VT 05701
802-773-7180

VIRGINIA STATE GOLF ASSN.
830 Southlake Blvd., Ste. A
Richmond, VA 23236
804-378-2300

WASHINGTON JUNIOR GOLF ASSN.
633 North Mildred, Ste. 3
Tacoma, WA 98406

WASHINGTON STATE GOLF ASSN.
155 NE 100 St., #302
Seattle, WA 98125
206-526-1238

WESTCHESTER GOLF ASSN.
49 Knollwood Rd.
Elmsford, NY 10523
914-347-2340

WESTERN GOLF ASSOCIATION (WGA)/EVANS SCHOLARS FOUNDATION
1 Briar Rd.
Golf, IL 60029
708-724-4600

WISCONSIN STATE GOLF ASSN.
P.O. Box 35
Elm Grove, WI 53122
414-786-4301

WOMEN'S SOUTHERN CALIFORNIA GOLF ASSN.
402 W. Arrow Hwy., Ste. #10
San Dimas, CA 91773
909-592-1281

WYOMING GOLF ASSN.
501 First Ave. S.
Greybull, WY 82426
307-568-3304

INTERNATIONAL ASSOCIATIONS

ASSOCIATION SUISSE DE GOLF
En Ballegue
Case Postale
1066 Epalinges
41-217843531 (Switzerland)

AUSTRALIAN GOLF UNION
Golf Australia House
155 Cecil St.
S. Melbourne, Victoria 3205
61-3-699-7944 (Australia)

BAHAMAS GOLF FEDERATION
P.O. Box N-4568
Nassau (Bahamas)

BERMUDA GOLF ASSN.
Box HM
433, Hamilton, HMBX (Bermuda)

BRITISH COLUMBIA GOLF
ASSN.
Ste. 185, Sperling Plaza 2
6450 Roberts St.
Burnaby, BC, V5G 4E1
604-294-1818 (Canada)

CANADIAN GOLF FOUNDATION
Golf House, 1333 Dorval Dr.
Oakville, ON, L6J 4Z3
416-849-9700 (Canada)

CANADIAN LADIES GOLF ASSN.
1600 James Naismith
Gloucester, ON, K1B 5N4
613-748-5642 (Canada)

DEUTSCHER GOLF VERBAND
EV.
Leberberg, 25; Postfach 2106
D-6200 Wiesbaden
49-6121526041 (Germany)

ENGLISH LADIES GOLF ASSN.
Edgbaston Club
Church Rd.
Birmingham B15-3TB
44-21-4562088 (England)

FEDERATION FRANCAISE DE
GOLF
69 Ave. Victor-Hugo
F-75783 Paris Cedex 16
33-14205135 (France)

GOLF ASSN. OF THE REPUBLIC
OF CHINA
71, Lane 369
Tunhua South Rd.
Taipei, Taiwan (106)

GOLFING UNION OF IRELAND
Glencar House 81, Eglinton Rd.
Donnybrook, Dublin 4
353-12694111 (Ireland)

GRAHAM MARSH JR. GOLF
FDN.
P.O. Box 455
South Perth, 6151 (Australia)

HELLENIC GOLF FEDERATION
P.O. Box 70003
GR-166 10 Glyfada, Athens
30-18941933 (Greece)

JAPAN GOLF ASSN.
606 6th Fl., Palace Bldg.
Marunouchi, Chiyoda-Ku
Tokyo (Japan)

JUNIOR GOLF AUSTRALIA
155 Cecil St.
S. Melbourne, Victoria
61-3-699-7944 (Australia)

KOREA GOLF ASSN.
Rm. 18, 13th Fl., Manhattan Bldg.
36-2 Yeo Eui Do-Dong
Seoul
82-2783-4748 (Korea)

MANITOBA GOLF ASSN.
200 Main St.
Winnipeg, MB, R3C 4M2
204-985-4057 (Canada)

NATIONAL GOLF FOUNDATION
JAPAN
3-3-4 Sendagaya Shibuya-ku
Tokyo
81-3478-4355 (Japan)

NEW SOUTH WALES GOLF
ASSN.
17-19 Brisbane St.
Darlinghurst, NSW 2010
61-2-264-8433 (Australia)

NOVA SCOTIA GOLF ASSN.
14 Limardo Dr.
Dartmouth, NS, B3A 3X4
902-465-7306 (Canada)

ONTARIO GOLF ASSN.
Golf House Ontario
RR #3
Newmarket, ON, L3Y 4W1
416-853-8511 (Canada)

PROFESSIONAL GOLFERS ASSN. OF AUSTRALIA
P.O. Box 345
Windsor, NSW 2756 (Australia)

QUEBEC GOLF ASSN.
3300 Cavendish Blvd., Rm. #250
Montreal, QB, H4B 2M8
514-481-0471 (Canada)

ROYAL AND ANCIENT GOLF CLUB OF ST. ANDREWS
St. Andrews
Fife KY16 9JD
011-44-334-72112 (Scotland)

ROYAL CANADIAN GOLF ASSN.
RR 2
Oakville, ON L6J 4Z3
416-844-1800 (Canada)

SCOTTISH LADIES' GOLFING ASSN.
Rm. 1010-Terminal Bldg.
Prestwick Airport
Prestwick, Ayrshire KA9 2PL
44-29279582 (Scotland)

THE GOLF FOUNDATION
Foundation House Hanbury Manor
Ware, Herts SG12-0UH
44-920-484044 (England)

THE INDIAN GOLF UNION
Tata Centre, 3rd Fl.
43 Chowringhee Rd.
Calcutta 700071 (India)

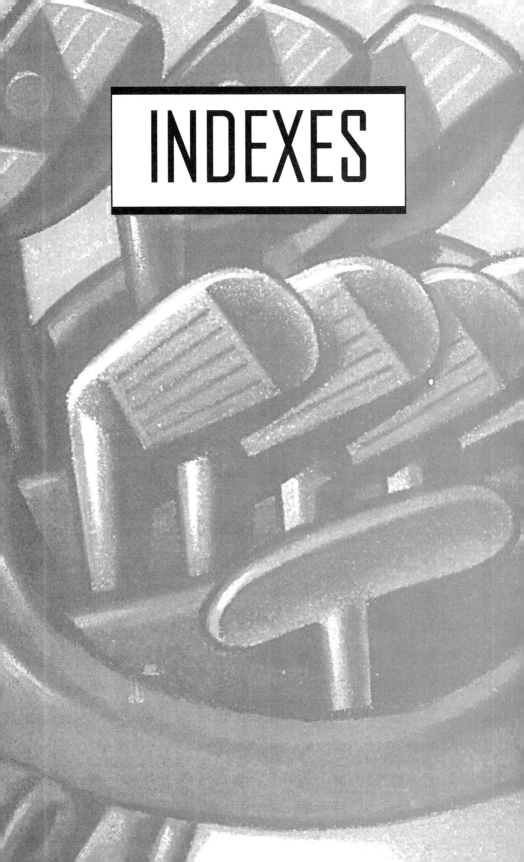

INDEXES

INDEX A

ALPHABETICAL LIST
OF ALL SCHOOLS

INDEX B

SHOW-ME

Instruction programs of the "Show-Me" variety tend to teach a method without completely rebuilding the swing from scratch. Instructors are generally of a slightly higher national profile (Chuck Hogan, Dave Pelz, Jim McLean [Doral], or Jim Flick), reflecting the success that their methods have had with touring professionals and via books and magazine articles. Instructors in this category tend to rely more on technical swing analysis and in many cases high-tech teaching methodologies.

Students who succeed here are typically average in confidence levels, and ready to make great changes in their swings if great improvements can result, but not so confident that rigorous swing analysis and correction will fall on deaf ears. These instructors also work quite well for beginners (since they rely more on teaching systems, making it easier to learn in the short duration of a golf school) as well as low-handicappers who can benefit from some of their more subtle analyses and corrections.

INDEX C

I-AM-ME

These schools typically work with what each student brings to the school, often avoiding complicated swing methods and mechanics for an overall development of the student's skills based on key strengths and weaknesses as discovered in the first day of instruction. The style of instruction tends to be quite friendly and often quite low-key. In most cases the successful teachers achieve their results through personal charisma and interaction as much as through indoctrination.

Students with above-average or below-average confidence levels in their games are typically most comfortable with this format. The highly confident student doesn't require (or may not want) a complete overhaul of the swing; less-confident students benefit from the "one step at a time" approach that builds on current strengths while attempting to correct major weaknesses. Older players also tend to benefit from this approach.

It's of interest that the largest of the golf instruction programs are of this low-key type. The schools represented here offer instruction programs in every region of the country, year-round, and offer a substantial variation in cost.

INDEX D

REBUILDERS

A small group of very high profile instructors teach highly technical (though often easy to understand) teaching philosophies and methods, and golfers will succeed in their programs if they are willing to try the entire system, even if it means rebuilding their entire swing or making major changes in their understanding of golf strategy. Teachers like David Leadbetter, Jimmy Ballard, Carl Welty, and others have received much attention in the press, and deservedly so, but students should be prepared for an intensive golf school experience and should desire major transformation and improvement in their games before contemplating these programs. They deliver the greatest results but are rigorous in their application of golf methods.

Students who succeed here tend to desire a radical transformation in their games—from beginners struggling to establish a handicap for the first time, to Nick Faldo reconstructing his swing to take his game to the next level.

INDEX E

SCHOOLS FOR WOMEN

The following schools are not the only programs that teach women. Rather, they cater especially to the needs of the female golfer and in some cases are exclusively for women or offer women-only programs, and they typically feature female instructors.

INDEX F

HI-TECH

The following schools offer highly innovative use of swing training aids and videotaped swing recording and analysis.

INDEX G

ON-COURSE EMPHASIS

The following programs place a special emphasis on situational instruction on the golf course, using real-life lies, conditions, and strategic problems.

INDEX H

RESORTS

Alabama
Marriott Grand (John Jacobs'), 65

Arizona
Arizona Golf Resort (Professional Golf School of America), 100
Gold Canyon Ranch (Bill Skelley), 34
McCormick Ranch (Chuch Hogan), 38
Marriott's Mountain Shadows (John Jacobs'), 69
Scottsdale Princess (Nicklaus/Flick), 91
Sedona (Chuck Hogan), 37
Tucson National (John Jacobs'), 66
The Wigwam (John Jacobs'), 65

California
Aviara (Aviara), 30
Chardonnay Club (John Jacobs'), 66
La Costa (La Costa), 86
Marriott's Desert Springs (John Jacobs'), 66
Marriott's Rancho Las Palmas (John Jacobs'), 66
Mission Hills (Ken Venturi), 85
PGA West (Dave Pelz, David Leadbetter, Swing's The Thing), 41
Pala Mesa (*Golf Digest*), 54
Pebble Beach (The Golf Clinic, Nicklaus/Flick), 49
Quail Lodge (Aviara, *Golf Digest*), 30
Rancho Bernardo (Ken Blanchard), 82
San Vicente Inn (America's Favorite), 21
Silverado (America's Favorite), 22
Singing Hills (The School of Golf), 116
Warner Springs Ranch (Riley), 105

Colorado

The Broadmoor (The Academy of Golf), 16
Copper Mountain (Bill Skelley), 35
Garden of the Gods (Academy of Golf Dynamics), 18
Lone Tree (America's Favorite), 22
Skyland Mountain (John Jacobs'), 66
Sonnenalp (*Golf Digest*), 55
Tamarron (Craft-Zavichas), 40

Florida

Bay Hill (Arnold Palmer), 27
Belleview Mido (United States), 116
Bluewater Bay (Bill Skelley), 36
Boca Raton (Dave Pelz), 42
Bonaventure (John Jacobs'), 66
The Breakers (Rick Smith), 103
Don Shula's (Bill Skelley), 35
Doral (Doral), 45
Grand Cypress (Grand Cypress), 62
Grand Palms (Roland Stafford), 107
Hollywood Beach (Professional Golf School of America), 100
Innisbrook (*Golf Digest*, The Golf Institute), 55
Marriott's Marco Island (John Jacobs'), 66
Marriott's Orlando World (John Jacobs'), 66
Naples Beach (Paradise), 94
Orange Lake (Swing's The Thing), 114
PGA National (The Academy of Golf, Nicklaus/Flick), 15
Palm Beach Polo (Jimmy Ballard), 64
Perdido Bay (Roland Stafford), 107
Saddlebrook (Arnold Palmer), 28
Spring Lake (United States), 117

Georgia

Chateau Elan (*Golf Digest*), 56
The Cloister (*Golf Digest*), 56
Stouffer Pine Isle (America's Favorite), 23

Hawaii

Waikoloa (Chuck Hogan, The Golf Clinic), 37